The Criminalization of Violence Against Women

Interpersonal Violence Series

SERIES EDITORS

Claire Renzetti, Ph.D.
Jeffrey L. Edleson, Ph.D.

Parenting by Men Who Batter: New Directions for Assessment and Intervention
Edited by Jeffrey L. Edleson and Oliver J. Williams

Coercive Control: How Men Entrap Women in Personal Life
Evan Stark

Childhood Victimization: Violence, Crime, and Abuse in the Lives of Young People
David Finkelhor

Restorative Justice and Violence Against Women
Edited by James Ptacek

Familicidal Hearts: The Emotional Styles of 211 Killers
Neil Websdale

Violence in Context: Current Evidence on Risk, Protection, and Prevention
Edited by Todd I. Herrenkohl, Eugene Aisenberg, James Herbert Williams, and Jeffrey M. Jenson

Poverty, Battered Women, and Work in U.S. Public Policy
Lisa D. Brush

Child Victims and Restorative Justice: A Needs-Rights Model
Tali Gal

Battered Women's Protective Strategies
Sherry Hamby

Men Who Batter
Nancy Nason-Clark and Barbara Fisher-Townsend

When Men Murder Women
R. Emerson Dobash and Russell P. Dobash

Comparative Perspectives on Gender Violence: Lessons From Efforts Worldwide
Edited by Rashmi Goel and Leigh Goodmark

Religion and Intimate Partner Violence: Understanding the Challenges and Proposing Solutions
Nancy Nason-Clark, Barbara Fisher-Townsend, Catherine Holtmann, Stephen McMullin

Violence Against Women in the 21st Century: Transnational Perspectives of Empowerment and Subjugation
Edited by Kristen Zaleski, Annalisa Enrile, Eugenia Weiss, Xiying Wang

State Sanctioned Violence: Advancing a Social Work Social Justice Agenda
Melvin Delgado

Collaborating for Change Transforming Cultures to End Gender-based Violence in Higher Education
Edited by Susan B. Marine and Ruth Lewis

Women, Intimate Partner Violence, and the Law
Heather Douglas

Urban Gun Violence Self-Help Organizations as Healing Sites, Catalysts for Change, and Collaborative Partners
Melvin Delgado

Islamophobia and Acts of Violence
Carolyn Turpin-Petrosino

Coercive Control in Children's and Mothers' Lives
Emma Katz

Coercive Control: How Men Entrap Women in Personal Life, Second Edition
Evan Stark

Children of Coercive Control
Evan Stark

The Criminalization of Violence Against Women: Comparative Perspectives
Heather Douglas, Kate Fitz-Gibbon, Leigh Goodmark, and Sandra Walklate

The Criminalization of Violence Against Women

Comparative Perspectives

EDITED BY

HEATHER DOUGLAS

KATE FITZ-GIBBON

LEIGH GOODMARK

AND

SANDRA WALKLATE

Oxford University Press is a department of the University of Oxford. It furthers
the University's objective of excellence in research, scholarship, and education
by publishing worldwide. Oxford is a registered trade mark of Oxford University
Press in the UK and certain other countries.

Published in the United States of America by Oxford University Press
198 Madison Avenue, New York, NY 10016, United States of America.

© Oxford University Press 2024

All rights reserved. No part of this publication may be reproduced, stored in
a retrieval system, or transmitted, in any form or by any means, without the
prior permission in writing of Oxford University Press, or as expressly permitted
by law, by license, or under terms agreed with the appropriate reproduction
rights organization. Inquiries concerning reproduction outside the scope of the
above should be sent to the Rights Department, Oxford University Press, at the
address above.

You must not circulate this work in any other form
and you must impose this same condition on any acquirer.

CIP data is on file at the Library of Congress
ISBN 978-0-19-765184-1

DOI: 10.1093/oso/9780197651841.001.0001

Printed by Integrated Books International, United States of America

CONTENTS

Acknowledgments ix
Contributors xi

Introduction: Whither Criminalization? 1
Heather Douglas, Kate Fitz-Gibbon, Leigh Goodmark, and Sandra Walklate

PART 1 The Criminalization Agenda: "New" Approaches to Old Problems

1. The Criminalization of Coercive Control: The Benefits and Risks of Criminalization From the Vantage of Victim-Survivors 21
   Kate Fitz-Gibbon, Sandra Walklate, Silke Meyer, and Ellen Reeves

2. The Criminalization of Psychological Violence in Brazil: Challenges of Legal Recognition and Unintended Consequences 43
   Thiago Pierobom de Ávila

3. Criminalization at the Margins: Downblousing, Creepshots, and Image-Based Sexual Abuse 61
   Clare McGlynn

4. Sexual Violence in Criminal Law: Presumptions, Principles, and Premises in Relation to the Crime of Negligent Rape 79
   Ulrika Andersson

5. Criminal Justice Responses to Domestic Violence in Fiji 97
Jojiana Cokanasiga

PART 2 Criminalization, Criminal Justice Challenges, and Consequences

6. Sentencing Aboriginal Women Who Have Killed Their Partners: Do We Really Hear Them? 115
Kyllie Cripps

7. *United States v. Maddesyn George*: The Consequences of Criminalization for Native Women in the United States 133
Leigh Goodmark

8. Prosecuting Intimate Partner Sexual Violence: Reforming Trial Process by Reimagining the Judicial Role 151
Elisabeth McDonald

9. "If It's Good for the Goose, It's Good for the Gander": Perceptions of Police Family Violence Policy Adherence in Victoria, Australia 171
Ellen Reeves

10. Operationalizing Coercive Control: Early Insights on the Policing of the Domestic Abuse (Scotland) Act 2018 189
Michele Burman, Oona Brooks-Hay, and Ruth Friskney

11. The Consequences of Criminalizing Domestic Violence: A Case Study of the Nonfatal Strangulation Offense in Queensland, Australia 209
Heather Douglas and Robin Fitzgerald

PART 3 Making Sense of Criminalization: Concepts, Context, Activism

12. Human Rights Penality, the Inter-American Approach to Violence Against Women, and the Local Effects of Centering Criminal Justice 231
Silvana Tapia Tapia

13. Intersectionality, Vulnerability, and Punitiveness: Claims of Equality Merging Into Categories of Penal Exclusion and Secondary Victimization 249
   Gema Varona

14. Dangerous Liaisons: Restorative Justice and the State 269
   Aparna Polavarapu

15. Bureaucratic Violence: State Neglect of Domestic and Family Violence Victims in Aceh, Indonesia 285
   Balawyn Jones

16. Reclaiming Justice: Understanding the Role of the State and the Collective in Domestic Violence in India 299
   Niveditha Menon

Index 317

ACKNOWLEDGMENTS

The editors wish to thank the research assistants who helped with formatting and checking final chapters: Roanna McClelland, Thomas Fletcher, and Tess Varney. They also wish to thank the Melbourne Law School Academic Research Service, who trained and provided support for the research assistants. This aspect of the work was supported by an Australian Research Council grant (DP200101020).

We are also particularly grateful to the contributors to this collection for their brilliant chapters during what has been an extremely challenging time for many people. While we weren't able to meet in person to exchange ideas and drafts, we thoroughly enjoyed the virtual sessions that we had with the authors and believe that these discussions enriched the final chapters. Thank you to all authors involved for finding the time and the writing space to contribute to this volume during this time of uncertainty.

Thanks also to Dana Bliss and Sarah Ebel from Oxford University Press, who believed in this project from the start and supported us throughout the publishing process.

CONTRIBUTORS

Ulrika Andersson, Professor, Faculty of Law, Lund University, Sweden. Her research focuses broadly on questions concerning law and power and engages with issues of sexuality and gender, including sexual violence and the criminal legal process.

Oona Brooks-Hay is a Reader in Criminology within the Scottish Centre for Crime and Justice Research (SCCJR) at the University of Glasgow, Scotland.

Michele Burman, CBE FRSE FAcSS, is Professor of Criminology within the Scottish Centre for Crime and Justice Research (SCCJR) at the University of Glasgow, Scotland.

Jojiana Cokanasiga, PhD Candidate, School of Social Science, The University of Queensland, Australia.

Kyllie Cripps, Professor, is an Indigenous academic, Director, Monash Indigenous Studies Centre, School of Philosophical, Historical, and International Studies and School of Social Sciences, Faculty of Arts, Monash University.

Thiago Pierobom de Ávila, Associate Professor of Law at UniCEUB, Brazil. Affiliated Researcher in the University of Lisbon and Monash Gender and Family Violence Prevention Centre, and a Senior Specialized Domestic Violence Prosecutor in Brasilia, Brazil.

Heather Douglas, AM, FASSA, Professor, Melbourne Law School, The University of Melbourne, Australia.

Robin Fitzgerald, School of Social Science, The University of Queensland, Australia. Associate Professor Fitzgerald is a criminologist with research interests in legal responses to crime, including domestic violence.

Kate Fitz-Gibbon, Professor of Social Sciences and Director, Monash Gender and Family Violence Prevention Centre, Faculty of Arts, Monash University, Australia.

Ruth Friskney is a Research Associate within the Scottish Centre for Crime and Justice Research (SCCJR) at the University of Glasgow, Scotland.

Leigh Goodmark is the Marjorie Cook Professor of Law and director of the Gender, Prison, and Trauma Clinic at the Francis King Carey School of Law, University of Maryland, United States.

Balawyn Jones is an academic at La Trobe Law School. She completed her PhD at Melbourne Law School (2022), researching domestic violence at the intersection of gender, religion, and law.

Elisabeth McDonald, MNZM, Adjunct Professor, University of Canterbury and the Institute of Judicial Studies, New Zealand. Elisabeth publishes and teaches in the areas of evidence and family and sexual violence.

Clare McGlynn, Professor of Law, Durham Law School, Durham University, UK, and coauthor of *Cyberflashing: Recognizing Harms, Reforming Laws* (2021).

Niveditha Menon is the Deputy Director at the Centre for Budget and Policy Studies (CBPS), Bangalore, India. She works in the area of gender, focusing on issues of violence, empowerment, and poverty.

Silke Meyer, Leneen Forde Chair of Child and Family Research, School of Health Sciences and Social Work, Griffith University, Australia.

Aparna Polavarapu, School of Law & SC Restorative Justice Initiative, University of South Carolina, United States.

Ellen Reeves, Research Fellow, Monash Gender and Family Violence Prevention Centre, Faculty of Arts, Monash University, Australia.

Silvana Tapia Tapia, Leverhulme Fellow, Birmingham Law School, United Kingdom. Until 2022 she served as Assistant Professor and Coordinator of Research at Universidad del Azuay's Law School, Ecuador.

Gema Varona, Professor of Victimology and Criminal Policy at the Faculty of Law and Senior Researcher at the Basque Institute of Criminology (University of the Basque Country).

Sandra Walklate, Eleanor Rathbone Chair of Sociology, Social Policy, and Criminology, University of Liverpool, England.

Introduction

Whither Criminalization?

HEATHER DOUGLAS, KATE FITZ-GIBBON, LEIGH GOODMARK, AND SANDRA WALKLATE ■

BACKGROUND

The collection in this book grew out of discussions that we, the editors, have been having for a long time about the role of criminal law as a response to violence against women. In most countries, a significant part of the policy agenda set by movements to end gender-based violence has been to prioritize state intervention in cases involving violence between intimate partners, sexual harassment in the workplace, and rape and sexual assault by both strangers and intimate partners. These interventions have taken various forms, including the passage of substantive civil and criminal laws governing intimate partner violence, rape and sexual assault, and sexual harassment; the development of civil orders of protection; and the implementation of procedures in the criminal legal system to ensure the effective intervention of police and prosecutors. Although states have taken divergent approaches to the passage and implementation of criminal laws and procedures to address violence against women, criminalization has been relied on as a primary strategy in most jurisdictions.

Over time, we have come to recognize the negative, but increasingly predictable, consequences that criminalizing violence against women has on women, their children, and their communities. These negative consequences include the disproportionate rates of incarceration of First Nations people (Douglas & Fitzgerald, 2018; Nancarrow, 2019) and people of color and the increasing criminalization of women who often have histories of victimization and are too frequently misidentified as perpetrators of violence (Goodmark, 2021, 2023; Reeves, 2021; Walklate & Fitz-Gibbon, 2021). Given that the negative consequences of criminalization are now familiar, it is no longer possible to argue they are unintended. They are to be expected.

While there are many criminalization-related topics that have animated our discussions, there are two recent and continuing global debates that stand out: the criminalization of coercive control and psychological abuse and the rapid, uneven rise in incarceration rates worldwide, particularly of women victim-survivors.

Criminalization of coercive control and psychological abuse as a strategy to respond to violence against women is being debated in many countries across the globe. In the United Kingdom, United States, and Australia, the criminalization of coercive control and nonphysical forms of abuse are high on national agendas (Wangmann, 2022). Debates about the criminalization of these forms of abuse have motivated renewed attention on the role of the criminal law as a response to violence against women. Although coercive control has been described and defined in different ways (Barlow & Walklate, 2022), Evan Stark's (2007) explanation is perhaps most cited in these recent debates. Stark (2007) described coercive control as a strategic pattern of behavior that is designed to exploit, control, create dependency, and dominate. He defined it as a liberty crime, the result being that the victim's everyday existence is micromanaged and her space for action in the world is limited and controlled by the abuser (Kelly et al., 2014). Such violence has significant impacts on women's "life projects" (Chapter 2). The criminalization of coercive control has the potential to criminalize forms of behavior not previously captured by the criminal law and therefore represents a significant expansion of the criminal law as a response to violence against women. For many people, including some victim-survivors who have campaigned for such laws (e.g., Gillespie, 2021), criminalizing coercive control is a positive development. Advocates for criminalization have argued that criminalizing coercive control ensures many of the invisible harms women experience as a result of intimate partner violence will be recognized and accounted for by the criminal law and therefore by the state (McMahon & McGorrery, 2016). Unlike most other offenses, criminalizing coercive control is designed to recognize *patterns* of abuse rather than one-off incidents of violence (Bettinson & Bishop, 2015) and has the potential to educate the public about this form of harm (Youngs, 2014; Chapter 1, this volume). However, others have urged caution and expressed concern about the criminalization of coercive control, explaining that it could be used to charge primary victim-survivors of intimate partner violence when they respond to such abuse and will be time consuming, complex, and difficult to successfully prosecute (see, inter alia, Tolmie, 2018; Walklate et al., 2018). The criminalization of coercive control is an expansion of state surveillance and power. Many women and their families have not benefitted from increased state surveillance (Bumiller, 2008). Such net widening often results in unequal application of the law; people from marginalized communities are likely to be overrepresented in charging rates and prosecutions. More specifically, evidence suggests marginalized women will be at heightened risk of being misidentified as perpetrators of coercive control (Goodmark, 2018; Gruber, 2020; Watego et al., 2021).

While incarceration rates of men in most countries continue to grow, in many jurisdictions women are the fastest growing segment of the incarcerated population (Fair & Walmsley, 2022). In Australia, the population of women in prison grew by 64% between 2009 and 2019, while the population of male prisoners grew by 45% (Australian Institute of Health and Welfare [AIHW], 2020). While First Nations people in Australia make up just 2.5% of the population, they make up over 20% of the Australian prison population, and First Nations women make up 33% of the female prison population in Australia (AIHW, 2020). Many people in custody are serving sentences for offenses related to domestic and family violence, but First Nations women are 39 times more likely than non–First Nations women to be convicted of a family violence–related offense (Chen, 2021). In the United States, the story is similar. In the United States, there has been a 500% increase in the number of people in prison since the 1980s (The Sentencing Project, 2022b). In the United States, Black people are almost five times more likely to be incarcerated than white people, and the rise of imprisonment of women has grown rapidly since 1980 (The Sentencing Project, 2022a). Throughout the 1990s states across the United States introduced mandatory arrest policies for crimes involving intimate partner violence. These policies contributed to increased arrests of both men and women, but research has since shown that they had the most impact on women, particularly women of color (Goodmark, 2018; Gruber, 2020, pp. 87–88; Richie, 2012).

The damaging impacts of imprisonment are now well known. Prison breaks up families. Employment postimprisonment is difficult to obtain and retain. Incarceration lessens people's self-respect, and some people acquire a wider knowledge of criminal activity in prison. Prisons are costly and highly detrimental to both physical and mental health (Liebling & Maruna, 2005). In the Australian context, Debbie Kilroy (2018, p. 264) described the ways in which prisons have "ravaged" First Nations families, with prison delivering a continuation of the same kinds of personal and institutional abuse incarcerated individuals experience outside of the prison system.

Arising out of these conversations about the impact of criminalization generally and the criminalization of coercive control specifically, we began to discuss the possibility of this collection at the beginning of 2021. Initially, we wrote to several of our colleagues around the world who were writing about criminal system responses to violence against women to test interest in the possibility of bringing together a collection of this scope. Responses were positive, and we initially hoped to meet in person together, but the Covid-19 pandemic intervened. Instead, we held several smaller online workshops to discuss possible contributions across the course of 2022.

In recognition of the continued high rates of the victimization of women, our focus in this book is on the criminalization of violence against women. Given violence against women is predominantly carried out by the woman's partner or former partner in her home, it is not surprising that many of the chapters in this collection focus on intimate partner violence; however, the situatedness of this form of violence within broader social norms and structures and in the shadow of state power is also considered in several contributions. When inviting contributions, we did not define the concept of criminalization, and the resulting contributions speak to a wide, or "thick" (McNamara et al., 2018, p. 93) understanding of criminalization generally as well as more focused debates surrounding the criminalization of specific forms of violence. The chapters examine the creation and enforcement of offenses, the setting and imposition of penalties and sentences, and the operation of criminal procedures more broadly, including how police and judicial officers use their powers in response to criminal charges. As a result, the contributions reflect a wide range of views. For some, questions persist about the extent to which male violence is met with impunity, resulting in calls for more, not less, criminalization (see also Women's Safety and Justice Taskforce, 2021, p. 41). In many countries, experimentation with the development of new forms of criminal offenses, sentencing, and police and judicial powers is central to the state response to violence against women. Offenses including coercive control and psychological abuse, forms of technology-facilitated abuse, and nonfatal strangulation have been introduced across several jurisdictions in recent years, and some of the contributions here engage with those reforms from a range of different perspectives.

Some contributions recognize the ongoing problems with criminalization but argue that criminalization itself is not the problem; rather, it is how the underlying rules and powers of the legal system are enforced and implemented that are responsible for the negative consequences experienced by women victim-survivors. Such implementation problems, as Rosemary Hunter (2006) has argued, are often encountered in feminist-informed law reforms. Nevertheless, some of our authors hold out hope that more extensive education and training of criminal legal system participants, including police, prosecutors, lawyers, and judicial officers, could change the way criminal laws are enforced and implemented, making it possible for criminalization to result in improved outcomes for women without the need to radically alter the criminalization approach. In other quarters, the movement to defund the police and abolish prisons is gaining ground where questions persist about the implementation and effectiveness of criminalization as a strategy and its impact on marginalized groups (Davis et al., 2022). Sometimes referred to as the "abolition movement," this broader ambition is to dismantle punitive state institutions (including not only the police and prisons, but also immigration and child protection systems) as the way of dealing with social problems and to redirect resources to mechanisms that address poverty and homelessness and to promote social cohesiveness (Baldry et al., 2015; Davis et al., 2022; Schenwar & Law, 2020).

Other contributions within this collection challenge this agenda, arguing that law will continue to have an impact on women's lives; if the law is not changed, it will continue to neglect women's injuries and fail to provide redress (McGlynn, 2022). Rather than throwing out criminalization as a strategy, Clare McGlynn, for example, argued for fundamental reform from the inside, calling for "more expressive, educative, and rehabilitative approaches" to criminal justice (2022, p. 2). What form these approaches could take is reflected in different ways across the chapters in this collection.

Despite the renewed debates about the role of criminalization as a response to violence against women, there are still many unresolved questions about this approach. Some of the questions that are addressed in this collection include the following: Is criminalization ever an appropriate response to violence against women—and if so, when? Is criminalization effective in curtailing violence? Who bears the consequences of criminalization, and when are those consequences justified? Should we be thinking about less, rather than more, criminalization or thinking about criminalization differently? What tensions or dilemmas emerge when criminal law, family law, and social policy speak or fail to speak to each other? What role do histories of colonization play in the approach to criminalizing violence against women? As Lacey (2013) reminded us, there is a political-economic framework underpinning the success or otherwise of any process of criminalization, and the comparative lessons emerging from this edited collection illustrate this observation well.

The answers to these questions depend on the diversity of aspirations about what criminalization can achieve and the history and context where these debates are playing out. It is clear that the criminalization path has been unfolding differently and in nuanced and nonlinear ways across the globe (Fitz-Gibbon & Walklate, 2021, p. ii). This collection uses a comparative lens to explore the scope, impact, and alternatives to criminalization in the response to different forms of violence against women in domestic contexts across the Global North and South. While we recognize the difficulties of transferring laws and policies across diverse communities and context, each with different resources, geography, and histories, we also recognize the importance of learning from each other, both regarding the approaches that might be promising in using criminalization to recognize and respond to the harms of violence against women and to learn from each other's missteps.

THIS COLLECTION: COMPOSITION AND CONNECTION

This book is structured in three sections. The first section broadly explores how criminalization is being used in new ways to deal with long-recognized as well as emerging forms of violence against women. The chapters included in this section grapple with when criminalization might be justified and highlight the benefits and risks of criminalizing particular forms of violence against women. As discussed, the nonphysical forms of abuse associated with intimate partner violence have often escaped the purview of criminal law, yet they are common (Boxall & Morgan, 2021), and victim-survivors often claim that their experiences of coercive and controlling behaviors were the "worst part" of their experience of abuse (Douglas, 2021; McGorrery & McMahon, 2021). Kate Fitz-Gibbon and colleagues (Chapter 1) draw on the voices of Australian victim-survivors to explore views on the criminalization of coercive control and what criminalizing coercive control may achieve. Their chapter draws out the complex expectations that victim-survivors hold for criminalization. While many victim-survivors expect denunciation and increased community awareness will result from criminalization, they are less confident that criminalization will deliver improved safety and justice outcomes for victim-survivors.

The criminalization of psychological violence in Brazil is explored by Thiago de Ávila in Chapter 2. de Ávila refers to psychological violence as a form of "symbolic violence" and recognizes that criminalization carries not only benefits, including greater recognition, but also risks, including the undermining of prevention strategies in favor of criminalization. Using the behavior of "downblousing," where someone takes an image or video down a woman's clothing to capture their breasts, cleavage, or bra (Law Commission, 2021, para. 2.26) as a case study, in Chapter 3 Clare McGlynn explores when such behavior should be criminalized. McGlynn highlights the continuum (Kelly, 1988) of behaviors underpinning women's experiences of downblousing and other forms of image-based abuse, at the same time observing that criminal law requires quite specific definitions of crime. Both de Ávila and McGlynn point out that the law's requirement for definitional specificity can invisibilize the experiences of some women victim-survivors when the violence and harm they experience does not neatly fit within criminal law definitions. Yet, McGlynn contends that new criminal offenses should be introduced in some cases in recognition of women's particular experiences of violence and harm as part of their search for justice.

Turning the focus to existing criminal law offenses, Ulrika Andersson is interested in how to best assess the operation of crimes that respond to violence against women. Using the crime of negligent rape as her exemplar, in Chapter 4 Andersson identifies three intertwined factors: legal presumptions (e.g., evidence and legal definitions); criminal and procedural principles (e.g., the burden of proof); and implicit premises (focused on gender and sexuality). Andersson argues these factors should be used to analyze and evaluate offenses that criminalize violence against women. In Chapter 5, Jojiana Cokanasiga considers how the introduction of criminal law is rooted in Fiji's colonial history. Her chapter highlights the stickiness of criminal law, showing that despite the introduction of domestic violence protection order laws in Fiji, police continue to default to punitive criminal responses when addressing intimate partner abuse.

The chapters in the second part of this collection directly confront the challenges and consequences of criminalization. In this section, the authors reflect on who bears the greatest burden of the impacts of criminalization, with the analyses demonstrating the range of ways in which legislative reform alone routinely fails to live up to its promise of justice and safety for women victim-survivors of violence. In Chapter 6, Kyllie Cripps highlights the heavy toll paid by First Nations women in Australia who are criminalized when they kill their partners to save themselves. Cripps demonstrates how legislative reforms appear on the surface to deliver justice (e.g., through expanded understandings of self-defense). Her analysis also finds, however, that these reforms are often ineffectual in practice and fail to "hear" women's stories, especially the stories of First Nations women in Australia and other colonized states. In Chapter 7, Leigh Goodmark extends this analysis to the United States, drawing attention to the experience of Maddesyn George of the Colville Nation tribe. Kristopher Graber, a white man and George's meth dealer, raped George, then came looking for her the next day. She shot him in self-defense. Goodmark's analysis explains how the criminalization of gender-based violence has failed to protect Native women, while creating a context where people like George are found to be "imperfect victims" (Goodmark, 2023) who cannot rely on the state to protect them but are punished when they act to protect themselves.

The three chapters that follow turn their attention to actors within the legal system, both judges and police, to explore how these actors contribute to the negative experiences of victim-survivors who engage with the criminal legal system. These chapters interrogate the possibility that the law is "good," but that system actors are failing to properly implement it. In Chapter 8, Elisabeth McDonald examines trials involving allegations of intimate partner rape to explore the impact of judges' behavior on the rape complainant's experience of the trial. McDonald argues that if judges used their powers in a uniform and consistent way to communicate with the complainant, control inappropriate questioning, and direct juries regarding the application of myths and stereotypes about rape, the complainant's experience would be improved. This argument is reminiscent of Ann Genovese's faith in the power of judges to be feminist. Regarding the possibility of feminist judging, Genovese has said:

> By taking law's doctrines and techniques seriously, feminist jurists have shown many times that to change law—to reform its practice or alter its perceptions—does not necessarily involve a polemical position that would force feminists to sit outside the door of the court. Instead, the task has been to master law, to understand its rehearsed movements and its rules of interpretation, as well as to monitor its lived effects. (Genovese, 2014, p. 378)

Ellen Reeves (Chapter 9) and Michele Burman and colleagues (Chapter 10) examine the adequacy of police responses in the context of violence against women. Reeves draws on interviews with magistrates and legal practitioners in Victoria, Australia, to better understand why police officers commonly misidentify victim-survivors of family violence as the primary perpetrators of violence. She finds that while some police apply risk assessment policies too rigidly, others attempt to circumvent risk minimization policies, relying on their own biases and stereotypes of who is a "genuine" victim. Reeves finds both approaches contribute to the misidentification problem, with women from marginalized backgrounds most likely to be misidentified. In Chapter 10 Burman and colleagues also highlight the gap between the aspirations of law and policy versus practical application. They report on their interviews with police officers in Scotland to consider how the new Scottish domestic abuse offense *Domestic Abuse (Scotland) Act 2018* has influenced police practice. They find police have mixed responses to the new law, considering it both welcome and a burden. While Burman and colleagues point to growing confidence of police to recognize the abusive behavior offense, the authors register their concerns about the broad investigation police must make to gather evidence of the abusive behavior and the increased impacts and burdens this evidence-gathering process places on survivors. In Chapter 11, the final chapter in this section, Heather Douglas and Robin Fitzgerald explore the implementation of the nonfatal strangulation offense in Queensland, Australia. Through an analysis of court and prosecution service data, the authors show that sentences of imprisonment are almost inevitable, and that First Nations Australians are disproportionately prosecuted for the new offense. The likelihood of incarceration has resulted in many victim-survivors attempting to withdraw from the prosecution. The authors argue not for the decriminalization of nonfatal strangulation, suggesting criminalization has been important in raising awareness of its harms, but for more creative approaches to sentencing that untangle criminalization from incarceration.

The chapters in Part III attempt to make sense of criminalization by interrogating the implications of legislating human rights standards and challenging the capability of the state to deliver justice to victim-survivors of intimate partner violence. In Chapter 12, Silvana Tapia Tapia argues that the human rights–focused criminalization of violence, or "human rights penalty," has failed to respond adequately to violence against women. Drawing on the case study of Ecuador, Tapia Tapia shows how human rights penalty has failed to reduce violence against women, has resulted in reduced services being available to victim-survivors, and has marginalized alternative approaches to justice that might better respond to their needs. Gema Varona (Chapter 13) similarly highlights the challenge of realizing human rights standards through legislation. Varona explores the ambivalent results of legislating intersectionality with the aim of achieving human rights for women in Spain. Varona shows how legislating intersectionality has resulted in it being an add-on rather than reconstitutive of identity in the way that Crenshaw (1991) intended. Understood in the way imagined by Crenshaw, intersectionality would ensure that the diversity of women's lives could be seen in full, and their experiences of violence could be properly understood. Instead, legislation has reduced intersectionality to a notion of formal equality that is ultimately of little assistance to many women victim-survivors and is, in some cases, detrimental.

In Chapter 14, Aparna Polavarapu considers state interventions in a different context. Polavarapu highlights the promise of restorative justice approaches in repairing the harm of gender-based violence and in preventing future harm. However, Polavarapu shows how the very success of restorative justice as an alternative to the traumatic criminal trial process has, ironically, led to some restorative justice programs collaborating with the criminal system and the state. She expresses caution about this direction. In Chapter 15, Balawyn Jones draws on fieldwork conducted in Banda Aceh, Indonesia, in developing the concept of bureaucratic violence. Among other things, bureaucratic violence is reflected in a lack of coordination between various parts of government that impedes the implementation of the law and ultimately results in the state failing to protect victims of domestic violence. Jones draws attention to Indonesia's failure to properly fund and support safe houses for victims or to provide perpetrator rehabilitation programs as aspects of bureaucratic violence. Jones argues that the state should be held accountable for the bureaucratic violence it inflicts when it fails to protect victims.

In the final chapter, Niveditha Menon also explores the role of the state and considers the importance of how we understand the concept of justice. In the context of India, Menon explains that government interest in listening to the voices of women appears to have waned, and government agencies have moved away from providing justice to women to enabling justice mechanisms. To show how this shift plays out, Menon explores the role of the police in returning "missing" women to their families (in circumstances where women have likely escaped violent households). Menon highlights the role of the police as, effectively, the executive arm of the state. Looking for justice elsewhere, Menon focuses on Nari Adalats (Women's Courts) as offering the potential to provide a space for women to find justice outside the state.

We are acutely aware that our structure only reflects some of the connections and engagements across and between the chapters. There are many other ways of connecting the chapters contained in this collection. For example, Varona (Chapter 13), Menon (Chapter 16), and Fitz-Gibbon and colleagues (Chapter 1) emphasize the role of women generally and victim-survivors particularly in articulating the kind of justice they want: a vision of justice that does not always match that presumed by advocates, policymakers, and those working within the criminal legal system. Several chapters, including Burman and colleagues (Chapter 10), Cokanasiga (Chapter 5), and Menon (Chapter 16) highlight the pivotal role of the police in implementing criminal responses and the consequences of police contact for women victim-survivors. Other chapters, notably the contributions of Cripps (Chapter 6) and Goodmark (Chapter 7), point to the challenges that different ways of thinking about what counts as justice pose for agendas focused on criminalization within conventional criminal systems. Further, the challenges posed for the practice of justice in terms of what counts as evidence (McGlynn Chapter 3) and/or proof (Andersson Chapter 4) add nuance to thinking about criminalization. Several chapters suggest thinking outside of the carceral box (Goodmark Chapter 7; Polavarapu Chapter 14; and Douglas and Fitzgerald Chapter 11). That women in a wide range of differently constructed jurisdictions continue to be constituted as the unexpected subjects of the law is also a central theme to several of these contributions (Menon, Chapter 16; Cripps Chapter 6). Thus, the ordering of this collection is not intended to be dispositive: The chapters should be read and considered within and across the three sections to provoke further thought and debate.

CONCLUSION

While the contributions in this collection arrive at diverse positions on the place and future of the criminalization of different forms of violence against women, the contributions are aligned insofar as they concur that criminalization on its own is an imperfect response. Indeed, some time ago Carol Smart (1989) urged feminists to decenter the law, and many of the contributions within this collection repeat that call. In so doing, the volume demonstrates the pitfalls of criminalization in different countries and the range of ways in which the recourse to criminal law—a primary response to violence against women for over four decades now—continues to fail the safety and justice needs of victim-survivors. We recognize that some voices continue to be missing or are invisibilized in these debates. While one collection cannot examine the diverse experiences of all communities globally, we have sought to bring an intersectional lens to these debates. Although many of our chapters reflect the experiences of cisgender women, for example, we recognize both implicitly and explicitly that trans women experience particularly high rates of violence and abuse (Messinger & Guadalupe-Diaz, 2020). Similarly, we are cognizant of the disparate impact of criminalization on communities as a function of identity, with low-income communities of color most likely to experience negative outcomes in interactions with the criminal system, at the same time looking to that system as one of the only, if not the only, responses available to address the violence they experience.

While the opening chapter of this collection draws directly from the voices of victim-survivors, in many instances the expansion of the criminal law has occurred *for* victim-survivors but largely without their direct input. The failure to both see and genuinely hear the justice and safety needs of victim-survivors has been a consistent shortcoming of law reform processes in this space. Questions remain, of course, concerning how to address this shortcoming in ways that are both effective and meaningful (Peacock, 2022). As MacIntyre (1988) pointed out some time ago, there are many justices and many rationalities. How to square the demands that the recognition of this creates within the confines of criminal justice remains moot.

By bringing together this collection our objective has been to advance the evidence base on which debates surrounding the criminalization of violence against women draw globally. While we acknowledge the importance of context and community, we also recognize the value of sharing learnings within and across jurisdictions. This collection seeks to do that. It also aims to offer a body of work that is neither entirely in support of nor opposed to criminalization as the primary response to violence against women. Debates surrounding the criminalization of different forms of violence against women sometimes lack nuance, with advocates, scholars, and practitioners feeling pressured to express unequivocal support for, or opposition to, criminalization. Our aim has been to create a space for contributors to explore the complexities and nuances of criminalization, its objectives, and its impacts. The goals of various sectors of the antiviolence community have typically been aligned: to enhance justice and safety outcomes for women victim-survivors. However, as the chapters contained within this collection demonstrate, achieving those goals using criminalization can be fraught, and the outcomes of criminalization are neither simple nor always straightforward. As a primary strategy, criminalization is failing to deliver for women victim-survivors. The question that lingers is to what extent states should steer away from the criminal law in devising improved responses to violence against women.

REFERENCES

Australian Institute of Health and Welfare (AIHW). (2020). The health and welfare of women in Australia's prisons. https://www.aihw.gov.au/reports/prisoners/health-and-welfare-of-women-in-prison/summary

Baldry, E., Carlton, B., & Cunneen, C. (2015). Abolitionism and the paradox of penal reform in Australia: Indigenous women, colonial patriarchy and co-option. *Social Justice*, 3(137), 168–169. https://www.jstor.org/stable/24361638#metadata_info_tab_contents

Barlow, C., & Walklate, S. (2022). *Coercive control*. Routledge.

Bettinson, V., & Bishop, C. (2015). Is the creation of a discrete offence of coercive control necessary to combat domestic violence? *Northern Ireland Law Quarterly*, 66(2), 179–197. https://heinonline.org/HOL/LandingPage?handle=hein.journals/nilq66&div=15&id=&page=

Boxall, H., & Morgan, A. (2021). Experiences of coercive control among Australian women. Australian Institute of Criminology. https://www.aic.gov.au/sites/default/files/2021-03/sb30_experiences_of_coercive_control_among_australian_women_v2.pdf

Bumiller, K. (2008). *In an abusive state: How neoliberalism appropriated the feminist movement against sexual violence*. Duke University Press.

Chen, D. (2021). Domestic violence responses for incarcerated Indigenous women in Australia & New Zealand. Indigenous Justice Clearinghouse. https://www.indigenousjustice.gov.au/wp-content/uploads/mp/files/publications/files/dv-responses-for-incarcerated-indigenous-women-final.pdf

Crenshaw, K. (1991). Mapping the margins: Intersectionality, identity politics, and violence against women of color. *Stanford Law Review*, 43, 1241–99. https://doi.org/10.2307/1229039

Davis, A., Dent, G., Meiners, E., & Ritchie, B. (2022). *Abolition. Feminism. Now*. Hamish Hamilton.

Domestic Abuse (Scotland) Act 2018. Scotland. https://www.legislation.gov.uk/asp/2018/5/contents/enacted

Douglas, H. (2021). *Women, intimate partner violence and the law*. Oxford University Press.

Douglas, H., & Fitzgerald, R. (2018). The domestic violence protection order system as entry to the criminal justice system for Aboriginal and Torres Strait Islander people. *International Journal for Crime, Justice and Social Democracy, 7*(3), 41–57. https://doi.org/10.5204/ijcjsd.v7i3.499

Fair, H., & Walmsley, R. (2022). World female imprisonment list. Institute of Crime Justice Policy Research. https://www.prisonstudies.org/sites/default/files/resources/downloads/world_female_imprisonment_list_5th_edition.pdf

Fitz-Gibbon, K., & Walklate, S. (2021). Why criminalise coercive control? The complicity of the criminal law in punishing women through furthering the power of the state. *International Journal for Crime, Justice and Social Democracy, 10*(4), 1–12. https://doi.org/10.5204/ijcjsd.1829

Genovese, A. (2014). Commentary: Goode and Goode. In H. Douglas, F. Bartlett, & T. Luker (Eds.), *Australian feminist judgments: Righting and rewriting law*. Hart Publishing.

Gillespie, E. (2021). Hannah Clarke's parents recognised for their coercive control campaign. SBS, 12 November. https://www.sbs.com.au/news/article/hannah-clarkes-parents-recognised-for-their-coercive-control-campaign/ijau9rr63

Goodmark, L. (2018). *Decriminalizing domestic violence: A balanced approach to intimate partner violence*. University of California Press.

Goodmark, L. (2021). Gender-based violence, law reform, and the criminalization of survivors of violence. *International Journal for Crime Justice and Social Democracy, 10*(4), 13–25. https://doi.org/10.5204/ijcjsd.1994

Goodmark, L. (2023). *Imperfect victims: Criminalized survivors and the promise of abolition feminism*. University of California Press.

Gruber, A. (2020). *The feminist war on crime: The unexpected role of women's liberation in mass incarceration*. University of California Press.

Hunter, R. (2006). Narrative of domestic violence. *Sydney Law Review, 28*(4), 733–776. http://classic.austlii.edu.au/au/journals/SydLawRw/2006/31.html

Kelly, L. (1988). *Surviving sexual violence*. Polity.

Kelly, L., Sharp, N., & Klein, R. (2014). *Finding the costs of freedom: How women and children rebuild their lives after domestic violence*. Solace Women's Aid. http://cwasu-org.stackstaging.com/wp-content/uploads/2019/07/Costs_of_Freedom_Report_-_SWA.pdf

Kilroy, D. (2018). Imagining abolition: Thinking outside the prison bars. *Griffith Review, 60*, 264–270. https://www.griffithreview.com/articles/imagining-abolition-sisters-inside-debbie-kilroy/

Lacey, N. (2013). The rule of law and the political economy of criminalisation: An agenda for research. *Punishment & Society, 15*(4), 349–366. https://doi.org/10.1177/1462474513500619

Law Commission. (2021). *Intimate Image Abuse: A consultation paper*. Law Commission.

Liebling, A., & Maruna, S. (2005). Introduction: The effects of imprisonment revisited. In A. Liebling & S. Maruna (Eds.), *The effects of imprisonment*. Routledge.

MacIntyre, A. (1988). *Whose justice? Which rationality?* University of Notre Dame Press

McGlynn, C. (2022). Challenging anti-carceral feminism: Criminalisation, justice and continuum thinking. *Women's Studies International Forum, 93*, 102614. https://doi.org/10.1016/j.wsif.2022.102614

McGorrery, P., & McMahon, M. (2021). Criminalising the "worst part": Operationalising the offence of coercive control in England and Wales. *Criminal Law Review, 11*, 957–965.

McMahon, M., & McGorrery, P. (2016). Criminalising coercive control: The next step in the prosecution of family violence. *Alternative Law Journal, 41*(2), 98–101. https://doi.org/10.1177/1037969X1604100206

McNamara, L., Quilter, J., Hogg, R., Douglas, H., Loughnan, A., & Brown, D. (2018). Theorising criminalisation: The value of a modalities approach. *International Journal for Crime, Justice and Social Democracy, 7*(3), 91–121. https://doi.org/10.5204/ijcjsd.v7i3.511

Messinger, A., & Guadalupe-Diaz, X. (2020). *Transgender intimate partner violence: A comprehensive introduction*. New York University Press.

Nancarrow, H. (2019) *Unintended consequences of domestic violence law: Gendered aspirations and racialised realities*. Palgrave.

Peacock, D. (2022). Moving beyond a reliance on criminal legal strategies to address the root causes of domestic and sexual violence. *Violence Against Women, 28*(8), 189–1907. https://doi.org/10.1177/10778012221086002

Richie, B. (2012). *Arrested justice: Black women, violence, and America's prison nation*. New York University Press.

Reeves, E. (2021). "'I'm not at all protected and I think other women should know that, that they're not protected either": Victim–survivors' experiences of "misidentification" in Victoria's family violence system. *International Journal for Crime Justice and Social Democracy, 10*(4), 39–51. https://doi.org/10.5204/ijcjsd.1992

Schenwar, M., & Law, V. (2020). *Prison by any other name: The harmful consequences of popular reforms*. New Press.

The Sentencing Project. (2022a). Incarcerated women and girls. https://www.sentencingproject.org/app/uploads/2022/11/Incarcerated-Women-and-Girls.pdf

The Sentencing Project. (2022b). Prison population over time. https://www.sentencingproject.org/research/

Smart, C. (1989). *Feminism and the power of the law*. Routledge.

Stark, E. (2007). *Coercive control: The entrapment of women in personal life*. Oxford University Press.

Tolmie, J. (2018). Coercive control: To criminalize or not to criminalize? *Criminology & Criminal Justice, 18*(1), 50–66. https://doi.org/10.1177/1748895817746712

Walklate, S., & Fitz-Gibbon, K. (2021). Why criminalise coercive control? The complicity of the criminal law in punishing women through furthering the power of the state. *International Journal for Crime, Justice and Social Democracy, 10*(4), 1–12 https://doi.org/10.5204/ijcjsd.1829

Walklate, S., Fitz-Gibbon, K., & McCulloch, J. (2018). Is more law the answer? Seeking justice for victims of intimate partner violence through the reform of legal categories. *Criminology and Criminal Justice*, *18*(1), 115–131. https://doi.org/10.1177/1748895818 7728561

Wangmann, J. (2022). Law reform processes and criminalising coercive control. *Australian Feminist Law Journal*, *48*(1), 57–86. https://doi.org/10.1080/13200 968.2022.2138186

Watego, C., Macoun, A., Singh, D., & Strakosch, E. (2021, May 25). Carceral feminism and coercive control: When Indigenous women aren't seen as ideal victims, witnesses or women. *The Conversation*. https://theconversation.com/carceral-feminism-and-coercive-control-when-indigenous-women-arent-seen-as-ideal-victims-witnesses-or-women-161091

Women's Safety and Justice Taskforce. (2021). *Hear her voice: Report 1*. Women's Safety and Justice Taskforce. https://www.womenstaskforce.qld.gov.au/__data/assets/pdf_f ile/0013/700600/volume-1-exectutive-summary-and-introduction.pdf

Youngs, J. (2014). Domestic violence and criminal law: Reconceptualising reform. *Journal of Criminal Law*, *79*(1), 55–70. https://doi.org/10.1177/0022018314566746

PART 1

The Criminalization Agenda

"New" Approaches to Old Problems

1

The Criminalization of Coercive Control

The Benefits and Risks of Criminalization From the Vantage of Victim-Survivors

KATE FITZ-GIBBON, SANDRA WALKLATE,
SILKE MEYER, AND ELLEN REEVES ■

INTRODUCTION

There has been significant debate and law reform activity over the last decade surrounding the adequacy of responses to nonphysical forms of domestic and family violence (DFV). Within this, coercive control has become a central focus, with policymakers, practitioners, advocates, and academics scrutinizing the degree to which current responses to coercive control—which in Australia remain largely outside of the realm of the criminal law—are adequate. Coercive control is a term used to capture the long-term, ongoing nature of a wide range of forms of violence that are not exclusively physical but can pervade an individual's daily life with devastating impact (Hamberger et al., 2017; Stark, 2007).

Debates surrounding whether coercive and controlling behaviors should form the focus of a stand-alone criminal offense have gained

Kate Fitz-Gibbon, Sandra Walklate, Silke Meyer, and Ellen Reeves, *The Criminalization of Coercive Control* In: *The Criminalization of Violence Against Women*. Edited by: Heather Douglas, Kate Fitz-Gibbon, Leigh Goodmark, and Sandra Walklate, Oxford University Press. © Oxford University Press 2024. DOI: 10.1093/oso/9780197651841.003.0002 momentum globally (Walklate & Fitz-Gibbon, 2019). Concerningly, these debates have largely occurred in the absence of any significant evidence detailing the views and experiences of victim-survivors of DFV. Given the well-documented reluctance of victim-survivors to engage in the criminal justice process (see, inter alia, Hoyle & Sanders, 2000; Nancarrow, 2019), the absence of victim-survivor voices represents a fundamental evidential gap in contemporary knowledge and has allowed an argument for criminalization to advance on behalf of, but not informed directly by, victim-survivors themselves.

Drawing on the findings of a national survey of victim-survivors' views on the criminalization of coercive control in Australia, this chapter addresses that gap in current understandings. Privileging the voices of victim-survivors of coercive control, we explore their views on the role of law, including their views on the benefits of criminalizing coercive control, perceived risks, as well as the (potential) impacts of criminalization on justice and safety outcomes for victim-survivors of DFV.

DEBATES SURROUNDING THE CRIMINALIZATION OF COERCIVE CONTROL

New criminal offenses of coercive control have been introduced to varying degrees over the last 10 years across the United Kingdom, Europe, and Australia (Barlow & Walklate, 2022). While these offenses have taken varied forms, at the core of each has been an argument that a new category of criminal offense is necessary to capture a pattern of abusive behaviors the law is otherwise incapable of responding to (Quilter, 2020).

In 2015, a new offense of "controlling or coercive behavior" was introduced in England and Wales (Section 76 of the Serious Crime Act 2015). This offense, as defined in law at present, is gender neutral and limited to behavior between persons in a current intimate relationship and/or who live together (Home Office, 2015). The offense covers a wide range of behaviors and draws directly on the work of Stark (2007). Early evaluations of the English legislation have pointed to problems for front-line police officers in "seeing" coercive control (Wiener, 2017) in practitioner understandings of coercive control more generally and problems associated with evidential difficulties (Bishop & Bettinson, 2018). Despite these mixed evaluations, similar offenses have continued to emerge in nearby jurisdictions, including Scotland (Domestic Abuse [Scotland] Act 2018; see also Burman et al., 2023) and Ireland (Section 39, Domestic Violence Act 2018).

In Australia, in the last 10 years there has been unprecedented attention on improving DFV policy and practices. There have been numerous reviews conducted at the national and state levels (see, inter alia, Royal Commission Into Family Violence, 2016; Special Taskforce on Domestic and Family Violence, 2015; Women's Safety and Justice Taskforce, 2021), which have revealed significant limitations in legal responses to DFV and the need to develop new policies and practices to better respond to perpetrators and ensure the safety of victim-survivors.

Within this political context and climate of reform, and in the wake of several high-profile intimate partner homicide cases (see, e.g., Bentley, 2022), there has been increasing debate surrounding the need to create a specific criminal offense of coercive control. While coercive and controlling behaviors are recognized as abuse in the definition of DFV in civil law in most Australian states and territories, Tasmania is the only Australian jurisdiction to date to have introduced a specific criminal offense to cover this form of DFV (McMahon & McGorrery, 2016).

The absence of coercive control in the form of a specific criminal offense across other Australian jurisdictions has animated significant calls for reform. Those advocating for criminalization have argued that the law sets the standard for acceptable and unacceptable behavior and that the lack of a criminal offense has limited women's help-seeking options and minimized perpetrator accountability (McMahon & McGorrery, 2020). Other advocates and scholars have urged caution, noting that law reforms introduced to improve responses to different forms of violence against women have historically brought about unintended consequences that have undermined women's access to justice (see, inter alia, Walklate et al., 2018). This remains an area of live debate and law reform discussion, with the Queensland and New South Wales governments recently committing to implementing an offense within the next 12 to 24 months (Caldwell, 2021; Department of Communities and Justice, 2021).

RESEARCH DESIGN

This chapter draws on data from a national survey of victim-survivor views on the criminalization of coercive control. The survey was aimed at adult Australians (aged 18 years and over) who had experienced coercive control in a DFV context. The survey combined a series of demographic questions with multiple-choice and open-ended questions. Participation in the survey was anonymous. The survey was administered via the Qualtrics platform online and was advertised on social media platforms (Twitter, LinkedIn) via relevant support services and community organizations and through the professional networks of the research team. All survey data were collected over a 6-week period in early 2021.[1]

1,261 individuals participated in the survey. In this chapter, we focus on female victim-survivor views on the criminalization of coercive control across Australia. Females comprised 81.2% of total survey respondents ($n = 1024$). Characteristics of the survey participant sample are presented in Table 1.1. Throughout this chapter, we present direct quotations to center the voices of victim-survivors; for each quotation we have identified the age range and sexual identity of the female participant.

VICTIM-SURVIVOR VIEWS ON THE CRIMINALIZATION OF COERCIVE CONTROL AS A CRIMINAL OFFENSE

The vast majority of survey participants supported the criminalization of coercive control. Table 1.2 presents responses to the multiple-choice question: "Which of the following statements matches most closely your views on making coercive control a criminal offense?"

Table 1.1 SURVEY PARTICIPANTS' CHARACTERISTICS

Demographic Category	Participants' Characteristics (%)
Sexual identity	Heterosexual (81%)
	Bisexual (9.5%)
	Queer (2%)
	Pansexual (2.5%)
	Lesbian (2%)
	Questioning (2%)
	Asexual (1%)
	Other (0.6%)
	Prefer not to say (2%)
Age	30 years old and under (8%)
	31–40 years old (23%)
	41–50 years old (35%)
	51–60 years old (24%)
	60 years or older (10%)
First Nations identity	Identified as Aboriginal and Torres Strait Islander (3%)
Disability	Identified as living with disability (18%)
Education (highest level of education)	Year 12 equivalent and less (16%)
	Technical and further education (TAFE) degree or undergraduate degree (47%)
	Postgraduate degree (34.5%)
Area of residence	Metropolitan (62%)
	Regional (26%)
	Rural (11%)
	Remote (less than 1%)

(*continued*)

Table 1.1 CONTINUED

Demographic Category	Participants' Characteristics (%)
State and territory lived in	Victoria (31%)
	Queensland (24%)
	New South Wales (23%)
	Western Australia (9%)
	South Australia (5.5%)
	Tasmania (3.8%)
	Australian Capital Territory (3%)
	Northern Territory (less than 1%)

Table 1.2 FEMALE PARTICIPANT VIEWS ON MAKING COERCIVE CONTROL A CRIMINAL OFFENSE (%, N)

Response Options	Participants	Participants Who Identified as Heterosexual	Participants Who Identified as Sexually Diverse
I believe coercive control should be a criminal offense	91.3%, 843	92%, 686	89%, 141
I do not believe coercive control should be a criminal offense	3.6%, 33	3%, 25	4.5%, 7
I do not have a view one way or the other	5.1%, 47	5%, 37	6.5%, 10

Victim-survivors who supported criminalization described this reform as "essential and very overdue," "vital and timely," and "imperative." Several participants communicated a sense of urgency surrounding the speed with which they would like to see this reform introduced. This sentiment is captured in the following quotations:

Do it ASAP please. (51–60, heterosexual)

It needs to be done NOW. It should have been done decades ago! (41–50, heterosexual)

We just need it criminalised urgently. So, we don't have more of these horrific deaths. (41–50, bisexual)

In contrast, those victim-survivors who opposed the criminalization of coercive control emphasized both the importance of focusing on other points of the system and the limits of criminal law reform. As captured in the remarks of one victim-survivor:

Because laws re gender-based violence already in existence do very little to keep victims safe. The system retraumatises and criminalises victims. A new, more complex law will not change this. . . . Marginalised people will get hurt and perpetrators will be emboldened further, just as they are with other DV and related laws. There are many more potent things we can do to address cc [coercive control]. (41–50, bisexual)

Survey participants who were in support of criminalization or who did "not have a view one way or the other" were asked what positive effect, if any, they thought an offense of coercive control would have. Participants were able to select as many options as applied. The results received are presented in Table 1.3.

Participants were most likely to believe that the criminalization of coercive control would improve community awareness that DFV is not only physical abuse/is more than physical types of violence and would send a clear message that this form of DFV was not acceptable. Participants were least likely to identify the delivery of improved safety outcomes and greater justice for victim-survivors as likely effects of the introduction of an offense of coercive control. The second half of this chapter examines the key themes to emerge from this question by unpacking the qualitative data received through open-ended survey questions.

Table 1.3 PARTICIPANT VIEWS ON WHAT EFFECT A CRIMINAL OFFENSE OF COERCIVE CONTROL WOULD HAVE (%, N)

Response Options	Female Participants	Female Participants Who Identified as Heterosexual (n = 829)	Female Participants Who Identified as Sexually Diverse (n = 179)
It will improve community awareness of this form of DFV	73.3%, 751	74%, 612	71.5%, 128
It will improve community awareness that DFV is not only physical abuse but also is more than physical types of violence	78.3%, 802	79%, 655	74%, 132
It will send a clear message that this form of DFV is not acceptable	76.2%, 780	77%, 639	72%, 129
It will allow police to respond to coercive control	73.1%, 749	74%, 615	66%, 118
It will ensure the criminal justice system takes coercive control seriously	71.5%, 732	72%, 598	67%, 120
It will improve victim/survivor safety	60.8%, 623	61.5%, 510	56%, 100
It will improve perpetrator accountability	65.5%, 671	66%, 549	61%, 109
It will allow the court to punish perpetrators for their behavior	65.4%, 670	66%, 550	60%, 107
It will bring greater justice for victim-survivors	60.4%, 619	61%, 504	57%, 102

Impact on Improving Community Awareness

One of the key benefits of criminalization identified by victim-survivors across this study was the opportunity to utilize a new criminal law to improve community awareness and understanding of nonphysical forms of intimate partner violence. Victim-survivors highlighted the need to raise community awareness of what is and is not acceptable behavior within the context of an intimate partner relationship and saw a new offense as a vital vehicle through which this could be achieved. As two victim-survivors explained:

> If it were criminalised, it would be well known that it's absolutely not ok. At present there are grey areas that our society finds acceptable ... mostly to do with skewed ideas on what constitutes a heathy [sic] relationship not to mention skewed ideas on what is acceptable for men and women. Criminalisation shows that on one level, we as a society know that coercive control is wrong. (41–50, heterosexual)

> I believe criminalising it will not only help the victims of the worst and most obvious instances of CC [coercive control], but in naming it and bringing awareness, it will educate many others and help the victims and perpetrators and couples of less extreme but still very damaging behaviour patterns understand that it is not acceptable behaviour. (51–60, heterosexual)

Importantly, victim-survivors emphasized the preventive element of raised community awareness as well as the potential to enhance informal support systems for victim-survivors. As two victim-survivors commented:

> I also feel if coercive control laws were in place—my situations would not have occurred because it would have been validated instead of silenced and been made invisible. (61 years or older, heterosexual)

> The best thing about creating the offence will be the discussion, lessons and community understanding of it. Knowing the behaviors

to look for would prevent victims staying in bad relationships and enable them to get help. I hope it would also discourage people when they realise that they are perpetrators, and they are the behaviours they frequently use against their partners and seek help for them to change. (61 years or older, heterosexual)

As captured here, there were several survey respondents who also identified raising awareness of unacceptable behaviors among perpetrators themselves as a benefit of criminalization.

Impact on Victim-Survivor Safety

Interestingly, despite 91.3% ($n = 843$) of the female sample supporting the criminalization of coercive control, only 60.8% ($n = 623$) of these participants and participants who did not "have a view one way or the other" believed that it would improve victim-survivor safety. Victim-survivors who did believe that the criminalization of coercive control would improve safety outcomes for victim-survivors expressed the view that it would enhance referral pathways and opportunities for victim-survivors to leave an abuser. Other victim-survivors identified the role of the criminal justice system in preventing escalation of violence and significant harms, as well as the need to ensure the law is equipped to hold coercive and controlling individuals criminally to account. As captured in the views of two victim-survivors:

> In many ways the scars are deeper than physical violence and I would like to see coercive control taken seriously. (61 years or older, heterosexual)

> The violence has to stop and the safety of victims has to be maintained with a legal system to make perpetrators accountable. (61 years or older, heterosexual)

As the two quotations demonstrate, a key benefit of criminal law reform in this space was seen to be the opportunity to enhance perpetrator accountability and to ensure serious responses to this form of DFV. We turn now to this focus.

Impact on Perpetrator Accountability and the Ability of the Justice System to Punish Perpetrators

Victim-survivors emphasized the opportunity that a new offense would offer in enhancing opportunities to hold perpetrators to account and to ensure that the outcomes of the justice system reflected the totality of victim-survivor experiences of DFV and the seriousness of that offending. As three victim-survivors explained:

> I may have if I would have thought that my claims were taken seriously and that there would have been some accountability for his actions. (51–60, heterosexual)

> I think it's important, I really think it will help, the DVO [domestic violence order] is such a craply [sic] policed act, like these guys get away with so many breaches I hear and I wasn't even successful at getting one unless I did it myself, we need some additional help!!!! (31–40, heterosexual)

> It needs to be taken more seriously. My life during this time affected my own mental health and is something that I still struggle with now. I feel that he walked away with no consequences for how my kids and I were treated. (51–60, heterosexual)

For some victim-survivors, criminalization of coercive control was viewed as an opportunity for their perpetrator to be punished by the system. Victim-survivors described why they supported an offense that would, in their view, increase the justice system's ability to punish perpetrators for this form of DFV:

> Anybody who treats one person badly to make them feel worthless deserves to be punished. (51–60, heterosexual)

> In terms of dark humour, if coercive control were criminalised, that would make my ex-husband who looks on himself as a "pillar of society," a criminal and I would find that highly amusing. (61 years or older, heterosexual)

There were, however, several participants who raised concerns about what impact criminalization and punishment would have on community populations overrepresented in the criminal justice system. These comments often focused specifically on the impact that widening the net of criminal behaviors would have on First Nations communities (see also Watego et al., 2021). As two victim-survivors commented:

> I am worried about the negative impacts on marginalised groups. I think we should be discussing defunding the police and looking at community options, not increasing the funding to a broken system. (31–40, queer)

> The criminal justice system currently incarcerates Indigenous Australians at one of the highest rates of any group in the world. Further criminalisation will only further colonisation. Criminalising coercive control is also going to impact people of colour who have much higher rates of criminalisation than white people. LGBTIQA+ communities will not be supported by criminalising coercive control. . . . I have zero faith in the police to support victim-survivors. (31–40, lesbian, queer)

This was the key reason that several victim-survivors did not support criminalization:

> Criminalising women is an issue. We see First Nations women and girls arrested for DFV, and this will be the same if CC is made an offence. (51–60, heterosexual)

Coercive control must not be criminalised. These laws will ensure the violence of policing continue against First Nations women. (51–60, heterosexual)

In addition to identifying the risks of overcriminalization, a number of victim-survivors raised concerns about how a new offense of coercive control may result in the misidentification of victim-survivors as the predominant aggressor. There has been increasing awareness in recent years of the risks and significant impacts of misidentification, whereby police misidentify a victim-survivor and/or where perpetrators directly apply for civil protection orders against victim-survivors in the courts (see also Chapter 9, this volume). Victim-survivors were particularly concerned that limited police understanding of nonphysical forms of violence would increase the risk of misidentification. As one victim-survivor explained:

I don't think the police could handle the ongoing and subtle nature of it. It would lead to women being falsely accused by abusers, who are really good at playing the victim. (51–60, heterosexual)

Several victim-survivors reflected specifically on their own experience, describing a fear that if an offense of coercive control had been in law at the time of their victimization that their perpetrator would have used it against them. As captured in the following quotation:

He would have used it against me due to my mental health. He probably would have been successful. He was allowed to hold me down while I was sedated by nursing staff after being told in a family meeting they were sending me home even after I'd stated the day before he wants me to die. He had the whole world believing I was mad, controlling, and violent. He'd call the police to arrest me on my mental health; he was successful. (41–50, heterosexual)

Other victim-survivors referred to the misidentification that already occurs in DFV matters, noting that the introduction of an offense of coercive control may increase the likelihood of misidentification. As one victim-survivor commented:

> I'm concerned that perpetrators will be able to turn it around and accuse victims like they currently do with dv and cause greater problems for women and children trying to survive abuse. (31–40, bisexual)

Recognition of the Limits of Law and the Negative Impacts of the Justice System on Victim-Survivors of DFV

Numerous victim-survivors expressed a recognition of the limits of the law in improving the safety of victim-survivors. This viewpoint is illustrated in the following three quotations:

> Until the justice system is reformed, and male abusers are actually held suitably accountable for their treatment of women, none of this will make a lickety-split of difference. (31–40, bisexual)

> We need better services and support for women escaping this abuse and strengthened ability to protect children from having to share custody with controlling abusive men. I don't think this type of law is what's going to help. (31–40, heterosexual)

> I'm not actually opposed to it being a criminal offence I'm unconvinced that it is the best strategy to make women like me safe or free. (51–60, prefer not to say)

Several victim-survivors identified a distrust of the ability of police officers to respond effectively and to enhance the safety of victim-survivors as central to why they felt the criminalization of coercive control would have limited impacts on victim-survivor safety. As two victim-survivors described:

> I don't believe the police would be supportive because it's a can of worms they never want to open. (51–60, heterosexual)

> I don't believe police and the justice system will be able to properly investigate, charge and prosecute coercive control. I do not believe that police or the justice system provide anything that helps victims ensure their wellbeing or safety. I believe that going through a police process ruins victims lives. I think it is irresponsible to ask victims to go to the police. (25–30, heterosexual)

Victim-survivors often reflected on their own experiences with the police as informing their views on the likelihood that an offense of coercive control would have positive impacts for victim-survivors. These reflections carried a strong focus on police training and the inadequacy of police responses that focus only on physical forms of DFV:

> Police are untrained even when it is law. They questioned me in front of my ex-partner. When police were called, I was told to keep quiet and even with everything that has happened the police will not take me seriously and will take his side every time whether the evidence is there or not. (31–40, heterosexual)

> The police don't act when there is physical violence and don't understand the dynamics of DV. Even with training I doubt that the criminal justice system and the actors within would have the understanding or ability to understand the dynamics of DV and how the law would be applied. (41–50, heterosexual)

Beyond policing, numerous victim-survivors reflected on the trauma of engaging with the criminal court process, recognizing that the criminalization of coercive control would likely necessitate victim-survivor input at trial. As three victim-survivors commented:

> I felt like I was going insane, and he had me believing I was. I'm not sure I'd be able to stand up and be cross examined with any sort of certainty. (31–40, heterosexual)

> The process would be so horrible because I was so mentally scattered and ashamed and easily upset/overwhelmed/teary. (25–30, heterosexual)

> The very nature of being cross examined is similar to gaslighting—abusive behaviours so I can imagine it could trigger significant trauma and other PTSD [post-traumatic stress disorder] symptoms such as disassociation—dysregulation for many people. (41–50, heterosexual)

The survey asked victim-survivors if they would have been willing to give evidence in court if a criminal offense of coercive control had been in place at the time of their victimization. Even when they had expressed support for criminalization, victim-survivors overwhelmingly expressed hesitance to provide evidence in court:

> At the time my self-esteem was so thoroughly destroyed that I would not have been able to. I would have thought that no one would believe me, and they'll believe him. Because he will present as confident and likeable, and I'd present as a crazy woman seeking to destroy a man's life and reputation. . . . He had made me believe that no one would believe me, after 20 years of that—I believed that too. (51–60, heterosexual)

> I was terrified for years and not in a fit mental state to do it. (51–60, heterosexual)

These views sat among a more general concern raised by victim-survivors about the challenge of "proving" coercive control beyond a reasonable doubt, the evidence standard required in Australian state and territory criminal justice systems. As two victim-survivors questioned:

Problem is—it's easy to show photos of bruises and broken bones. How do you explain a broken brain? (41–50, heterosexual)

I think it would be hard to prove—it would be "he said, she said." If there no [sic] physical violence and the person was fairly isolated in the first place, it could be hard to prove.... I just don't believe it will help a lot of women. (31–40, bisexual)

Even among some victim-survivors who expressed overall support for the criminalization of coercive control, questions were raised about how it would be evidenced in court. Another victim-survivor questioned:

It needs to happen. But the courts are not ready for it, they are already clogged up. So they need to be prepared for it and magistrates need to be educated.... They won't cope with coercive control without education, and this will be even more damaging to victims.... My big question is, how do you prove coercive control? Far too often I hear stories of the abuser playing the victim and slapping their victim with a retaliatory VRO [violence restraining order]. How will it work with coercive control? (41–50, heterosexual)

Several other victim-survivors expressed their resistance to providing evidence in court and acknowledged the traumatic nature of such processes. As two victim-survivors commented:

No way. I would not have been able to do this at the time. I was a complete mess at the time of leaving. Also, I would be absolutely terrified of seeing him. Even three years on I would be scared to see him. (31–40, pansexual)

If I was asked to voluntarily take the stand I would not of done it. I was still too scared of him and what would happen if I made him angry. Even with AVOs [apprehended violence orders] and police support it doesn't stop the years of fear they put you through. (41–50, heterosexual)

These views reflect the findings of numerous studies that have documented the trauma experienced by victim-survivors of different forms of gender-based violence through the court process, particularly during cross-examination (see, inter alia, Antonsdottir, 2018; Jordan, 2001; McBarnet, 1983).

Support for Criminalization Alongside a Recognition of the Risks

There were a number of survey respondents who described their own unwillingness to engage with the criminal justice system, or their own negative experiences of doing so, but still expressed support for the criminalization of coercive control. These victim-survivors believed that the criminalization of coercive control may improve the justice system responses for *other* victims of coercive control, despite their own unwillingness to engage with the system again, regardless of future reforms. This viewpoint is well captured in the reflections provided by one participant:

> Coercive control is so difficult to prove. He lies. I perceive that it would be hard for me to be believed that it was abusive behavior. The one thing I have going for my current FV court case is a recording he made of himself in private conversation with someone, by mistake at the end of a "shareholder meeting" when he didn't hit "Leave." He said many things like I've got an unfortunate mental disorder, "separation means she's in a lifeboat and if it sinks, she drowns" and he repeatedly said, "she scared," "she's frightened" and that's "scared talking" and she's going to get nothing (financially) and many other things. If I didn't have this recording, that got into his mind and where he took delight in causing me fear and his intention to make me financially destitute, I would not have much confidence in going through the family violence jurisdiction. The burden of proof for the

criminal jurisdiction is much higher. But if the law recognized the criminality of this behavior, women and children would be safer, the police would be empowered, and public awareness of this type of "invisible" abuse would be heightened. (51–60, heterosexual)

Other victim-survivors acknowledged the limits of the justice system and the risks that victim-survivors face during the legal process but held the view that the current system has to change, and that the criminalization of coercive control is a key step in this process:

Although I know there are risks for women to criminalising coercive control, I do think something has to change as currently women (and children) are not protected from men who use coercive control. (41–50, heterosexual)

I do genuinely fear for true victims being mistaken as the abuser, which is clearly evident with Indigenous women, but there needs to be a law against coercive control and serious training for police to understand what they're dealing with. (31–40, heterosexual)

CONCLUSION

This chapter presents the findings of a national study examining victim-survivor views on the criminalization of coercive control in Australia. The findings demonstrate strong support among victim-survivors surveyed for the criminalization of coercive control; however, the analysis of justifications for criminalization revealed complexities in the views held on the objectives of criminal law reform as well as the risks of criminalization. Survey respondents recognized the limits of the law and in many cases reflected on their own traumatic experiences of engaging with the criminal justice system; however, there was still an overarching desire to support reforms that *may* improve the delivery and accessibility of the justice system for future victim-survivors of DFV. Importantly, victim-survivors viewed the law as a key vehicle for enhancing community awareness of coercive and controlling behaviors.

These insights are essential in highlighting the areas of gray that have emerged in the criminalization of coercive control debate, whereby a nuanced analysis of victim-survivor experiences belies the complexity of understanding their views on this topic, the perceived benefits of criminalization alongside the fears of engaging with justice processes. Importantly, these viewpoints are arguably not unique to the criminalization of coercive control and assist in better understanding victim-survivors' confidence in, and views on, the role of criminalization more broadly. These acknowledgments are essential for understanding the safeguards that will need to be put in place alongside the introduction of any new criminal offenses.

Victim-survivors emphasized that the steps taken to criminalize coercive control must be informed by lived experience and those with DFV expertise to ensure that the reforms introduced are evidence based and trauma informed. As one victim-survivor commented:

> I think it's important to realise that there are valid concerns and risks in this approach, but I think they are outweighed by the benefits. If legislation is introduced, I hope it will be developed very carefully in consultation with survivors and IPV experts, including international experts from jurisdictions where cc [coercive control] legislation has already been introduced. (41–50, prefer not to say)

While it is not within the scope of this chapter to unpack the difference in views within and across different cohorts of victim-survivors who participated in this research, this chapter has sought to tease out the range of lived experience-informed views on the criminalization of coercive control. It demonstrates that there is no singular victim-survivor viewpoint or experience on this topic, and in doing so, highlights the importance of ongoing engagement with victim-survivors.

NOTE

1. Ethics approval for this study was received from the Monash University Human Research Ethics Committee.

REFERENCES

Antonsdottir, H. F. (2018). "A witness in my own case": Victim–survivors' views on the criminal justice process in Iceland. *Feminist Legal Studies, 26*, 307–330. https://doi.org/10.1007/s10691-018-9386-z

Barlow, C., & Walklate, S. (2022). *Coercive control*. Routledge.

Bentley, J. (2022, June29). *Findings of inquest into the death of Hannah Ashlie Clarke, Aaliyah Anne Baxter, Laianah Grace Baxter, Trey Rowan Charles Baxter, and Rowan Charles Baxter*. Coroners Court of Queensland.

Bishop, C., & Bettinson, V. (2018). Evidencing domestic violence, including behaviour that falls under the new offence of "controlling or coercive behaviour." *International Journal of Evidence & Proof, 22*(1), 3–29. https://doi.org/10.1177/1365712717725535

Burman, M., Brooks-Hay, O., & Friskney, R. (2023). Operationalizing coercive control: Early insights on the policing of the Domestic Abuse (Scotland) Act 2018. In H. Douglas, K. Fitz-Gibbon, S. Walklate, & L. Goodmark (Eds.), *The criminalization of violence against women: Comparative perspectives*. Oxford University Press.

Caldwell, F. (2021, December 2). New DV offence of coercive control set to become law in Queensland. *Sydney Morning Herald*.

Department of Communities and Justice. (2021, December 18). Government to criminalise coercive control. [Media release]. NSW Government.

Domestic Violence Act (IR) s 39 (2018). https://www.irishstatutebook.ie/eli/2018/act/6/section/39/enacted/en/html

Domestic Abuse (Scotland) Act (2018). https://www.legislation.gov.uk/asp/2018/5/contents/enacted

Hamberger, K., Larsen, S. E., & Lehrner, A. (2017). Coercive control in intimate partner violence. *Aggression and Violent Behavior, 37*, 1–11. https://doi.org/10.1016/j.avb.2017.08.003

Home Office. (2015). *Controlling or coercive behaviour in an intimate or family relationship: Statutory guidance framework*. Home Office.

Hoyle, C., & Sanders, A. (2000). Police response to domestic violence: From victim choice to victim empowerment? *British Journal of Criminology, 4*(1), 14–36. https://doi.org/10.1093/bjc/40.1.14

Jordan, J. (2001). World's apart? Women, rape and the police reporting process. *British Journal of Criminology, 41*(4), 679–706. https://doi.org/10.1093/bjc/41.4.679

McBarnet, D. (1983). Victim in the witness box—Confronting victimology's stereotype. *Contemporary Crisis, 7*(3), 293–303. https://doi.org/10.1007/BF00729162

McMahon, M., & McGorrery, P. (2016). Criminalising emotional abuse, intimidation and economic abuse in the context of family violence: The Tasmanian experience. *University of Tasmania Law Review, 35*(2), 1–22.

McMahon, M., & McGorrery, P. (Eds.). (2020). *Criminalising coercive control: Family violence and the criminal law.* Springer.

Nancarrow, H. (2019). *Unintended consequences of domestic violence law: Gendered aspirations and racialised realities.* Palgrave MacMillan.

Quilter, J. (2020). Evaluating criminalisation as a strategy in relation to non-physical family violence. In M. McMahon & P. McGorrery (Eds.), *Criminalising coercive control* (pp. 111–131). Springer.

Reeves, E. (2023). "If it's good for the goose, it's good for the gander": Perceptions of police family violence policy adherence in Victoria, Australia. In H. Douglas, K. Fitz-Gibbon, S. Walklate, & L. Goodmark (Eds.), *The criminalization of violence against women: Comparative perspectives.* Oxford University Press.

Royal Commission Into Family Violence. (2016). *Report and recommendations.* State of Victoria.

Serious Crime Act (E&W) s 76 (2015). https://www.legislation.gov.uk/ukpga/2015/9/section/76/enacted

Special Taskforce on Domestic and Family Violence. (2015). *Not now, not ever: Putting an end to domestic and family violence in Queensland.* Queensland Government.

Stark, E. (2007). *Coercive control: How men entrap women.* Oxford University Press.

Walklate, S., & Fitz-Gibbon, K. (2019). The criminalisation of coercive control: The power of law? *International Journal for Crime, Justice and Social Democracy, 8*(4), 94–108. https://doi.org/10.5204/ijcjsd.v8i4.1205

Walklate, S., Fitz-Gibbon, K., & McCulloch, J. (2018). Is more law the answer? Seeking justice for victims of intimate partner violence through the reform of legal categories. *Criminology and Criminal Justice, 18*(1), 115–131. https://doi.org/10.1177/1748895817728561

Watego, C., Macoun, A., Singh, D., & Strakosch, E. (2021, May 25). Carceral feminism and coercive control: When Indigenous women aren't seen as ideal victims, witnesses or women. *The Conversation.* https://theconversation.com/carceral-feminism-and-coercive-control-when-indigenous-women-arent-seen-as-ideal-victims-witnesses-or-women-161091

Wiener. C. (2017). Seeing what is "invisible in plain sight": Policing coercive control. *Howard Journal of Crime and Justice, 56*(4), 500–515. https://doi.org/10.1111/hojo.12227

Women's Safety and Justice Taskforce. (2021). *Hear her voice: Report one—Addressing coercive control and domestic and family violence in Queensland.*

2

The Criminalization of Psychological Violence in Brazil

Challenges of Legal Recognition and Unintended Consequences

THIAGO PIEROBOM DE ÁVILA ■

INTRODUCTION

There is a global move toward the recognition of domestic violence as a violation of women's rights that requires effective prevention policies (World Health Organization & London School of Hygiene and Tropical Medicine [WHO & LSHTM], 2010). In Brazil (2006), the Maria da Penha Law (MPL) created a broad system of civil and criminal integrated interventions to confront physical, psychological, sexual, patrimonial, and moral forms of domestic violence against women.

Psychological violence is a form of symbolic violence, an impervious, insidious, and invisible relation of power that removes victim agency and voice (Thapar-Björkert et al., 2016). While physical assault is more explicit and usually recognized as violence, psychological violence is more subtle and not immediately recognized. Since gender violence derives from power relations, naturalized by sociocultural stereotypes that entitle men to exercise authority and discipline over women, psychological violence is probably the most ordinary manifestation of gender violence (Silva et al., 2007). A Brazilian study found that 88% of femicides analyzed were preceded by acts of control or stalking, and 73% were preceded by threats (Ávila et al., 2021).

The recognition of psychological violence aims to protect the basic human right of women "to a life free from violence, both in the public and private spheres," as stated in the Belem do Pará Convention (Organization of American States [OAS], 1994, Article 3). This form of violence may have a significant impact on women's life projects. Victimization research with 10,000 women found that, in some places, about 48% of women had experienced some form of psychological harm due to domestic violence (Carvalho & Oliveira, 2017). In Europe, 43% of women have experienced psychological violence from a partner (European Institute for Gender Equality [EIGE], 2022). Psychological violence is a form of slow violence (Wonders, 2018), a progressive, silent, and invisible violence made of a succession of small acts of manipulation and coercive control, that reduces women's resistance as a strategy to avoid the escalation of violent acts. This phenomenon was defined as "relational anaesthesia" by Ravazzola (1997).

Abuse produces cumulative effects on women's psychological integrity. Emotional damage associated with abusive relationships includes crying; distress; flashbacks; nightmares; insomnia; irritability; eating disorders; hypervigilance; fear of walking in public spaces; chronic pain; fear of starting new relationships; inability to make relevant decisions; loss of concentration and memory; reduced work capacity (absenteeism, unemployment); alcoholism; suicidal thoughts; and other disorders (Pinheiro, 2019; Ribemboim, 2012; Silva et al., 2007; WHO & LSHTM, 2010; Zanello, 2018).

Many countries have criminalized acts similar to psychological violence. Portugal criminalized "domestic violence," comprising "physical or psychological abuse" (Portuguese Penal Code, Article 152), in 2007. In Spain, a similar crime is defined as to "cause psychic disgrace" or "hit or mistreat another person without causing injury" in intimate partner relations (Spanish Penal Code, Article 153). In England, § 76 of the Serious Crime Act 2015 created the offense of "controlling or coercive behaviour in an intimate or family relationship." In France, there is the crime of "marital harassment" (French Penal Code, Article 222-33-2-1), which requires repeated acts that degrade someone's living conditions, generating a change in physical or mental health. Many European countries criminalize psychological violence under a specific domestic violence crime with a broad definition (EIGE, 2022).

In Brazil (2006), despite the inclusion of psychological violence as grounds for civil interventions, there was no corresponding crime. In 2021, stalking and psychological violence were criminalized in Brazil, with more severe penalties than prior existing crimes, such as death threats. This criminal innovation was received with enthusiasm by legal practitioners, but skepticism by feminist movements. Preliminary research showed an inability of police and prosecutors to recognize these new crimes and provide adequate response (Prosecution Office of the Federal District of Brazil, 2022a). This chapter discusses the challenges of defining subtle forms of psychological violence in criminal law, the legal system's resistance to provide adequate recognition, and the possible unintended consequences of criminalization.

THE CIVIL DEFINITION OF PSYCHOLOGICAL VIOLENCE IN BRAZIL

The MPL creates a legal subsystem organized around three areas of violence against women (Brazil, 2006, Article 5): domestic, family, and intimate partner relations. Article 7 of MPL describes five types of violence from which women are entitled to legal protection: physical, psychological, sexual, patrimonial, and moral. The law has a broad definition of psychological violence (Brazil, 2006, Article 7, Item II):

II—psychological violence, understood as any conduct that causes emotional damage and a decrease in self-esteem or that harms and disturbs their full development or that aims to degrade or control their actions, behaviours, beliefs and decisions, through threat, embarrassment, humiliation, manipulation, isolation, constant surveillance, persistent persecution, insult, blackmail, violation of their privacy, ridicule, exploitation and limitation of the right to come and go or any other means that harm their psychological health and self-determination.

Until 2020, Brazil did not criminalize stalking or coercive control. Most acts of stalking could be considered "tranquillity disturbance" (a misdemeanor) and coercive control (if associated with explicit and serious threats) could be prosecuted as "illegal constraint" (Brazil, 1940, Article 146). Considering stalking a misdemeanor had the collateral effect of degrading the seriousness of this form of violence. This is especially the case when stalking was not followed by explicit threats. In these circumstances, some legal practitioners believed that "he is just walking around her house" and did not recognize the symbolic violence of surveillance. Furthermore, the criminal case law on "illegal constraint" requires an explicit threat and usually fails to recognize more subtle forms of constraints derived from gender relations. This conservative operation of criminal legal theory led to most forms of psychological violence being excluded from criminal prosecution.

Despite the legal intention to expand access to protection regardless of criminal definitions, civil protection for psychological violence was still restricted. According to the MPL, the victim would go to a police station, file a complaint, and the police officers should offer the victim an intervention order request and send this request to the court in up to 48 hours (Brazil, 2006, Article 12, Item III). However, police were unwilling to receive intervention order requests in cases that did not involve violence that rose to the level of crime (Fernandes et al., 2021). Most specialized courts denied protection when there was no criminal charge or when the women did not provide authorization to prosecute (Ávila & Garcia, 2022; Diniz & Gumieri, 2016; Pasinato et al., 2016).

THE CRIMINALIZATION OF PSYCHOLOGICAL VIOLENCE

Brazil (2021a, 2021b) created two new crimes: persecution (threatening their physical or psychological integrity, restricting their ability to move around or, in any way, invading or disturbing their sphere of freedom or privacy) and psychological violence against women, defined in the penal code as (Brazil, 1940, Article 147-B):

> Cause emotional harm to a woman that impairs and disturbs her full development or that aims to degrade or control her actions, behaviours, beliefs, and decisions, through threats, embarrassment, humiliation, manipulation, isolation, blackmail, ridicule, limitation of the right to go and come or any other means that causes harm to their psychological health and self-determination.

Both crimes are forms of psychological violence, as defined in Article 7 of MPL, and are not limited to the context of family and intimate partner violence. For example, stalking or psychological violence can occur in community, religious, educational, or work relations. The new definition of psychological violence may even comprise violence perpetrated by agents of public institutions, police, justice officers, or the so-called obstetric violence (neglecting or disrespecting autonomy of a pregnant, parturient, or postpartum woman).

The crime of psychological violence is exclusively applied to violence against women. This gender perspective in the criminalization aims to highlight the subtle and sophisticated forms of violence perpetrated against women because they are women. It recognizes that gender relations create invisible constraints subjectively internalized by women related to the existential need to be in an intimate partner relation, to raise children, and to be the main carer of family members. These functions of partner, mother, and carer create a female identity as a being for others, not herself (Zanello, 2018).

CHALLENGES TO LEGAL RECOGNITION

Psychological violence requires a new and complex investigation paradigm, one that is active, sensitive, comprehensive, and dynamic. This generates several problems.

The first problem is related to receiving the information since the woman may not recognize she is in an abusive relationship. She may accept and even justify the perpetrator's acts, especially if her references of relationships (in her childhood or community) normalize the abuse. Thus, disclosure of the violence usually requires some psychological preparation by the woman to be able to recognize the abuse and to substantiate her report of the acts of violence. Proving psychological violence can be difficult. Forensic experts in psychology are only found in bigger cities (state capitals). If the justice system considers a forensic psychosocial report essential to prove the crime of psychological violence, in most medium and small cities psychological violence would never be recognized as a crime. Legal experts have argued that a forensic report is not essential evidence and could be replaced by the victim's or family member's testimony or reports from specialized services (Ávila et al., 2022; National Commission of Domestic Violence Prosecutors [COPEVID], 2022; Fernandes et al., 2021). Requiring a forensic report could also have the collateral effect of stigmatization, reinforcing stereotypes of women being hysterical, unbalanced, or mentally ill. Relying only on women's testimony can be risky, however; losing her cooperation would lead to an absence of evidence.

Police effectiveness also requires proper training for officers, who may lack an understanding of psychological violence. For example, police officers may not see the use of aggressive or imposing communication, restricting the use of some types of clothes, or forbidding a woman to have political, philosophical, or religious beliefs as violence. Threats may not be explicit, such as the use of a generic intimidating expression ("you will see what I will do"). Police might not recognize as psychological violence threatening the woman to stop having contact with her children or illicitly suppressing rights related to her children (failing to pay alimony, failing to carry out the visitation) as well as promises that the woman will never see her children again if she separates (Ávila et al., 2022).

Recognizing manipulation requires special sensitivity (Ávila et al., 2022). Manipulation may be carried out by silence or relational indifference; blaming the woman for not complying with gender stereotypes (not taking care of the house or children, not being in an affective relationship, not being sexually available); telling the woman that if she leaves the affective relationship, she will not be able to have another; inducing decisions against the woman's will by lying; or promises of suicide in case of breakup of relationship. Blackmail may also be disguised with apparently legitimate legal claims (i.e., requesting shared custody as a strategy to maintain abusive control over women or promising to file various lawsuits or representations for institutions to disturb the victim). Recognizing social isolation as an abusive act also requires special sensitivity since often the woman will comply with the abusive requests of the offender to isolate herself without explicit threats. Self-submission to social isolation is obtained by abusing a woman's emotional dependence, for example, with the insinuation that her partner will break off the relationship if she does not comply. This emotional dependence is an expression of unequal gender relations since women are immersed in a social culture that considers intimate partner relations central to the female existence (Zanello, 2018).

Recognizing psychological violence requires police and justice professionals to see beyond individual acts, putting in perspective the abusive relational pattern and the series of micro subtle acts of control. This gender sensitivity requires new investigative skills. Police must actively work to investigate the crime and will need to connect individual complaints with a history of violence and with other ongoing criminal investigations (Burman et al., 2023). A report of what seems to be a minimal moral offense might follow a series of previous acts of humiliation or ridicule that are already causing significant emotional damage, rising to the level of psychological violence. When the abusive relation is ongoing, the escalation of violence after the complaint may change the police's understanding of the initial report. When there are multiple complaints, police may need to unify all investigations to provide an accurate overview of the abusive relationship. This active, sensitive, comprehensive, and dynamic paradigm of criminal investigation is similar to other very complex investigations, as in organized crime, where police must actively research to discover the existence of illicit acts and must pursue an ongoing crime (Ávila, 2016). These investigations may drain police resources from other more serious and less complex cases.

Finally, another challenge to the legal recognition of the crime may be a restrictive interpretation of emotional harm as only covering psychic harms. Emotional harm is related to abusive suffering, the willful infliction of pain and anguish, with the potential to influence a woman's cognitive, social, emotional, and affective development, even without an International Classification of Diseases (*ICD*) report (Fernandes et al., 2021, p. 11). On the other hand, psychic harm is related to causing a psychological disease, with a medical report discriminating the *ICD* code (Fernandes et al., 2021). Machado (2013, p. 189) argued that: "Psychic violence would cause a medical pathology; while the psychological violence could not generate any type of somatic pathology, being restricted to the field of suffering that cannot be qualified as a disease." This distinction is essential for the effectiveness of the new crime since the production of the psychiatric report may have traumatizing effects on the woman, and it may be very hard to prove a strong causal link between fragmented acts of coercive control and the psychiatric disease. If it is possible to prove the production of a mental disease, thus a health problem, it would be the case to consider the crime of "bodily injury" since the legal definition of this crime comprises offending someone's health (Brazil, 2006, Article 129, *caput*; Fernandes et al., 2021). For example, generation of a post-traumatic stress disorder (*ICD-11*, 6B40) should be considered an injury to health, thus a battery.

POTENTIAL BENEFITS AND RISKS ON THE CRIMINALIZATION OF PSYCHOLOGICAL VIOLENCE

The criminalization of psychological violence not only has possible benefits, but also carries risks. A possible benefit of the criminalization of psychological violence is to have a standard definition of such violence. Naming is a strategy to give visibility, using law as a symbolic counternarrative (Machado, 2020). Elevating psychological violence to a crime may raise public awareness of the seriousness of this violence and induce justice professionals to grant intervention orders in these cases (see EIGE, 2022, p. 74). It may also promote networking with women's support services.

On the other hand, legal enunciation risks narrowing the definition of a complex phenomenon with multiple and dynamic manifestations. The crime of psychological violence is narrower than the civil definition in the MPL. In the civil definition of psychological violence, emotional harm is only one of the many forms of violence. It also does not require that a woman experience "decreased self-esteem."

Furthermore, the criminalization of psychological violence may hide other, more serious crimes since the crime considers acts within a limited time, usually some months up to a year before the police complaint. A longer analysis of the cumulative effects of abuse could include other forms of impairment of woman's life possibilities, leading up to a "slow femicide" (Walklate et al., 2020).

According to Castilho (2016), the criminalization of psychological violence could enhance the quality of statistics related to the different types of violence against women. This strategy has already been used in the criminalization of femicide (Pasinato & Ávila, 2023). Before the criminalization of psychological violence, there were no statistics on this form of violence. After criminalization, police and prosecution began producing data that indicate a striking lack of ability to recognize this type of violence. During 2021, there were 27,722 complaints about stalking and 8,390 complaints on the new crime of psychological violence in Brazilian police stations (Brazilian Public Security Forum [FBSP], 2022). These complaints are not translating into perpetrators being held criminally accountable. In the Federal District of Brazil, during the first 10 months of the new law, from August 2021 to May 2022, there were 238 police complaints of psychological violence, but only 4 cases were substantiated and prosecuted (Prosecution Office of the Federal District of Brazil, 2022a). To have a perspective on these data, during 2021 there were 15,928 reports of domestic violence in the federal district's police stations (Prosecution Office of the Federal District of Brazil, 2022b).

The progressive narrowing of the concept in criminal law along with resistance and lack of sensitivity of criminal agencies to recognize this violence may have the opposite effect of reinforcing the invisibility of psychological violence, however. According to Foucault (2001), what law recognizes as truth is the fruit of the political frame in which legal practitioners are immersed. When the legal system repeatedly denies the recognition of psychological violence, it may be creating a new discursive truth that denies the existence of such violence.

When law promises protection but the conservative operation of the criminal system disregards women's experiences, saying control is not violence, reducing the seriousness of abuse, or finding there was not enough evidence of emotional damage, it may frustrate women's expectations and produce revictimization. Women may be blamed for not breaking off an abusive relationship or returning to their abusers (Walklate & Fitz-Gibbon, 2021). They may also be criticized if not complying with the stereotype of an "abused woman"; in some cases, defense attorneys have confronted women with their posts on social media showing them smiling or going to the cinema as evidence of the lack of emotional damage. Reacting to violence or not complying with gender stereotypes may also be considered violation of this "ideal victim" position (Christie, 2018), even though feminist research has long proved that abused women react to and challenge gender stereotypes (Gregori, 1993). Furthermore, victims usually have the burden of cooperating with criminal investigations; since the investigation of psychological violence is very complex, it is not uncommon for women to be called multiple times to clarify specific points in the investigation as it evolves; provide additional evidence on each act of violence (psychological reports, analysis of messages in cell phones, video recordings from safety cameras); identify additional witnesses; and confirm new information provided by them. Weariness with continuous cooperation may lead some victims to disengage with police, especially if they have already solved their problem outside the criminal system.

The creation of a crime "only against women" may highlight the gender relations behind these forms of coercive control. It may also reduce the risk of turning criminal law against women. But the criminal definition does not exclude the possibility that a woman will be charged with perpetrating psychological violence against another woman (mother to daughter, or between sisters). On the other hand, the creation of a crime in which only women may be victims may increase prejudice, essentializing women as victims per nature, reducing empowerment (Pasinato & Ávila, 2023).

Racism and social exclusion of Black and poor women create more intense forms of abuse (Flauzina, 2015; Ribeiro, 2018). Failing to incorporate the intersectional and decolonial perspectives will broaden the invisibility of violence. For example, the racist shared representation of Black women as less beautiful may create more intense forms of emotional dependence, as the offender may argue she would never find another partner. The lower incomes of Black women create stronger forms of economic dependence. Poor women living in violent communities may need a man in the house to reduce the risk of social violence, forcing the women to tolerate violent behaviors from the partner. Black women are already exposed to exponential forms of violence derived from the intersection of gender, race, and class, which may blur the recognition of more subtle forms of psychological violence.

This law reform was pushed by criminal agencies and politicians from both the conservative wing and the parliamentary female bench, which usually promotes women's rights. Feminist movements were not invited to participate in the legislative process and watched with suspicion the increase of punishment for psychological violence, believing it could have some positive impact on recognition, but also fearing the scrapping of prevention policies. Criminalization may reinforce the centrality of the criminal system as the main locus to promote women's rights, fostering a punitive drift and undermining the centrality of prevention (Vasconcelos, 2015). Indeed, besides the new criminalization, there is an ongoing process of scrapping prevention policies in Brazil. In 2020, only 4.4% of the budget for women's policies was spent (Brazilian Chamber of Deputies News Agency, 2020). In 2022, there was a reduction of 33% of the budget from the previous year (Institute of Socioeconomic Studies [INESC], 2021).

Since psychological violence is the most ordinary form of gender violence, its criminalization strengthens the state's power over women's lives (Walklate & Fitz-Gibbon, 2021).

Criminalization has critical consequences for human rights since the criminal system is also a source of violation of rights through police brutality, overcrowded prisons, and revictimization of women. From 2013 to 2021, there were 43,171 people killed by police officers, and 84% of those killed were Black (FBSP, 2022). There are 820,689 people in prison, but only 634,469 places, and prison conditions are notoriously unhealthy (FBSP, 2022). Extensive research (see Montenegro, 2015; Pasinato, 2012) has documented that women feel revictimized in their interactions with criminal agencies: victim blaming, the banalization of violence, the obligation to comply with multiple subpoena orders to provide testimony, "condução coercitiva" to courts (literally, "coercive driving" by police officers when failing to attend a subpoena order), the risk of being accused of false reporting of crime when they change testimony to support a partner or when they do not remember details of the crime, aggressive questioning in court by defense attorneys, frustration with acquittals for lack of evidence, and disregarding victim's testimony by employing gender stereotypes.

Criminalization creates new spaces for revictimization, obliging the woman to comply with a punitive system when her problems may have already been solved by other interventions (civil jurisdiction or social or family support). In addition, research indicated that an ongoing judicial procedure dissociated from preventive interventions may work as a trigger for new acts of violence; that risk may escalate to femicide (Ávila

& Magalhães, 2022). As Pasinato and Ávila (2023, p. 72) argued: "Just creating new crimes is an easy solution since it does not compromise the budget, but it may create a smoke screen that transfers responsibility from the Executive to the Judiciary and inflates conservative drifts."

CONCLUSION

Despite the civil definition of psychological violence, justice professionals were resistant to grant intervention orders when there was no correspondence with a crime. The criminalization of psychological violence aims to raise public awareness and foster sensitivity by justice professionals, highlighting with an "only-against-women" crime the gender relations behind ordinary control, producing better statistics, integrating with protective services, and, it is hoped, providing accountability. Since the law requires mandatory police investigation, it may help women to bring to light this invisible and insidious form of violence. The main current challenge is to create a new criminal investigation paradigm, one that should be active in assessing forms of violence that may be invisible for the victim herself, sensitive to validate women's experiences on violence and to recognize subtle forms of abuse and control, comprehensive to comprise a panoramic view of multiple complaints, and dynamic to follow ongoing violence.

The criminalization of psychological violence has potential benefits and risks (see Table 2.1).

Critics argue that instead of criminalizing psychological violence to promote public awareness and induce support for women, society and the justice system should evolve to support and promote women's dignity. Since law reform is recent and institutions are still adapting, the criminalization of psychological violence may yet fulfill its promised advancements. Brazilian women are still waiting for the Belem do Para Inter-American Convention's promises of a life free of all forms of violence to come true.

Table 2.1 POTENTIAL BENEFITS AND RISKS OF THE CRIMINALIZATION OF PSYCHOLOGICAL VIOLENCE

Potential Benefits	Potential Risks
Raises visibility of the seriousness	Narrows the definition
Highlights gender relations by a crime only against women	Essentializes women in the position of victims per nature
Induces recognition by police and justice	Transfers the power of definition from feminist activism to criminal agencies
Promotes better statistics	Nonrecognition reinforces invisibility
Induces better reception and treatment of women and integration with prevention services	Produces revictimization in interactions
Promotes better accountability	Reinforces a punitive drift
	Smoke screen undermines the centrality of prevention polices

REFERENCES

Ávila, T. P. (2016). *Investigação criminal [Criminal investigation]*. Juruá.

Ávila, T. P., & Garcia, M. B. (2022). Análise quanto aos diferentes padrões decisórios de medidas protetivas de urgência nos 20 Juizados de VDFCM do Distrito Federal durante o ano de 2019 [Analysis of decision standards on intervention orders in the 20 specialized courts of domestic violence against women of the Federal District of Brazil]. MPDFT. http://ibdfam.org.br/assets/img/upload/files/Relato%CC%81rio%20 de%20Pesquisa%20-%20MPUs%20no%20DF%202019%20-%20v9.pdf

Ávila, T. P., & Magalhães, T. Q. S. (2022). Itinerários processuais anteriores ao feminicídio: os limites da prevenção terciária [Legal interventions prior to femicide: The limits of tertiary prevention]. *Brazilian Journal of Criminal Sciences, 187*, 355–395.

Ávila, T. P., Silva C. C., Nunes M. S., Lima D. V., Pinto G. G., Chaves, I. A. S., Amorim Filho, J., Baumfeld, L. S., & Fonseca, R. S. (2022). *Diretivas resultantes da oficina sobre violência psicológica [Directives for the crime of psychological violence]*. MPDFT. https://www.mpdft.mp.br/portal/images/pdf/nucleos/nucleo_genero/publicacoes/ Diretivas_oficina_sobre_violencia_psicologica.pdf

Ávila, T. P., Medeiros, M. N., Chagas, C. B., & Vieira, E. N. (2021). Fatores de risco de feminicídio no Distrito Federal [Risk factors for femicide in the Federal District of Brazil]. *Brazilian Journal of Criminal Sciences, 180*, 297–328.

Brazil. (1940). National Congress. Decree-Law 2,848, from December 7, 1940. Penal Code. http://www.planalto.gov.br/ccivil_03/decreto-lei/del2848compilado.htm

Brazil. (2006). National Congress. Law 11,340, from August 7, 2006. Maria da Penha Law. http://www.planalto.gov.br/ccivil_03/_ato2004-2006/2006/lei/l11340.htm

Brazil. (2021a). National Congress. Law 14,132, from March 31, 2021. Creates the crime of persecution on Article 147-A of Brazilian Penal Code. https://www.planalto.gov.br/ccivil_03/_ato2019-2022/2021/lei/l14132.htm

Brazil. (2021b). National Congress. Law 14,188, from July 28, 2021. Creates the crime of psychological violence on Article 147-B of Brazilian Penal Code and other provisions. https://www.planalto.gov.br/ccivil_03/_ato2019-2022/2021/lei/l14188.htm

Brazilian Chamber of Deputies News Agency. (2020). The government spent only BRL 5.6 million out of a total of BRL 126.4 million planned on policies for women. https://www.camara.leg.br/noticias/668512-governo-gastou-apenas-r-56-milhoes-de-um-total-de-r-1264-milhoes-previstos-com-politicas-para-mulheres

Brazilian Public Security Forum [FBSP]. (2022). *Anuário Brasileiro de segurança pública 2022 [Brazilian annuary of public safety 2022]*. FBSP. https://forumseguranca.org.br/wp-content/uploads/2022/06/anuario-2022.pdf?v=5

Burman, M., Brooks-Hay, O., & Friskney, R. (2023). Operationalizing coercive control: Early insights on the policing of the Domestic Abuse (Scotland) Act 2018. In H. Douglas, K. Fitz-Gibbon, L. Goodmark, & S. Walklate (Eds.), *The criminalization of violence against women: Comparative perspectives*. Oxford University Press.

Carvalho, J. R., & Oliveira, V. H. (2017). *Pesquisa de Condições Socioeconômicas e Violência Doméstica e Familiar contra a Mulher PCSVDFMulher: Violência Doméstica e seu Impacto no Mercado de Trabalho e na Produtividade das Mulheres [Survey of socioeconomic conditions and domestic and family violence against women—PCSVDFMulher: Domestic violence and its impact on the labor market and women's productivity]*. Federal University of Ceará. https://www.institutomariadapenha.org.br/assets/downloads/relatorio_II.pdf

Castilho, E. W. (2016). Violência Psicológica [Psychological violence]. In T. K. F. G. Barbosa (Ed.), *A mulher e a justiça: Violência doméstica sob a ótica dos direitos humanos [Woman and the justice: Domestic violence in regard of human rights]* (pp. 35–61). AMAGIS.

Christie, N. (2018). The ideal victim. In: M. Duggan (Ed.), *Revisiting the "ideal victim"—Developments in critical victimology* (pp. 11–23). Bristol University Press.

Diniz, D., & Gumieri, S. (2016). Implementação de medidas protetivas de urgência da Lei Maria da Penha no distrito federal entre 2006 e 2012 [Implementation of Maria da Penha Law's intervention orders in the federal district between 2006 and 2012]. In A. C. C. Pareschi, C. L. Engel, & G. C. Baptista (Eds.), *Direitos Humanos, grupos vulneráveis e segurança pública [Human rights, vulnerable groups and public security]* (pp. 205–231). Ministry of Justice.

European Institute for Gender Equality (EIGE). (2022). Combating coercive control and psychological violence against women in the EU member states. https://eige.europa.eu/publications/combating-coercive-control-and-psychological-violence-against-women-eu-member-states

Fernandes, V. D. S., Ávila, T. P., & Cunha, R. S. (2021). Violência psicológica contra a mulher: comentários à Lei n. 14.188/2021 [Psychological violence against women: comments on Law 14,188/2021]. https://meusitejuridico.editorajuspodivm.com.br/2021/07/29/comentarios-lei-n-14-1882021/

Flauzina, A. L. P. (2015). Lei Maria da Penha: Entre os anseios da resistência e as posturas da militância [Maria da Penha Law: Between resistance's yearnings and activism]. In A. L. P. Flauzina, F. Freitas, H. Vieira, & T. Pires (Eds.), *Discursos negros: legislação penal, política criminal e racismo [Black speeches: Criminal law, policy and racism]* (pp. 115–144). Brado Negro.

Foucault, M. (2001). Truth and juridical forms. In J. D. Faubion (Ed.), *Essential works of Foucault, 1954–1984: vol. 3 Power* (pp. 1–89). London: Penguin.

France (1992). French Penal Code, from July 22, 1992. https://www.legifrance.gouv.fr/codes/texte_lc/LEGITEXT000006070719/

Gregori, M. F. (1993). *Cenas e queixas: Um estudo sobre mulheres, relações violentas e a prática feminista [Scenes and complaints: A study on women, violent relations and feminist practice]*. Paz e Terra.

Institute of Socioeconomic Studies [INESC]. (2021). Análise do Projeto de Lei Orçamentária Anual: PLOA 2022 [Analysis of the annual budget bill: PLOA 2022]. https://www.inesc.org.br/wp-content/uploads/2021/09/PLOA-2022-Analise-do-Inesc_V09.pdf

Machado, I. V. (2013). *Da dor no corpo à dor na alma: uma leitura do conceito de violência psicológica da lei Maria de Penha [From body pain to soul pain: A reading on the concept of psychological violence of the Maria da Penha Law]* [PhD thesis]. Federal University of Santa Catarina. https://repositorio.ufsc.br/handle/123456789/107617

Machado, L. Z. (2020). Feminicídio: Nomear para existir [Femicide: Naming to exist]. In F. C. Severi, E. W. V. Castilho & M. C. Matos (Eds.), *Tecendo fios das críticas feministas ao Direito no Brasil II: direitos humanos das mulheres e violências [Feminist critics to Law in Brazil II: Women's humans rights and violence]* (vol. 2, pp. 106–143). FDRP/USP.

Montenegro, M. (2015). *Lei Maria da Penha: Uma análise criminológico-crítica [Maria da Penha Law: A critic criminological analysis]*. Revan.

National Commission of Domestic Violence Prosecutors [COPEVID]. (2022). Statement 56. https://www.mpdft.mp.br/portal/images/pdf/nucleos/nucleo_genero/enunciados_copevid_nov_2021.pdf

Organization of American States (OAS). (1994). Inter-American Convention on the Prevention, Punishment, and Eradication of Violence against Women. Convention of Belém do Pará. https://www.oas.org/juridico/english/treaties/a-61.html

Pasinato, W. (2012). *Acesso à justiça e violência contra a mulher em Belo Horizonte [Justice access and violence against woman in Belo Horizonte City]*. Annablume/FAPESP.

Pasinato, W., & Ávila, T. P. (2023). Criminalization of femicide in Latin America: Challenges of legal conceptualization. *Current Sociology*, *71*(1), 60–77. https://doi.org/10.1177/00113921221090252

Pasinato, W., Garcia, I. J., Vinuto, J., & Soares, J. E. (2016). Medidas protetivas para as mulheres em situação de violência [Intervention orders for women facing domestic violence]. In A. C. C. Pareschi, C. L. Engel, & G. C. Baptista (Eds.), *Direitos Humanos, grupos vulneráveis e segurança pública [Human rights, vulnerable groups and public security]* (pp. 233–265). Ministry of Justice.

Pinheiro, C. (2019). *Manual de psicologia jurídica [Handbook on legal psychology]* (5th ed.) Saraiva.

Portugal (1995). Decree Law 48, from March 15, 1995. Portuguese Penal Code. https://www.pgdlisboa.pt/leis/lei_mostra_articulado.php?nid=109&tabela=leis

Prosecution Office of the Federal District of Brazil. (2022a). *Preliminary statistics on the crime of psychological violence: Procedure 8191.090801/2022-84*.

Prosecution Office of the Federal District of Brazil. (2022b). Relatório estatístico de violência doméstica 2021 [Statistic report on domestic violence 2021]. https://www.mpdft.mp.br/portal/images/pdf/nucleos/nucleo_genero/estatisticas/Estatistica_VD_2021_NG_MPDFT.pdf

Ravazzola, M. C. (1997). *Historias infames: Los maltratos en las relaciones [Infamous stories: Maltreatment in relations]*. Paidós.

Ribeiro, D. (2018). *Quem tem medo do feminismo negro? [Who fears black feminism?* Cia das Letras.

Ribemboim, C. G. (2012). *Referências técnicas para atuação de psicólogas(os) em programas de atenção à mulher em situação de violência [Technical references for the performance of psychologists in programs for the care of women in situations of violence*. Federal Council of Psychology. https://site.cfp.org.br/wp-content/uploads/2013/05/referencias-tecnicas-para-atuacao-de-psicologas.pdf

Silva, L. L., Coelho, E. B. S., & Caponi, S. N. C. (2007). Violência silenciosa: violência psicológica como condição da violência física doméstica [Silent violence: Psychological violence as a condition of domestic physical violence]. *Interface*, *11*(21), 93–103. https://doi.org/10.1590/S1414-32832007000100009

Spain (1995). Organic Law 10, from November 23, 1995. Spanish Penal Code. https://www.boe.es/buscar/act.php?id=BOE-A-1995-25444

Thapar-Björkert, S., Samelius, L., & Sanghera, G. S. (2016). Exploring symbolic violence in the everyday: Misrecognition, condescension, consent and complicity. *Feminist Review*, *112*(1), 44–162. https://doi.org/10.1057/fr.2015.53

United Kingdom (2015). Serious Crime Act 2015, from March 3, 2015. https://www.legislation.gov.uk/ukpga/2015/9/contents/enacted

Vasconcelos, F. B. (2015). *Punir, Proteger, Prevenir? A Lei Maria da Penha e as limitações da administração dos conflitos conjugais violentos através da utilização do Direito Penal [Punish, protect, prevent? Maria da Penha Law and the limits of solving intimate partner violence through criminal Law]* [PhD thesis]. Pontifical Catholic University of Rio Grande do Sul.

Walklate, S., & Fitz-Gibbon, K. (2021). Why criminalise coercive control? The complicity of the criminal law in punishing women through furthering the power of the state. International Journal for Crime, Justice and Social Democracy, 10(4), 1–12. https://doi.org/10.5204/ijcjsd.1829

Walklate, S., Fitz-Gibbon, K., McCulooch, J., & Maher, JM. (2020). *Towards a global femicide index: Counting the costs*. Routledge.

Wonders, N. A. (2018). Climate change, the production of gendered insecurity and slow intimate partner violence. In: K. Fitz-Gibbon et al. (Eds.), *Intimate partner violence, risk and security: Securing women's lives in a global world* (pp. 34–51). Routledge.

World Health Organization & London School of Hygiene and Tropical Medicine (WHO & LSHTM). (2010). *Preventing intimate partner and sexual violence against women: Taking action and generating evidence*. WHO.

Zanello, V. (2018). *Saúde mental, gênero e dispositivos: cultura e processos de subjetivação [Mental health, gender, and devices: Culture and process of subjectivation]*. Appris.

3

Criminalization at the Margins

Downblousing, Creepshots, and Image-Based Sexual Abuse

CLARE MCGLYNN ■

INTRODUCTION

Downblousing is when someone (usually a man) takes an image or video, usually from above, down a woman's clothing to capture their breasts, cleavage, or bra (Law Commission, 2021, para. 2.26). Commonly, this takes place in public, with men positioning themselves at vantage points above women on public transport, in shopping centers, or the workplace where they are able to take images "down" a woman's clothing, hence the terminology "downblousing." This behavior is undoubtedly intrusive, breaching a woman's privacy and autonomy, and is exactly the kind of conduct that means women have to engage in "safety work" while out in public to try to protect themselves from harassment and abuse (Vera-Gray & Kelly, 2020). But is it behavior that justifies criminal sanctioning?

This chapter considers this question. It examines, first, what we know about the nature, harms, and prevalence of downblousing. It then provides the first detailed examination of downblousing laws across a number of jurisdictions, identifying the scope of these provisions and

Clare McGlynn, *Criminalization at the Margins* In: *The Criminalization of Violence Against Women*. Edited by: Heather Douglas, Kate Fitz-Gibbon, Leigh Goodmark, and Sandra Walklate, Oxford University Press. © Oxford University Press 2024. DOI: 10.1093/oso/9780197651841.003.0004 their application to a range of behaviors. This analysis is then considered in the broader context of debates on the role of criminalization in challenging violence against women and girls.

In relation to terminology, while it is undoubtedly the case that the use of the term *downblousing* may minimize and trivialize the practice, it is used pragmatically here as it is the term adopted in academic writing, in public debates, and by policymakers. The use of this term is also distinguishable from the adoption of other sensationalizing terms, such as "revenge porn," which is inherently victim blaming and in respect of which many victims are on record as finding the use of the term as traumatic (McGlynn et al., 2019).

DOWNBLOUSING: NATURE, HARMS, AND PREVALENCE

Defining Downblousing and Creepshots

The first challenge in this field is to define what is meant by the term *downblousing*. The English Law Commission provided the following definition: "the taking of images, usually from above, down a female's top in order to capture their bra, cleavage and/or breasts" (Law Commission, 2021, p. xi). This definition comes closest to emphasizing that it is the surreptitious and nonconsensual nature of the act that generates the label and its inclusion in discussions of harassment and abuse. It is also one that explains the use of "down" in the term. It covers some of what might be seen as paradigmatic cases of downblousing, such as images captured from a high vantage point in a public space, such as a balcony in a shopping center, standing on public transport taking an image of a seated woman, an image of a woman leaning over that reveals more of her breasts than is the case when normally seated, and so on. Gillespie expanded our understanding of what might constitute downblousing by also referring to so-called "nip-slip" photographs, where the top of a dress slips or where the buttons of a shirt become undone, allowing a glimpse of the breast (Gillespie, 2019). Such images are a particularly common feature of paparazzi images of celebrities. These are all examples of where the woman has not voluntarily chosen to reveal her breasts, cleavage, or underwear in the way depicted, and the image has been taken without her consent.

Few other discussions of downblousing provide any definition of the term, with most debate considering downblousing and upskirting together, with the latter the principal focus, or it is image-based sexual abuse in general that dominates. There is, therefore, little clarity about overlaps between what might be considered to be downblousing images compared with any other image taken of a woman's breasts or cleavage without their consent. For example, a woman may choose to wear in public a low-cut top that displays her cleavage and bra. Taking a photograph of such a woman, including a close-up of her chest, is not commonly criminalized unless also accompanied by some form of harassment. The capturing of such an image may still be experienced as intrusive, coming within the genre labeled as "creepshots" (Hargreaves, 2018), but it is an "ordinary" image taken in public of a woman who has voluntarily chosen to display her cleavage or bra.

In considering the scope of downblousing, the English Law Commission discussed such "creepshots" and gave examples of images taken of clothed women that are shared on creepshot groups' forums, such as women in gym kit or zoomed in photos of them in leggings (Law Commission, 2022, para. 3.92). It rightly identified the problematic nature of such practices, referring to the existence of these forums as demonstrating a "sense of entitlement to women's bodies" (Law Commission, 2022, para. 3.92) and citing work of others arguing that these forums adversely impact women's rights to dignity and respect (Chan, 2020). However, such creepshots seem qualitatively different from images being taken without consent that reveal breasts, cleavage, or underwear in ways that were otherwise not visible, though delineating the distinctions in any particular case is not always going to be obvious.

While these differences between varying types of images of breasts, cleavage, and bras are not generally acknowledged in scholarly or public discussions, they are critical when it comes to considering criminal legal responses. Accordingly, McGlynn and Rackley have suggested categorizing images of breasts and downblousing into three distinct behaviors (Law Commission, 2022, para. 3.106; McGlynn & Rackley, 2021), namely (a) an image of a woman who is voluntarily choosing to show some underwear and/or cleavage (even though she may not be expecting to have images of her underwear/cleavage taken and/or shared); (b) an image taken (e.g., from a balcony or standing position on public transport of a seated woman) *down* a woman's top showing partially exposed breasts and/or underwear; and (c) an image of a woman's breasts, cleavage, or bra that would not otherwise be visible and exposes the breasts in a manner not of her choosing, such as if she was wearing a loose-fitting top and an image revealed her breasts as she bent down, including so-called "nip slips."

Requiring such specific definitions exemplifies the dissonance between women's experiences of violating behaviors and abuse and legal frameworks seeking to categorize and regulate specific conduct. It is such dissonance more broadly that led to the development of the concept of "image-based sexual abuse," a term covering all forms of the taking, creating, or sharing of intimate images without consent and therefore including downblousing (McGlynn & Rackley, 2017). This term challenges conventional criminal law conceptions of harmful conduct, drawing on women's experiences of abuse that transcend existing criminal legal categories, and also reflects understanding that these forms of abuse as being on a continuum of experiences (Kelly, 1988; McGlynn et al., 2017). Nonetheless, while understanding downblousing as a continuum of behaviors is helpful, in terms of drafting and adopting criminal laws, the challenges of specificity remain and are considered further below after examining the prevalence and harms of the various forms of downblousing.

The Prevalence of Downblousing

The English Law Commission recently examined the issue of downblousing and attempted to uncover information about its nature, harms, and prevalence. It stated that downblousing "seems to be extremely common" (Law Commission, 2021, para. 2.27), referring to a study by the Australian eSafety Commission that found that the most common form of intimate image abuse for women aged 18 and over was images of their cleavage (20%) (eSafety Commission, 2017). A subsequent Australian study found that 1 in 10 women respondents said that an image had been taken of their cleavage without their consent (Henry et al., 2019).

However, what is unclear from these studies is the type of image being reported and whether it is a "creepshot" of a woman who is voluntarily choosing to reveal her cleavage (Type a above), an image of the breasts that would not otherwise have been visible (Type c above), or some other image. The studies referred to "cleavage" images, classifying these as downblousing. It is not clear, therefore, whether the stated commonality of downblousing involves surreptitious taking of images, or are the type of creepshots referred to above. In a more recent survey of 245 Australians, 1 in 5 reported they had witnessed an instance of downblousing (Flynn et al., 2022). Although the term *downblousing* is used in this study, again it is not clear exactly what type of downblousing images are being included.

My point here is not to downplay what might be the prevalence of the continuum of behaviors labeled downblousing, but that identifying some of the specific behaviors that might be subject to criminal sanction is difficult. Further, these studies provided particular data, but the incidence of downblousing behaviors will likely also be included in other surveys and studies where participants are asked about experiences of any intimate or sexual videos being taken without their consent. Such studies, while not separating out downblousing, provide further indicative data on experiences of image-based sexual abuse, with one study across New Zealand, Australia, and the United Kingdom finding that one in three participants had experienced someone taking such an image without their consent (Henry et al., 2021, p. 11).

In addition, when considering the commonality of these experiences, it is also important to recognize that just as there is considerable underreporting of violence against women and girls, this will also be the case for online and image-based sexual abuse. There are high levels of hidden victimization as many women simply do not know that images of them have been taken without their consent. This is particularly likely with downblousing, which can be perpetrated via hidden cameras and where material is shared in groups and internet forums where victims are unaware their images have been taken and distributed. The reported incidence of abuse, therefore, is likely to be a considerable underestimate.

We can also glean more information about the prevalence of this form of abuse from examining the internet forums where many of these images are traded and shared. The English Law Commission noted the prevalence of many online forums where images of downblousing and upskirting are traded and shared, referring to one that had 180,000 members (Law Commission, 2021, para. 2.29). Any internet search for information on downblousing brings up pages and pages of links to various forums where men trade such images and share advice on how to get the "best" surreptitious images. Hall et al., in their examination of online forums trading and sharing upskirting and downblousing material, showed how those posting and responding online frame their activities as "artistic and technical," providing guidance on where and how to get the "best" shots (Hall et al., 2022). In their broader study of gendered digital violence, they conceptualized this form of abuse as "homosociality" and "crafts*man*ship" (original emphasis) and highlighted how the intrusion into the woman's personal and body space seems to be part of the attraction for many of the men (Hall et al., 2023). Homosocial misogyny, they suggested, is reproduced through women as currency, initially close-up, then at a relative distance, in a dispersed way among an online community of men (Hall et al., 2023). Further, we know that most perpetrators of image-based sexual abuse are men, with studies finding motivations, including seeking power and control, misogyny and masculine entitlement, sexual gratification, a "prank," distress, humiliation, and to build up social capital (Hall et al., 2023; Henry et al., 2021; Mortreux et al., 2019). This underscores that it is long-standing gender inequality that underpins much of this behavior, particularly evident in what is referred to as the "collector culture" where men are trading and sharing intimate images without consent across internet forums and private groups (Moore, 2022; Plaha, 2022).

The Harms of Downblousing

Just as the incidence of downblousing is difficult to separate from other forms of online and image-based abuse, the same is true when considering the harms of such behaviors. We know that image-based sexual abuse can have devastating and life-shattering impacts for some victim-survivors (Bates, 2017; McGlynn et al., 2021; Ruvalcaba & Eaton, 2020), but there is little empirical evidence about any specific harms from downblousing.

What we do know is that downblousing is another form of public behavior that is part of women's broader experiences of harassment, or intrusion, in public spaces (Vera-Gray, 2017a). These are behaviors that, collectively, have an impact on women's freedom and limit their "space for action" (Kelly, 2003; Vera-Gray, 2017b), particularly when in public. In addition, as identified in relation to the online forums and communities engaging in trading and sharing of intimate, sexual images, including downblousing material, there is a broader social impact on women, with their privacy and autonomy invaded as part of a broader culture of masculinity. While Hall et al. framed this as "polite" misogyny (Hall et al., 2022), as men referred to the "beauty" of the images they have surreptitiously captured, it remains misogyny. It is also argued that as with upskirting, downblousing is a "gross invasion of privacy and a form of street harassment that leaves women feeling vulnerable in public spaces, impacting on their quality of life, access to public space and feelings of security" (McGlynn & Downes, 2015).

Therefore, while it is difficult to get a sense of the nature of the harms of downblousing specifically, we can identify the broader social and cultural harms of this practice and how they play a role in women's collective experiences of public sexual harassment and intrusion. It is also evident that deliberately taking images of women's breasts without their consent invades their privacy and autonomy and constitutes a form of image-based sexual abuse that can occasion considerable adverse impacts. In addition, the widespread taking and trading of downblouse images online contribute to a climate of misogyny. Nonetheless, as identified above, there remain challenges if criminal sanctions are to be considered for some forms of downblousing.

CRIMINALIZING DOWNBLOUSING: PRIVACY VIOLATIONS, PERPETRATOR MOTIVES, AND HARMS TO VICTIMS

Criminalization of Privacy Violations

Whether to criminalize acts of downblousing is not a new issue (Gillespie, 2008; McGlynn & Downes, 2015). In 2015, the Australian Capital Territory amended its voyeurism legislation to criminalize both "upskirting" and "downblousing" so that it now includes an offense under Section 61B(5) of the Crimes Act 1900 where someone observes or captures visual data of another person's breasts and a reasonable person would, in all the circumstances, consider the observing or capturing of visual data to be an invasion of privacy (McIlroy, 2015). In addition, New South Wales has criminalized filming another person's "private parts" when this is without consent and a reasonable person would reasonably expect the person's private parts could not be filmed, with "private parts" including the breasts of a female, transgender, or intersex person (Crimes Act 1900, Sections 91L and 91N). These changes were introduced and specifically identified downblousing as an issue.

What is important to note about these two provisions is that while the scope of the material potentially included is wide, covering a woman's "private parts," including images of her breasts, the offense is limited to where it is reasonable to conclude the person's privacy has been invaded. While obviously variable depending on the circumstances, this does suggest that it is the surreptitious and nonconsensual nature of the behavior that is being criminalized, with "reasonableness" standards playing a key role in delineating between criminal and other conduct.

Both of these Australian examples focused the boundaries of criminalization on approaches to what constitutes a privacy invasion and where the women had "protected" particular body parts from view. It is Type b downblouse images that challenge these definitions. As noted above, an image of a woman's cleavage or bra, for example, when taken at a particular angle, may indeed reveal more than she might have expected and in a manner not anticipated and is likely to be experienced as a privacy violation. But whether it is such a violation as to cross a boundary into unreasonableness is less clear, and it is perhaps likely that Type b images are not covered, although those involving a clear surreptitious or clandestine taking of images (Type c) are likely included.

Criminalization on Proof of Victim Harm

A different approach to policing the boundaries of downblousing abuses can be seen in Ireland, where legislation in 2020 created new image-based sexual abuse offenses, including downblousing. The offense is made out where images are taken without the victim's consent, but this is a criminal offense only if the act "seriously interferes with that other person's peace and privacy or causes alarm, distress or harm to that other person" (Harassment, Harmful Communications and Related Offences Act 2020, Sections 1–3). In Ireland, therefore, the offense requires (among other criteria) proof that either the privacy violation is "serious" or the victim was directly caused harm. The privacy element is obviously similar to the Australian jurisdictions mentioned above, although here there is an added threshold of "serious" invasion of privacy.

However, the Irish provision also provides another route to criminal sanction: proof that the victim actually suffered harm. This is an interesting provision because, generally, requiring such proof from a victim is itself intrusive (Gavey & Farley, 2020) and suggests that the harm manifests only where there is evidence of direct harm, as opposed to the harm being a violation of autonomy, rights, and dignity, no matter whether there are other consequential harms (McGlynn et al., 2021). However, in this particular case of downblousing, it does provide an alternative route to sanction that might otherwise not be available where the law interprets the privacy invasion as not sufficiently serious. Where societal understandings of harm frequently fail to recognize women's experiences, particularly of online abuse, this may provide a redress option where victims seek criminal justice sanctions.

Motive-Based Criminalization

Another approach is that adopted in Northern Ireland and Hong Kong, where criminalization is premised on proof of specific perpetrator motives. In 2022, Northern Ireland introduced new voyeurism laws that criminalize some forms of upskirting and downblousing. The legislation was introduced as part of a package of reforms to laws on trafficking and sexual offending, with the Department of Justice justifying the downblousing (and upskirting) measures on the basis that they would provide "added protection" against these "highly intrusive behaviours" (Department of Justice, 2021). While this legislation was notable for being the first jurisdiction in the United Kingdom to criminalize downblousing, the law has many thresholds to be satisfied before prosecution, meaning that there are unlikely to be many prosecutions. In particular, for the nonconsensual recording of a woman's breasts (whether exposed or covered with underwear) or the underwear covering her breasts to constitute a criminal offense it must be proven that the perpetrator was motivated by sexual gratification; or an intention to cause the victim distress, alarm, or humiliation; or were reckless to causing such harm and the victim has actually been harmed (Justice (Sexual Offences and Trafficking Victims) Act (Northern Ireland) 2022, Section 1).

This follows an approach adopted in 2021 in Hong Kong. Interestingly, when Hong Kong first considered reform, its Law Reform Commission did not include downblousing provisions in its recommendations on image-based sexual abuse (Law Reform Commission, 2019). One of the committee members stated that "there was not as strong a consensus about downblousing, compared to upskirting among panel members. The group held different views and thresholds as to what kind of photos depicting breasts would be regarded as unacceptable" (quoted in Crofts, 2020, p. 523). This position was challenged in subsequent debates, with the Legislative Council ultimately determining that downblousing should be included in new criminal laws due to its "prevalence" (Legislative Council, 2021, p. 9). Nonetheless, there was concern that downblousing was "more susceptible to argument and misunderstanding" and therefore it was necessary to "define the scope of the proposed offence precisely in order to avoid inadvertent contravention and false accusations" (Legislative Council, 2021, p. 9). The offense, therefore, requires proof of either a sexual purpose or seeking dishonest gain (Crimes (Amendment) Ordinance 2021, Clause 3).

Interestingly, while both Northern Ireland and Hong Kong seek to limit the scope of the measures by requiring proof of perpetrator motives, there is little overlap in which purposes are considered to be most culpable. Both include a sexual gratification motive, but Hong Kong is concerned with financial and dishonest gain, which would not be criminal in Northern Ireland, which focuses on intent to cause harm, which is not featured in Hong Kong law. The result is that the law in each country is complex, requiring quite specific knowledge of the provisions to understand exactly what conduct is included, as well as introducing evidential thresholds that will limit investigations and prosecutions. We know from laws on nonconsensual distribution of intimate images that requiring proof of specific motivations hinders prosecutions both because it is an additional threshold, meaning that police and prosecutors are less likely to take forward the case due to resource constraints, and there is often no such evidence, even if it can be assumed that perpetrators were so motivated (McGlynn et al., 2019; Rackley et al., 2021). While the Northern Irish provision does extend to a reckless knowledge of likelihood of causing harm, therefore being broader than the English law on upskirting on which it is based, to satisfy this element there must also be actual evidence from the victim of the adverse impacts on them.

Criminalizing Images of Breasts Otherwise Not Visible

Another way to limit the scope of laws targeting downblousing is to constrain the scope of the types of images covered. While each of the countries considered above has particular definitions of the types of images covered, they are generally broad definitions of body parts and intimate images, with the constraints focusing on other elements of the offense. While Northern Ireland also requires proof of specific motives, it does also limit the scope of the offense by reference to the type of image in question. It only covers images of breasts or underwear "in circumstances where the breasts or underwear would not otherwise be visible." This avoids problems of being overinclusive, such as images of Type a where a woman has voluntarily chosen to display her breasts, cleavage, or underwear. It covers Type c where she has clearly not exercised a choice to reveal herself in the manner captured by the photography or filming. In relation to Type b, where images may be taken "down" a top from a specific vantage point, I would suggest they are not covered as the images are not revealing something that was not "otherwise visible." Anyone standing up on public transport, for example, may have been able to view the cleavage or bra; it was visible depending on where someone was positioned.

This is similar to the provision in Singapore where it is an offense to "intentionally or knowingly record without another person's (B) consent an image of B's genital region, breasts if B is female, or buttocks (whether exposed or covered), in circumstances where the genital region, breasts, buttocks or underwear would not otherwise be visible" (Penal Code 1871, Section 377BB). It also resembles laws recently adopted in Austria and Germany where the taking of intimate images without consent, including downblouse material, is criminalized only where the victim had protected the particular body parts from public view or the victim was in a dwelling or room specifically protected from public sight (Rigotti & McGlynn, 2022).

CHALLENGES OF CRIMINALIZATION AT THE MARGINS

The discussion thus far reveals the challenges of policing the boundaries between conduct that may be unacceptable and intrusive, but is not subject to criminal sanction, and identifying conduct that is rightly criminalized. In the context of online violence against women and girls, and image-based sexual abuse in particular, downblousing provides a very clear example of the challenges of law reform.

These challenges therefore raise broader questions about the role of the criminal law in tackling violence against women and online abuse. In recent years, there has been growing resistance among some feminists to the use of the criminal law and criminal justice system to tackle violence against women (McGlynn, 2022). This "anticarceral" feminist positioning is stated to be in contrast to "carceral feminism," a term first developed to critique the use of criminal responses to sex trafficking (Bernstein, 2007, 2012) and now used more generally to refer to "decades of feminist antiviolence collaboration with the carceral state or that part of the government most associated with the institutions of police, prosecution, courts, and the system of jails, prisons, probation and parole" (Kim, 2018, p. 220). There are many elements to this anticarceral feminist critique, but of particular relevance here is the call to feminists to "adopt an unconditional stance against criminalization, no matter the issue" (Gruber, 2020, p. 197) and that feminists "should not propose new substantive offenses" (Gruber, 2020, p. 18).

The clear implication of Gruber's analysis is that behaviors such as image-based sexual abuse, including downblousing, should not be criminalized. While there are legitimate concerns about some such laws, what is less clear is why women who have experienced online abuse such as intimate image abuse are not to have an option of criminal redress, should they so choose, but those who experience more conventional forms of sexual violence are able to avail themselves of existing criminal laws. The privileging of existing criminal offenses and harms risks reinforcing current criminal law categories and conventions that fail to understand and recognize women's experiences and how abuse has evolved, particularly with new technology (McGlynn & Johnson, 2021). These debates over creating new criminal offenses emphasize that existing categories of criminal law were not designed with women's experiences of harm to the fore. Therefore, while the anticarceral feminist rejection of criminalization chimes with similar concerns about "overcriminalization" (Husak, 2008) more generally, what is neglected is that society has tended to "undercriminalize" harms primarily experienced by women (Franks, 2017, p. 1305). Therefore, while anticarceral feminism is seeking to reduce harm and violence by disengaging with the state and criminal justice systems, it risks reifying the criminal law status quo without opportunity for change or reform. It risks setting in stone historical, often highly stereotypical, assumptions about the nature and extent of sexual violence and does not yet provide an answer to why some survivors should be able and entitled to pursue redress through criminal justice systems but not those who experience "newer" forms of abuse.

I have argued that there are justifications for the criminalization of some forms of image-based sexual abuse, requiring the adoption of new criminal offenses, in recognition of women's experiences of harms and some women's search for justice via the criminal justice system (McGlynn, 2022). Nonetheless, what we can take from these feminist debates is the need for caution and careful delineation of conduct that justifies criminal legal sanction. While some areas of image-based sexual abuse are rightly subject to the criminal law, such as nonconsensual distribution of sexual images, due to their clearly identifiable behaviors and life-shattering impacts on many victims, these facets of the abusive conduct are not always present in relation to other abuses, such as some forms of downblousing.

The common use of the term *downblousing* itself spans a broad range of behaviors, all of which are intrusive, but not all of which cross over into criminal wrongdoing. Differentiating between criminal and noncriminal conduct has required a variety of legal responses, often complex and often involving intrusive evidential requirements from victims. Whereas many legislative differences regarding the criminalization of other forms of image-based sexual abuse are commonly based on perceptions of seriousness, such as requiring malicious intent, in the case of downblousing there has been little focus on this behavior specifically, and the differing legislative responses are largely due to the complexity of specifying the wrongdoing. The analysis presented here is an attempt to unpack what we understand by downblousing and to provide some clarity around possible criminalization. It suggests that images taken of a woman in public who has voluntarily chosen to reveal her cleavage, breasts, and/or bra (Type a) should not be subject to criminal sanction. This is because such images are similar to other 'creepshots' taken in public that are not commonly criminalized, even if experienced as intrusive. Images that reveal a woman's breasts, bra, or cleavage that would not otherwise have been visible (Type c) and are taken without consent are a legitimate target for criminal sanction. There are similarities with other forms of image-based sexual abuse, such as upskirting (McGlynn & Rackley, 2017). More challenging, however, are images that show the breasts, cleavage, or bra in a manner that the woman did not anticipate and may also be experienced as intrusive, but are also similar to "ordinary" public photography (Type b). On balance, the latter should not be subject to criminal sanction.

These are challenging decisions, and the resulting legal complexity does not always assist easy understanding of the boundaries of the law. But the ingenuity of perpetrators of violence and abuse of women and girls, coupled with ever-changing and advancing forms of technology, means that the criminal law will continue to be challenged about its response. If we are to continue to support those women who choose a criminal justice response to abuse, we must undertake the necessary careful analysis of legal responses and make difficult decisions on the margins of abuse and the role of crimnalization.

ACKNOWLEDGMENTS

I am very grateful to Magdalena Furgalska and Laura Hepworth for their excellent research assistance that has informed this chapter. Carlotta Rigotti and Erika Rackley have also helped to shape the analysis offered, with all errors remaining my own.

REFERENCES

Bates, S. (2017). Revenge porn and mental health: A qualitative analysis of the mental health effects of revenge porn on female survivors. *Feminist Criminology*, *12*(1), 22–42. https://doi.org/10.1177/1557085116654565

Bernstein, E. (2007). The sexual politics of the "new abolitionism." *Differences: A Journal of Feminist Cultural Studies*, *18*(3), 128–151. https://doi.org/10.1215/10407391-2007-013

Bernstein, E. (2012). Carceral politics as gender justice? The "traffic in women" and neoliberal circuits of crime, sex, and rights. *Theory and Society, 41*, 233–259. https://doi.org/10.1007/s11186-012-9165-9

Chan, R. (2020). Creepshots—A persistent difficulty in the Australian privacy landscape. *University of Tasmania Law Review, 39*(2), 83–98.

Crimes Act 1900.

Crimes (Amendment) Ordinance 2021.

Crofts, T. (2020). Criminalization of voyeurism and "upskirt photography" in Hong Kong: The need for a coherent approach to image-based abuse. *Chinese Journal of Comparative Law, 8*(3), 505–537. https://doi.org/10.1093/cjcl/cxaa031

Department of Justice. (2021). *Justice (sexual offences and trafficking victims) bill— Explanatory and financial memorandum*. Northern Ireland.

eSafety Commission. (2017). *Image-based abuse—National survey: Summary report*.

Flynn, A., Cama, E., & Scott, A. J. (2022). Image-based abuse: Gender differences in bystander experiences and responses. *Trends and issues in crime and criminal justice* [No. 656]. Australian Institute of Criminology.

Franks, M. A. (2017). Redefining "revenge porn" reform: A view from the front lines. *Florida Law Review, 69*(5), 1251–1337.

Hall, M., Hearn, J., & Lewis, R. (2022). "Upskirting," homosociality, and craftmanship: A thematic analysis of perpetrator and viewer interactions. *Violence Against Women, 28*(2), 532–550. https://doi.org/10.1177/10778012211008981

Hall, M., Hearn, J., & Lewis, R. (2023). *Digital gender-sexual violations: Violence, technologies, motivations*. Routledge. https://doi.org/10.4324/9781003138273

Husak, D. (2008). *Overcriminalization: The limits of the criminal law*. Oxford University Press.

Gavey, N., & Farley, J. (2020). Reframing sexual violence as "sexual harm" in New Zealand policy: A critique. In M. G. Torres & K. Yllö (Eds.), *Conceptualizing sexual violence in marriage: Research and policy* (pp. 229–248). Routledge. https://doi.org/10.4324/9780429322037

Gillespie, A. (2008). "Up-skirts" and "down-blouses": Voyeurism and the law. *Criminal Law Review, 5*, 370–382.

Gillespie, A. (2019). Tackling voyeurism: Is the Voyeurism (Offences) Act 2019 a wasted opportunity? *Modern Law Review, 82*(6), 1107–1131. https://doi.org/10.1111/1468-2230.12441

Gruber, A. (2020). *The feminist war on crime: The unexpected role of women's liberation in mass incarceration*. University of California Press. https://doi.org/10.1525/9780520973145

Hargreaves, S. (2018). "I'm a creep, I'm a weirdo": Street photography in the service of the male gaze. In B. C. Newell, T. Timan, & B. Koops (Eds.), *Surveillance, privacy and public space* (pp. 179–198). Routledge. https://doi.org/10.4324/9781315200811

Harassment, Harmful Communications and Related Offences Act 2020 (Ireland).

Henry, N., Flynn, A., & Powell, A. (2019). *Image-based sexual abuse: Victims and perpetrators. Trends and issues in crime and criminal justice* [No. 572]. Australian Institute of Criminology.

Henry, N., McGlynn, C., Flynn, A., Johnson, K., Powell, A., & Scott, A. J. (2021). *Image-based sexual abuse: A study on the causes and consequences of non-consensual nude or sexual imagery*. Routledge. https://doi.org/10.4324/9781351135153

Justice (Sexual Offences and Trafficking Victims) Act 2022 (Northern Ireland).
Kelly, L. (1988). *Surviving sexual violence*. Polity.
Kelly, L. (2003). The wrong debate: Reflections on why force is not the key issue with respect to trafficking in women for sexual exploitation. *Feminist Review, 73*(1), 139–144. https://doi.org/10.1057/palgrave.fr.9400086
Kim, M. (2018). From carceral feminism to transformative justice: Women-of-color feminism and alternatives to incarceration. *Journal of Ethnic and Cultural Diversity in Social Work, 27*(3), 219–233. https://doi.org/10.1080/15313204.2018.1474827
Law Commission. (2021). *Intimate image abuse: A consultation paper*.
Law Commission. (2022). *Intimate image abuse: A final report*.
Law Reform Commission. (2019). *Voyeurism and non-consensual upskirt-photography*.
Legislative Council. (2021). *Report of the Bills Committee on Crimes (Amendment) Bill 2021 Paper No. CB(2)1443/20-21*.
McGlynn, C. (2022). Challenging anti-carceral feminism: Criminalisation, justice and continuum thinking. *Women's Studies International Forum, 93*. https://doi.org/10.1016/j.wsif.2022.102614
McGlynn, C., & Downes, J. (2015, April15). We need a new law to combat "upskirting" and "downblousing." *Inherently Human*. https://inherentlyhuman.wordpress.com/2015/04/15/we-need-a-new-law-to-combat-upskirting-and-downblousing
McGlynn, C., & Johnson, K. (2021). *Cyberflashing: Recognising harms, reforming laws*. Bristol University Press. https://doi.org/10.51952/9781529217643
McGlynn, C., Johnson, K., Rackley, E., Henry, N., Gavey, N., Flynn, A., & Powell, A. (2021). "It's torture for the soul": The harms of image-based sexual abuse. *Social and Legal Studies, 30*(4), 541–562. https://doi.org/10.1177/0964663920947791
McGlynn, C., & Rackley, E. (2017). Image-based sexual abuse. *Oxford Journal of Legal Studies, 37*(3), 534–561. https://doi.org/10.1093/ojls/gqw033
McGlynn, C., & Rackley, E. (2021). Policy briefing on Law Commission consultation on intimate image abuse. http://claremcglynn.files.wordpress.com/2021/05/mcglynn rackley-stakeholder-briefing-5-may-2021-final-1.pdf
McGlynn, C., Rackley, E., & Houghton, R. (2017). Beyond "revenge porn": The continuum of image-based sexual abuse. *Feminist Legal Studies, 25*(1), 25–46. https://doi.org/10.1007/s10691-017-9343-2
McGlynn, C., Rackley, E., Johnson, K., Henry, N., Flynn, A., Powell, A., Gavey, N., & Scott, A. (2019). *Shattering lives and myths: A report on image-based sexual abuse*. Durham University.
McIlroy, T. (2015, February 17). Changes to crimes act ban up-skirting and down-blousing. *Canberra Times*. https://www.canberratimes.com.au/story/6071779/changes-to-crimes-act-ban-up-skirting-and-down-blousing/
Moore, A. (2022, January 6). "I have moments of shame I can't control": The lives ruined by explicit "collector culture." *The Guardian*. https://www.theguardian.com/world/2022/jan/06/i-have-moments-of-shame-i-cant-control-the-lives-ruined-by-explicit-collector-culture
Mortreux, C., Kellard, K., Henry, N., & Flynn, A. (2019). *Understanding the attitudes and motivations of adults who engage in image-based abuse*. eSafety Commission.
Penal Code 1871 (Singapore).
Plaha, M. (2022, August 22). Inside the secret world of trading nudes. *BBC News*. https://www.bbc.co.uk/news/uk-62564028

Rackley, E., McGlynn, C., Johnson, K., Henry, N., Gavey, N., Flynn, A., & Powell, A. (2021). Seeking justice and redress for victim-survivors of image-based sexual abuse. *Feminist Legal Studies, 29*, 293–322. https://doi.org/10.1007/s10691-021-09460-8

Rigotti, C., & McGlynn, C. (2022). Towards an EU criminal law on violence against women: The ambitions and limitations of the commission's proposal to criminalise image-based sexual abuse. *New Journal of European Criminal Law, 13*(4), 452–477. https://doi.org/10.1177/20322844221140713

Ruvalcaba, Y., & Eaton, A. (2020). Nonconsensual pornography among U.S. adults: A sexual scripts framework on victimization, perpetration, and health correlates for women and men. *Psychology of Violence, 10*(1), 68–78. https://doi.org/10.1037/vio 0000233

Vera-Gray, F. (2017a). *Men's intrusion, women's embodiment: A critical analysis of street harassment*. Routledge. https://doi.org/10.4324/9781315668109

Vera-Gray, F. (2017b). Outlook: Girlhood, agency, and embodied space for action. In B. Formark, H. Mulari, & M. Voipio (Eds.), *Nordic girlhoods: New perspectives and outlooks* (pp. 127–135). Palgrave Macmillan. https://doi.org/10.1007/978-3-319-65118-7

Vera-Gray, F., & Kelly, L. (2020). Contested gendered space: Public sexual harassment and women's safety work. *International Journal of Comparative and Applied Criminal Justice, 44*(4), 265–275. https://doi.org/10.1080/01924036.2020.1732435

4

Sexual Violence in Criminal Law

Presumptions, Principles, and Premises in Relation to the Crime of Negligent Rape

ULRIKA ANDERSSON ■

INTRODUCTION

During the #metoo movement in the autumn of 2017, stories about sexual assault, including rape, garnered attention worldwide. While to some it might seem as if all these stories came out of nowhere, in fact, over the last several decades, countless rape cases have been highlighted and debated in the media all over the world. At least since the 1970s, criminal law treatment of sexual violence has attracted both attention and critique, in Sweden and internationally. Such critique has concerned, among other things, the definition of rape and other sexual crimes; evidentiary requirements for convictions; the assessment of evidence, including the credibility assessment of the complainant's story; and the treatment of victims during the criminal legal process. Voices in the debate come from many spheres, including the media, legal scholarship, legal practitioners, feminist academics, and the general public (Andersson, 2004; Brownmiller, 1976; Lacey, 1998; Leijonhufvud, 2105; Skilbrei & Stefansen, 2020; Stang Dahl, 1994; Sutorius & Kaldal, 2003). The issue at the heart of the critique is that not enough cases of sexual violence proceed to trial and then on to possible conviction (see also Chapter 8 in this volume).

In Sweden and the Nordic countries, discussion has centered primarily on whether and how the criminal justice system can improve its treatment of sexual violence. An example is the latest amendment to the Swedish rape law, introduced in 2018, which this chapter discusses (Proposition: 2017/18:177). In the United States, a debate is presently ongoing about the legitimacy of the criminal justice system itself, where critics take the point of view that it is basically discriminatory and racializing and reproduces socioeconomic inequality (Davis, 2020). My starting assumption is that it is both possible and desirable to examine and review the criminal justice system in order to improve it, while at the same time taking a critical stance toward the system itself in order to question whether it can achieve or contribute to justice (cf. Andersson & Wegerstad, 2022; McGlynn, 2022; Wegerstad, 2021).

In this chapter I analyze the recent criminalization, introduced in 2018, of negligent rape in Sweden. My aim is to contribute to the discussion of criminalization as it relates to violence against women while taking a broad view of criminalization that includes not only criminalization per se but also the application of law. Multiple scholars have highlighted the contextuality of law in general and criminal law in particular and have argued for taking a wider analytical perspective. Lacey emphasized the importance of a broad perspective on criminalization, above all stressing the inclusion of the application of law in any analysis of criminalization (Lacey, 2009). Further, as Gotell has shown with reference to Canadian sexual offense laws, law reforms take place within a context of multiple interests, and changes in law can lead to nonintended consequences when they are applied and interpreted by the courts (Gotell, 2015; cf. Smart, 1995; see also McGlynn, 2010, and Wegerstad, 2021). Both Hydén and Banakar addressed the fact that the application of law depends on various societal factors (Banakar, 2015; Hydén, 2011). Inspired by these scholars and based on my own research, I apply a perspective that focuses on presumptions, principles, and premises. I argue that all three parameters need to be taken into account in any analysis of the criminalization of violence against women and sexual violence: both in evaluations of legal protection in relation to existing legislation or new laws and when deciding on new law reforms (Andersson, 2004, 2011, 2021).

In this chapter I analyze a recent law reform in Sweden that created the new crime of negligent rape. I first give an account of my analytical framework, followed by a description of the new crime as defined in Swedish law. I then analyze two cases from the Supreme Court of Sweden from the perspective of presumptions, principles, and premises, and last I offer some concluding thoughts.

ANALYZING SEXUAL VIOLENCE IN CRIMINAL LAW: PRESUMPTIONS, PRINCIPLES, AND PREMISES

Briefly, the aforementioned critique of the criminal law treatment of sexual violence involves on the one side issues of legal certainty for the defendant and on the other legal protections for the victim. These issues of legal certainty and legal protection can in turn each be considered in relation to three factors. First are the central legal *presumptions*: the criminal legal definitions and evidentiary issues. The definitions of the offenses state the conditions that must be proven in the legal process beyond a reasonable doubt in order to obtain conviction and are clearly crucial. In addition, evidentiary issues in a broad sense are highly important and affect the outcome of the legal process. Evidentiary issues include the preliminary investigation that presents the evidence, the assessment of evidence, and, evidently, how and when the high standard of proof is fulfilled.

Second, legal *principles* define the framework of the legal process and position the issues that must be considered. Such principles include the principle that the accused is innocent until proven guilty and the principle of guilt, that is, that criminal liability requires intent or negligence. These principles affect, for example, how evidence is assessed and what must be proven to establish guilt on the part of the defendant (Andersson, 2004; Bladini, 2013).

Finally, implicit *premises*, such as conceptions of gender and sexuality, play a vital role in how criminal definitions of sexual violence are designed and applied. Earlier studies have shown how these premises shape, both explicitly and implicitly, the application of criminal sexual offense laws (Andersson 2004, 2011, 2019, 2021; Bladini & Svedberg Andersson, 2021). An example is the recurrent questioning by courts about why complainants did not try to leave the place where the criminal event happened, resist, or shout for help (Andersson, 2004). A recent study of cases of negligent rape confirmed these implicit premises and showed that evaluations of the complainant's credibility and witness statements expressed emotions and stereotypes about gender and sexuality, specifically pertaining to rape myths, which in turn led to inconsistent outcomes. At the same time, the new rape law challenges some fundamental assumptions about gender and sexuality, indicating that it may invite discursive shifts and enhanced reflexivity in legal reasoning (Wallin et al., 2021; see also Bladini & Svedberg Andersson, 2021).

I proceed from the assumption that it is crucial to consider each of these three intertwined parameters in any analysis of the criminalization of violence against women, including sexual violence—and, actually, in any analysis of criminalization at all (Andersson, 2019, 2021; Bladini & Svedberg Andersson, 2021; Gotell, 2015; Lacey, 1998; McDonald, Chapter 8 in this volume; McGlynn, 2010; Wegerstad, 2021).

NEGLIGENT RAPE: A NEW SWEDISH CRIME

Historically, Swedish law has construed rape as a sexual act associated with force or exploitation. In practice, however, establishing whether force was used has generally been seen as related to the will or consent of the complainant (Andersson, 2004; cf. Bladini & Svedberg Andersson, 2021). Internationally, as well, rape law has always included the element of the will or consent of the complainant to some extent (Andersson, 2004; Brownmiller, 1976; McGlynn & Munro, 2010; Temkin et al., 2018).

Sweden introduced nonvoluntariness as a basis for the definition of rape only very recently (Proposition: 2017/18, 177). Until July 1, 2018, the decisive criterion in the provisions on rape was force or exploitation, whereas

English law, for example, focuses on the victim's will, or lack of consent (Burman, 2010; McGlynn & Munro, 2010). Thus, the elements of force or exploitation have until recently set the legal boundaries for rape offenses in Sweden. Yet despite this focus on force and exploitation, in practice, consent and will have dominated the legal assessments and argumentation (Andersson, 2004).

Current Swedish rape legislation makes the nonvoluntariness of the complainant the prerequisite for rape. The new legal definition of rape is thus more centered on the will of the complainant, following common law, but the focus is specifically on the will, or more properly the voluntariness of the complainant, rather than consent (Burman, 2010; Wallin et al., 2021).

The 2018 amendment also introduced *negligent rape* as a new crime under Swedish law. This new crime is subsidiary to ordinary rape, which requires intent, and differs only when it comes to the requirement of gross negligence in relation to nonvoluntariness. In practice, the introduction of negligent rape seems to have shifted the focus of judicial questions and assessment of the evidence away from force and violence and toward matters of intent and negligence (Wallin et al., 2021).

Swedish law distinguishes between two kinds of negligence: conscious, or advertent, negligence and unconscious, or inadvertent. This is the case also in other civil law systems (Wegerstad, 2022). Conscious or advertent negligence is equivalent to recklessness in common law (Bennet, 2022). In relation to rape, conscious negligence means that the defendant was aware of a risk that the complainant's participation could be nonvoluntary but did not think that was in fact the case. If the defendant had known that the complainant did not want to participate, the defendant would have stopped (Asp et al., 2013; Wallin et al., 2021; Wegerstad, 2022). Conscious negligence thus has a common denominator with the lowest form of intent, conditional or reckless intent: In both cases, the defendant perceives that there is a risk that the complainant is not participating voluntarily. Reckless intent requires that the defendant perceives a risk that the victim is not participating voluntarily but is indifferent to that risk and would have done it anyhow. In a rape case, a negligent defendant can be held liable only if negligent rape is criminalized (Asp et al., 2013; Bennet, 2022; Wallin et al., 2021; Wegerstad, 2022).

When it comes to "unconscious negligence," the defendant's behavior is assessed not only subjectively but also against an objective standard. The crime of negligent rape, by including unconscious negligence, made it possible to convict those who were truly ignorant of the risk of nonvoluntary participation and thus extended the scope of criminal liability considerably (Wegerstad, 2022). Despite this demarcation of the criminalized area via the new crime of negligent rape, however, there has not yet been an explicit discussion in Swedish case law about this objective standard in relation to sexual behavior. As mentioned, the amendment entered into force in 2018, and since then there have been only two Supreme Court rulings on negligent rape: the two cases I take up in this article. The second of these, discussed below, deals explicitly with unconscious negligence, but the Supreme Court did not address the question of the objective standard.

Assessing unconscious negligence is usually described as a two-step process: The defendant *should* have been aware of the risk that the complainant was not participating voluntarily and *could* have done something to become aware of it. First, the court must find out whether the defendant breached a duty of care, that is, if the defendant was careless. This means considering what could be expected from a sensible and diligent person with regard to the concrete circumstances and the context. Next, it must be established that there is something the defendant *could* have done to meet the required standard of care and also that the defendant *should* have done this, such as asking the complainant whether their participation was voluntary. This normally includes an evaluation of the defendant's degree of negligence in relation to the expressed voluntariness of the victim (Bennet, 2022; Proposition: 2017/18, 177; Wallin et al., 2021; Wegerstad, 2022). One example mentioned in the preparatory works is if the complainant acts as if she was clearly drunk and the defendant should have realized she might be in a vulnerable situation, thus not participating voluntarily (Proposition: 2017/18, 177, 85). Finally, as already mentioned, the negligence must be gross, in other words, clearly reprehensible, in order to lead to criminal liability (cf. Halley, 2016; Rosenbaum, 2008).

In the following section, I analyze two cases from the Swedish Supreme Court. For each case, I first describe the event in question and then summarize the statements of the parties. Finally, I analyze the court's judgments in relation to the relevant presumptions, principles, and premises.

RECENT CASE LAW: TWO CASES FROM THE SWEDISH SUPREME COURT

Since the introduction of the crime of negligent rape in 2018, the Swedish Supreme Court has ruled in two cases involving the offense: one in 2019 about conscious negligence (B 1200-19) and, most recently, one in April 2022 (B 779-21) about unconscious negligence.

In the first case (SC19), the parties involved had not met in person before, but had communicated for some time on the Internet. They had talked about various things, and the defendant had proposed they should have sex. On the night of the event in question, they had agreed that the defendant would visit the complainant and stay overnight. The complainant texted the defendant saying that she didn't want to have sex, and he replied something like "OK." When the defendant arrived, the complainant had left the door open and gone to bed and was lying in bed under the duvet in her panties. The defendant undressed but kept his underpants on and went to bed. He stayed overnight and left the next morning (para. 8).

According to the *complainant*, she had dozed off and reacted when the defendant started touching her breasts and her lower abdomen. She froze and did not know what to do. Throughout the entire course of events—during which he put his fingers into her vagina and then had intercourse with her—she remained lying in the same position, on her stomach with her face turned away from him. She did not show in any way that she wanted to participate, and she resisted when at some point he tried to turn her around. She did not take her panties off and did not know how they came to be taken off. The defendant ejaculated, and when he was done, he lay down next to her. At around half past three in the morning, she spoke on the phone with a friend and told her what had happened (para. 10).

The *defendant* gave a different version of events. According to him, the complainant first rolled toward him but nothing physical happened between them then. He did not know if she was awake, but he felt she wanted to have sex. Then she turned around and laid with her face turned away from him. After a while he started to touch her back and breasts, not thinking about what she wanted and inserted his fingers into her vagina. Because he did not get a no, he continued and touched her in the area around her panties, her hand helping him to take her panties off. When they later had vaginal intercourse, he did not ejaculate, they did not say anything, and the complainant was completely passive, but he understood her to be agreeing with what was happening. After a while, however, he said it did not feel good; it appeared that maybe she did not want to, and it did not feel right to either of them, so he ended the intercourse. The complainant did not seem to be sad afterward. Later, he texted her to ask what she thought of the day before, and in another text, he apologized because he knew what he had done was wrong (para. 11).

As for the *presumptions* in this case, first, the definition of the crime, the criminalized area. In this case, the requirement of gross negligence in relation to the complainant's voluntariness, clearly affected the application of the law. The court's account of the applicable law was more or less in line with the preparatory works (para. 27–28). Further, in its assessment of negligence, the court first established that reckless intent was not proven, primarily because of the fact that the defendant

> interrupted the intercourse when he noticed that it did not feel good; however, doubt remains as to whether [the defendant] at the time of the act was indifferent to the fact that the complainant did not participate voluntarily in the manner required for intent.

The court found, however, that the defendant was aware there was a risk the complainant was not taking part voluntarily because of her text message saying she did not want to have sex (para. 38, 43), and that he was aware of this when he was performing the sexual acts, which meant that conscious negligence was proven. The argumentation is very short but clearly confirmed that conscious negligence generally indicates gross negligence, the prerequisite for negligent rape, and that this situation was no exception; on the contrary, the defendant here was consciously taking a risk (para. 44).

Another important presumption involved the evidentiary issues. The ones at stake were about assessing the evidence (para. 30–32), starting with the complainant's story. The court noted that the complainant's story was clear and coherent, and there were no contradictions, but that some parts were difficult to explain. In the main, it said, the complainant's story appeared to be reliable. Her story was further indirectly supported by two witnesses whom she had told about the event shortly after it happened. The court also placed emphasis on the fact that the complainant had texted the defendant saying that she did not want to have sex (although it is possible to change one's mind), and that both parties had said that the complainant had mainly been passive during the event. In a first step, taking the complainant's story and the mentioned evidence into account, the court found it to be proven beyond reasonable doubt that the complainant did not participate voluntarily. In the next step, the court evaluated the defendant's story to check if it could change this assessment. In its evaluation of the defendant's story, the court placed emphasis on his "short answers without details" (para. 34) and his contradictory information, which it called "difficult to interpret (*svårtolkade*)" (para. 35). Overall, the defendant's story did not affect the court's evaluation, and the court found it to be proven beyond reasonable doubt that the defendant had "performed intercourse and put his fingers into the complainant's vagina without her participating voluntarily" (para. 36).

The evaluation of the evidence in this case was clearly in line with current case law in that it involved an assessment of the stories of the parties as well as the supportive evidence (para. 30–36). Thus, the enforcement of the new crime of negligent rape was characterized by the same evidentiary issues normally at stake in rape cases: The complainant's story is the main evidence and normally needs to be supported by other forms of evidence (NJA 1991 s. 83/2005 s. 712/2010 s. 671/2017s. 316—cases from the Supreme Court).

In relation to the relevant presumptions, one more statement by the court should be mentioned. The definition of rape, including negligent rape, states that consideration must be given to whether the complainant expressed voluntariness, either in words or in some other way. The sentence as it stands is the result of a compromise struck during the legislative process (Lagrådet, 2018-01-23; Proposition: 2017/18:177; Statens offentliga utredningar [SOU], 2016:60). The interpretation of this sentence is somewhat specified in the court's assessment, that passivity can be an expression of voluntariness, but the room for this interpretation is limited (para. 15).

Turning to *principles*, at the heart of the assessments in this case was the principle that the accused is innocent until proven guilty with the high standard of proof in relation to intent, exemplifying the frequent intertwining between presumptions and principles common to these sorts of cases.

Finally, as regards *premises*, the court explicitly rejected a common blame-the-victim-narrative: namely, if you have gotten into bed with someone without your clothes on, this means you have said yes to sex. This is not the case, the court declared: "This does not mean the complainant also participated voluntarily in the sexual acts" (para. 33; cf. Andersson, 2019). This is an example of the observation made by Wallin et al. that fundamental assumptions about gender and sexuality are being challenged through the application of the new rape law (Wallin et al., 2021).

The second negligent rape case (SC21) involved a couple who had been going out for a period of months and had met seven times before the event in question. The couple were not in an established relationship, but rather were friends who had sex. On the evening in question, they met in the man's apartment. He was drunk and more than usually violent. The two went to bed (para. 16). According to the *complainant*, they began having consensual sex, but when the defendant put his hands around her throat, she put her hands on his shoulder and he stopped (para. 16). Later, the complainant was awakened in the middle of the night by the defendant guiding her hand to his penis. She was tired and confused but did not want to upset him, so she decided to perform oral sex on him just to get it over with. She didn't recognize his behavior, saying that he was more aggressive than usual and "took hold of her hair like a ball," holding hard and firmly pushing her head down to his penis. She performed oral sex but not voluntarily; rather, the defendant was in control and had to use force. When he released his hold slightly, she became passive. She was basically passive throughout, feeling afraid that he would be angry if she objected. After the oral sex, the defendant tried several times to penetrate the complainant before finally succeeding, while she remained passive. The penetration was very painful. The complainant fell asleep and woke up with the defendant urinating inside her, after which he went to the bathroom. When he came back, he said he was sorry (para. 17).

The *defendant* said he had been very drunk and could not remember much. He did, however, remember the first act of sexual intercourse, when he took his hands from around the complainant's throat after she protested. Regarding the sexual acts that took place later, after they had been asleep, he had a vague memory of holding the complainant's hair as she performed oral sex on him. He had not meant to control her, just to be the one steering or guiding. If she had told him to stop, he said, he would have done so (para. 18).

As regards evidentiary issues, the court found it to be proven beyond a reasonable doubt that the complainant had not participated voluntarily in either the sexual intercourse or the oral sex (para. 19). As regards the oral sex, the court stated that under the terms of the rape paragraph (Swedish Criminal Code, chap. 6:1), she had been partially forced into the act by means of violence. However, the court also asserted that it had not been proven that the defendant was aware of the risk that the complainant's participation was nonvoluntary, which, as mentioned, is the first step in assessing negligence:

> The fact that the complainant was to a great extent passive, as well the violence used, suggests to some extent that the defendant should have understood the complainant was not participating voluntarily. At the same time, there were no other signs that her participation was not voluntary, as compared to the earlier act of sexual intercourse, when the defendant put his hands around her neck and she

indicated to him that she did not want that. Given the other evidence that has come forward, including about the relationship between the parties and their sexual relationship, the investigation does not provide sufficient support for the idea that the defendant should have understood that the complainant, the second time, was not voluntarily participating in the sexual intercourse and the oral sex. In any case, any negligence that might have been at hand was not so clearly reprehensible that it should be considered as gross and lead to criminal liability. (para. 21)

The defendant was acquitted, thus underscoring the *principle* that the accused is innocent until proven guilty, with the high standard of proof, and the principle of guilt, which means intent or negligence must be established to reach a conviction. It is quite contradictory here that the court asserted on the one hand that violence occurred and the complainant was passive, and on the other hand that the defendant was not expected to understand that the complainant was not taking part voluntarily.

Between the lines we can read an expectation that the complainant should have showed the defendant that she did not like the violence and forceful treatment the second time around either: an expectation that can be associated with implicit *premises* surrounding gender and sexuality and reinforces the notion of availability of femininity (cf. Andersson, 2004). This reading is consistent with the fact that the court did not talk about an objective standard of care: quite remarkable, given that this was the Supreme Court's first ruling on unconscious negligence explicitly relating to carelessness (Proposition: 2017/18, 177, 85).

NEGLIGENT RAPE: PRESUMPTIONS, PRINCIPLES, AND PREMISES

Regarding legal *presumptions*, the recent criminalization of negligent rape, involving a new crime definition in relation to the guilt requirement, obviously affected the application of the law and the outcome in the two cases discussed above. As already mentioned, negligent behavior in relation to rape was not criminalized in Swedish law prior to 2018. Moreover, in sexual offense cases, evidentiary matters are most commonly decisive for the outcome (Andersson, 2004; BRÅ 2019: 9; BRÅ 2020: 6). In these two cases, however, the evidentiary matters go in slightly different directions. The assessment of the evidence was explicitly at stake in the first case, but not in the second. In the first case, as mentioned, the assessment of the complainant's story was in line with case law. In the second case, the assessment in the Supreme Court, at least explicitly, mainly had to do with assessing the defendant's negligence. The assessment of negligence, however, was clearly intertwined with issues of evidence as well. Thus, the court stated that, given the parties' relationship and their sexual history together, there was no clear support in the investigation for the conclusion that the defendant should have understood that "this time" the complainant was not taking part voluntarily (para. 21).

As far as *principles* are concerned, it is clear that in these two cases, the court's reasoning relied respectively on the principle that the accused is innocent until proven guilty and the principle of guilt. In the first case, the principle of the presumption of innocence appears in the court's careful assessment of the evidence and its emphasis on a high standard of proof. In the second case, the principle of guilt lies at the heart of the court's argument when it stressed that negligence must be "obviously reprehensible" to be seen as gross and lead to criminal liability (para. 21).

I interpret the court's reasoning regarding the relationship and sexual relations between the parties as an expression of premises relating to gender and sexuality, specifically the idea that feminine sexuality primarily involves being passive and available. Particularly, the court's stressing that the complainant should have clarified her unwillingness "this time," also indicates an expectation of availability (e.g., Andersson, 2021; Edgren, 2019).

As mentioned above, the court's reasoning and argumentation in the first case (SC19) was very much in line with the rape amendment and its intent, according to the preparatory works, in relation to unconscious negligence. The court also confirmed that the act of unconscious negligence had to be clearly reprehensible in order to be punishable (para. 20).

The same point was repeated in the second case (SC21, para. 11), but here, another interesting argument was added:

> Generally speaking ... there is only limited scope to assess unconscious negligence as gross. It must therefore be about a marked and significant departure from the requirement of due diligence which can be asked in the present situation. The negligence must appear conspicuously reprehensible. (para. 12)

In my view, the court here underlined and, in relation to the preparatory works and the first case (SC19), slightly tightened the demand for reprehensibility: from "clearly" reprehensible to "conspicuously" (*påfallande*; para. 12). The argumentation further illustrates how the presumptions (here, the definitions and evidence issues), principles (here, the principle that the accused is innocent until proven guilty and the principle of guilt), and premises (here related to gender and sexuality) are clearly intertwined. Presumptions, principles, and premises are all at stake in the assessment of negligence here.

In conclusion, this analysis of the application of the crime of negligent rape, from the perspective of legal presumptions, criminal and procedural principles, and implicit premises, clearly illustrates the complexity of legal certainty and legal protection when it comes to sexual violence. The practice of criminal law could be described as a function of these three intertwined factors, so the criminalization of sexual violence, and perhaps of other types of offenses as well, should therefore be analyzed and evaluated from the standpoint of all of these three factors, rather than just in relation to one of them.

REFERENCES

Andersson, U. (2004). *Hans (ord) eller hennes? En könsteoretisk analys av straffrättsligt skydd mot sexuella övergrepp*. Bokbox.
Andersson, U. (2011). Våld mot kvinnor i straffrätten: utsatta individer i strukturell och diskursiv belysning. In E.-M. Svensson (Ed.), *På vei: kjønn og rett i Norden* (pp. 404–419). Makadam.

Andersson, U. (2019). The visible vagina: Swedish legal narratives about rape through the lens of gender, place and vulnerability. In U. Andersson, M. Edgren, L. Karlsson, & G. Nilsson (Eds.), *Rape narratives in motion* (Palgrave Studies in Crime, Media and Culture) (pp. 101–118). Palgrave Macmillan.

Andersson, U. (2021). The body and the deed. Places of rape in Swedish court narratives. *Gender and Women Studies*, 4(1), 2–12.

Andersson, U., & Wegerstad, L. (2022). Straffsystemets janusansikte. Rättvisa i #metoo-relaterade domar om våldtäkt och förtal. In H. Ganetz, K. Hansson, & M. Malin Sveningsson (Eds.), *Maktordningar och motstånd. Forskarperspektiv på #metoo i Sverige* (pp. 93–123). Nordic Academic Press.

Asp, P., Ulväng, M., & Jareborg, N. (2013). *Kriminalrättens grunder* (2nd ed.). Iustus.

Banakar, R. (2015). *Normativity in legal sociology: Methodological reflections on law and regulation in late modernity*. Springer International Publishing.

Bennet T. (2022). Criminal law. In M. Bogdan & C. Wong (Eds.), *Swedish legal system* (pp. 141–185). Norstedts Juridik

Bladini, M. (2013). *I objektivitetens sken: en kritisk granskning av objektivitetsideal, objektivitetsanspråk och legitimeringsstrategier i diskurser om dömande i brottmål*. Makadam.

Bladini, M., & Svedberg Andersson, W. (2021). Swedish rape legislation from use of force to voluntariness—Critical reflections from an everyday life perspective. *Bergen Journal of Criminal Law & Criminal Justice*, 8(2), 31. https://doi.org/10.15845/bjclcj.v8i2.3241

BRÅ 2019:5. Indikatorer på sexualbrottsutvecklingen 2005–2017.

BRÅ 2019:9. Våldtäkt från anmälan till dom: en studie av rättsväsendets arbete med våldtäktsärenden.

BRÅ 2020:6. Den nya samtyckeslagen i praktiken. En uppföljning av 2018 års förändringar av lagreglerna rörande våldtäkt.

Brownmiller, S. (1976). *Against our will: Men, women and rape*. Penguin.

Burman, C. (2010). Rethinking rape law in Sweden: Coercion, consent or non-voluntariness? In C. McGlynn & V. Munro (Eds.), *Rethinking rape law: International and comparative perspectives* (pp. 196–208). Routledge.

Davis, A. Y. (2020). Struggle, solidarity, and social change. In G. Chandra & I. Erlingsdottir (Eds.), *The Routledge handbook of the politics of the #MeToo movement*. Taylor & Francis eBooks (pp. 27–33). Routledge.

Edgren, M. (2019). Conditional vulnerability: Rape narratives in Swedish courts, 1990–2014. In U. Andersson, M. Edgren, L. Karlsson, & G. Nilsson (Eds.), *Rape narratives in motion*. Palgrave Studies in Crime, Media and Culture (pp. 43–69). Palgrave Macmillan.

Gotell, L. (2015). Reassessing the place of criminal law reform in the struggle against sexual violence. In A. Powell, N. Henry, & A. Flynn (Eds.), *Rape justice: Beyond the criminal law* (pp. 53–71). Palgrave Macmillan UK.

Halley, J. (2016). Currents: Feminist key concepts and controversies. The move to affirmative consent. *Signs: Journal of Women in Culture and Society*, 42(1), 257–279. https://doi.org/10.1086/686904

Hydén, H. (2011). Looking at the world through the lens of norms. In K. Papendorf, S. Stefan Machura, & K. Andenaes (Eds.), *Understanding law in society* (pp. 120–159). LIT Verlag, Developments in Socio-legal Studies.

Lacey, N. (1998). Unspeakable subjects, impossible rights: Sexuality, integrity and criminal law. *Canadian Journal of Law and Jurisprudence*, *11*(1), 47–68. https://doi.org/10.1017/S0841820900001685

Lacey, N. (2009). Historicising criminalisation: Conceptual and empirical issues. *Modern Law Review*, 72 (6), 936–60.

Lagrådets yttrande 2018-01-23.

Leijonhufvud, M. (2015). *Svensk sexualbrottslag: En framåtblickande tillbakablick*. Norstedts Juridik.

McGlynn, C. (2010). Feminist activism and rape law reform in England and Wales: A Sisyphean struggle? In C. McGlynn & V. Munro (Eds.), *Rethinking rape law: International and comparative perspectives* (pp. 139–153). Routledge.

McGlynn, C. (2022). Challenging anti-carceral feminism: Criminalisation, justice and continuum thinking. *Women's Studies International Forum*, 93, 102614. https://doi.org/10.1016/j.wsif.2022.102614

McGlynn, C., & Munro, V. (2010). *Rethinking rape law: International and comparative perspectives*. Routledge.

Proposition 2017/18:177 En ny sexualbrottslagstiftning byggd på frivillighet. Governmental bill 177 (2017).

Rosenbaum, D. (2008). Strict liability and negligent rape: Or how learned to start worrying and question the criminal justice system. *Cardozo Journal of Law & Gender*, *14*(3), 731–758.

Skilbrei, M.-L., & Stefansen, K. (Eds.). (2020). *Rape in the Nordic countries*. Routledge.

Smart, C. (1995). *Law, crime and sexuality. Essays in feminism*. SAGE Publications.

Stang Dahl, T. (1994). *Pene piker haiker ikke: artikler om kvinnerett, strafferett og velferdsstat*. Universitetsforlaget.

Staten offentliga utredningar (SOU) 2016:60 Ett starkare skydd för den sexuella integriteten.

Sutorius, H., & och Kaldal, A. (2003). *Bevisprövning vid sexualbrott*. Norstedts juridik.

Temkin, J., Gray, M. J., & Barret, J. (2018). Different functions of rape myth use in court: Findings from a trial observation study. *Feminist Criminology*, *13*(2), 205–226. https://doi.org/10.1177/1557085116661627

Wallin, L., Uhnoo, S., Wettergren, Å., & Bladini, M. (2021). Capricious credibility— Legal assessments of voluntariness in Swedish negligent rape judgements. *Nordic Journal of Criminology*, *22*(1), 3–22. https://doi.org/10.1080/2578983X.2021.1898128

Wegerstad, L. (2021). Theorising sexual harassment and criminalisation in the context of Sweden. *Bergen Journal of Criminal Law & Criminal Justice*, *9*(2), 61–81.

Wegerstad, L. (2022). Sense and caution: A comparative perspective on Sweden's negligent rape law. In E. Hoven & T. Weigend (Eds.), *Consent and sexual offences. Comparative perspectives* (pp. 119–126). Nomos.

CASES

Judgment from the Swedish Supreme Court, July 11th 2019, case B 1200–19 (SC19).
Judgment from the Swedish Supreme Court, April 7th 2022, case B 779–21 (SC21).
Nytt Juridiskt Arkiv (NJA).
1991 s. 83.
2005 s. 712.
2010 s. 671.
2017 s. 316.

5
Criminal Justice Responses to Domestic Violence in Fiji

JOJIANA COKANASIGA ■

INTRODUCTION

Countries in the Pacific have some of the highest rates of violence against women (VAW) in the world; it is estimated that two in every three Pacific women are impacted by gender-based violence, which is twice the global average (Fiji Women's Crisis Centre [FWCC] and U.N. Women Fiji MCO, 2019). Rates of women experiencing intimate partner violence average 63% across Melanesian countries, 44% across Micronesia, and 43% across Polynesia (Secretariate of the Pacific Community, 2021).

Continued attention to the problem of VAW has led to a growing commitment to addressing domestic violence (DV) through various policy and legislative changes (Connelly & Cavanagh, 2007). In 1992, VAW was recognized in General Recommendation Number 19 of the Committee on the Elimination of Discrimination Against Women (CEDAW) and thereby international law (Committee on CEDAW, 1992).

Commitments to international human rights conventions such as the CEDAW meant that national legislation must be enacted to address the growing problem of VAW in the Pacific. Pacific states have implemented a range of policy and legal responses to addressing VAW. Most of this was

Jojiana Cokanasiga, *Criminal Justice Responses to Domestic Violence in Fiji* In: *The Criminalization of Violence Against Women*. Edited by: Heather Douglas, Kate Fitz-Gibbon, Leigh Goodmark, and Sandra Walklate, Oxford University Press. © Oxford University Press 2024. DOI: 10.1093/oso/9780197651841.003.0006 possible through global and regional feminist and human rights efforts that created an impetus for states to align themselves to global human rights standards and address the problem (Jivan & Forster, 2009).

Domestic violence laws provide an avenue through civil procedure to address DV. While domestic violence orders (DVOs) are designed so they can be obtained easily through a civil procedure, it is the breach of the DVO that results in a criminal penalty. Bates and Hester (2020, p. 134) observed:

> Over the past two decades there has been a shift in emphasis in the design of protection orders—from being purely civil law measures, towards orders being increasingly issued as part of criminal proceedings, and by criminal justice agents. Over time, this has resulted in a proliferation of different protection orders, and in the "hybridisation" of criminal and civil measures to protect victims from domestic abuse.

There is a lack of literature on legal responses to DV cases in Fiji especially given the context of the historical experiences of colonialism in Fiji and the implementation of human rights ideals coupled with the onset of feminist calls for the criminalization of DV. In the 1990s, there were increasing calls from feminist and human rights groups in Fiji to "ensure that DV is treated as a specific, separate, and serious offence that deserves special consideration" (FWCC, 1998). Prior to the enactment of the DV legislation in 2009 (Domestic Violence Act 2009, Fiji), Fiji, similar to other Pacific Island countries, ratified various international human rights conventions but had not reformed domestic law.

Fiji ratified CEDAW in 1995 (Office of the High Commissioner for Human Rights, n.d.) and, following that, was required to provide monitoring and implementation reports to CEDAW. Following ratification and at the start of the twenty-first century, many Pacific Island governments began to actively enact and implement DV legislation. Along with Fiji, other Pacific Island states that also ratified CEDAW were also obligated under CEDAW to enact laws and policies addressing gender-based violence (Jivan & Forster, 2009, p. 2). There was no or little consideration of the effect of colonial legal frameworks on DV responses. These are important considerations when thinking about improving DV responses in Fiji and in Pacific communities as legal frameworks in the Pacific were introduced and incorporated by colonial administrations. Cunneen and Tauri (2016, p. 66) observed:

> Defining and understanding crime through the broader lens of colonisation enables a better appreciation of contemporary Indigenous priorities for reform and change within criminal justice systems. It also enables a more thoughtful consideration of indigenous solutions to social disorder and dislocation which enhance Indigenous authority and lie outside state priorities of criminalisation.

Therefore, understanding the application and impact of legal responses to DV in the Pacific needs to be assessed not only in the context of Pacific cultures but also their colonial experiences. At the outset, "colonial law imposed criminal and penological concepts that were foreign to Indigenous peoples" (Cunneen & Tauri, 2016, p. 47). DV responses have been advocated and applied through an international liberal human rights approach, fueled by a strong feminist movement. In the Pacific, they are expected to be applied within hybridized structures of customary and colonially imposed laws and regulations, which are a predominant feature of Pacific Islands' legal systems (Corrin, 2017; Jivan & Forster, 2009).

Generally, there has been a failure to consider the experiences of Indigenous peoples through the criminal justice process in the Pacific. This is not surprising as colonial administrators effectively subsumed, if not abolished, customs and traditions when enacting new rules and regulations. As such, the consideration of Indigenous ways of addressing conflicts has largely been neglected (Cunneen & Tauri, 2016). However, feminists have also viewed culture as a problem when discussing non-Western women's experience with violence (George, 2016, p. 90). Given the continuing challenge faced by Indigenous peoples in accessing protection under the DV laws (Cunneen, 2007; Douglas & Fitzgerald, 2018), it is important to consider how Indigenous concepts and approaches may contribute to improving responses to DV. Studies in developed countries like Australia, for example, found that Aboriginal and/or Torres Strait Islander communities faced challenges when accessing DVOs. Cunneen (2007) discussed the lack of involvement of Indigenous people in the DVO process, especially where they were named as aggrieved or respondent in a DV case. He found that this was not the same situation with non-Indigenous applications for DVOs (Cunneen, 2007, p. 12). A comparison between Indigenous and non-Indigenous applications may not be an issue in Fiji; however, Indigenous peoples in Fiji must contend with understanding new concepts, especially considering human rights and feminist ideals about the criminalization of DV, which is a strong feature of the domestic violence protection order (DVPO) system in Fiji.

Colonial rule in Fiji was contentious and gendered. Criminal law introduced through the colonial administration applied differently to women as compared to men, and Indigenous women were particularly disadvantaged, especially when they were charged with offenses (Etherington, 1996, p. 52). The Fijian way of life became subsumed into colonial rules and regulations, and the lives of women were regulated by native regulations as well as the general law of the colony (Knox-Mawer, 1961, p. 644). As such, the history of the criminal justice system in Fiji was highly discriminatory to women, and many of the laws that formed part of the criminal justice process continued in existence until the early twenty-first century.

During the colonial era, policing featured predominantly as a means by which colonial administrations governed Indigenous people. The colonial state imposed an administrative order and a legal framework, including a system of courts and police. Cunneen and Tauri added that "criminalisation and punishment were central to how colonial administrations governed Indigenous people" (2016, p. 52). Following independence, Pacific Island states began their decolonization process, with many retaining colonial laws. Dinnen (2019, p. 273) explained that while decolonization has occurred in parts of the Pacific, this was mainly driven by the United Nations and, to a degree, colonial powers themselves following World War II.

This is particularly the case for Fiji, which gained independence from Britain and joined the United Nations in the same month of the same year, in October 1970. Fiji became actively engaged in peacekeeping in the lead-up to independence and after; however, many of the institutions established during the colonial era remained after independence. Jivan and Forster pointed out that many Pacific nations continue to operate with "outdated legislative frameworks, reflective not of local values or contemporary international norms, but rather of the mid-20th century values of the former colonial powers" (2009, p. 2). Dinnen observed that "significant numbers of Melanesians continue to live under what many view as de facto colonial rule, including in West Papua, and in the French territory of New Caledonia" (2019, p. 273).

In the context of Fiji, colonially inherited criminal laws continued in existence until 2009, when there was a move to remove dated colonial legislation. Fiji's Domestic Violence Act (Fiji DV Act) was enacted in 2009, and the Penal Code was repealed and replaced with the new Crimes Act 2009 and the Sentencing and Penalties Act 2009. However, other native laws of colonial construction still exist in Fiji that directly and indirectly affect women. This is important to mention here as studies tended to show a connection between colonization and gendered violence as "the colonial state was built as a power structure operated by men, based on continuing force" (Connell, 2014, p. 556). As such, colonial structures, especially in which the criminal justice process operates, have the potential to influence responses to DV, especially in formerly colonized countries. It is therefore crucial to ensure that DV laws are not operating within structures that may disadvantage victims of DV, which in the Pacific are predominantly women.

RESPONDING TO DV IN FIJI

Domestic violence is an ongoing problem in Fiji. Studies showed that about "64% of Women in Fiji experience physical and/or sexual intimate partner violence in their lifetime" (FWCC, 2013). Prior to the enactment of

DV laws, DV cases in Fiji were dealt with under criminal law and grouped under the general categories of common assault and assault occasioning actual or grievous bodily harm, making it very difficult to gauge the actual incidence and prevalence of DV-related crimes of assault and grievous bodily harm in Fiji (FWCC, 1998). This led to the FWCC submitting a draft legislation on DV to the Fiji Law Reform Commission in the late 1990s. The FWCC argued that the primary importance of putting such legislation in place is to provide a legal mechanism for the purposes of protection from violence within the home and family environment (FWCC, 1998).

The FWCC lobbied to improve responses to DV, highlighting that Fiji's criminal legislation did not distinguish between DV and other types of assault, and the nature of the criminal charge depended on the degree of injury inflicted. Further, criminal offenses addressing DV such as common assault and assault occasioning actual bodily harm were reconcilable offenses (meaning that where the perpetrator and victim showed the court they had reconciled, the perpetrator escaped conviction and sentence) under Section 163 of the Criminal Procedure Code. The Fiji DV Act was enacted in 2009 and established Fiji's DVPO system. The enactment of the Fiji DV Act was a result of a long tussle to finally have the state recognize and respond to DV. Prior to the passing of DV laws, the legal situation in Fiji was such that DV criminal cases that went to court rarely resulted in custodial sentences, with sentences being suspended or typically low (FWCC, 1998).

A DVO is a "civil order designed to protect the applicant from future harm and where the respondent has contravened conditions of a DVO, this may result in the respondent being charged with a criminal offence of contravention of the DVO" (Douglas & Fitzgerald, 2018, p. 43). The objective of the protection order system is to provide immediate protection to applicants of a DVO. DVOs in Fiji are called domestic violence restraining orders (DVROs), and anyone in a family or domestic relationship can apply for a DVRO to be protected from violence perpetrated within the home or family relationship, whether de facto or legal. Under the Fiji DV Act, anyone can apply for protection from DV. For example, an adult or a child (through an adult) can apply for a DVRO. The police can also apply for a DVRO on behalf of an adult and for a child (Fiji DV Act 2009, Section 19).

In Fiji, both the Family and Criminal Divisions of the Magistrate's Court has jurisdiction to issue a DVRO (Fiji DV Act 2009, Section 8). However, in the context of the Family Court, the application for a DVRO can be initiated by the parties to a Family Court proceeding or by the Family Court itself. Given the duty enshrined in most DV laws for police to protect against DV, applications are mostly initiated within the Criminal Court system as they often accompany a criminal charge [Fiji DV Act 2009, section 8(2)]. DV under Fiji's DV law is broadly defined to include physical abuse and nonphysical abuse, such as fear and apprehension of threats and damage to property (Fiji DV Act 2009, Section 3). There are also standard nonmolestation orders that apply to every DVRO. There are also various standard conditions available for regulating the behavior of respondents for the protection of victims of DV (Fiji DV Act 2009, Section 27).

Existing Data

In Fiji, DVROs can be applied for at the Criminal and the Family Divisions of the Magistrate's Court. Existing data highlight that nine out of ten of all DVRO applications in Fiji were initiated in the Criminal Division of the Magistrate's Court, and one out of ten were initiated in the Family Division of the Magistrate's Court (Fiji Women's Rights Movement [FWRM], 2019).

> In 2017, 4,027 DVRO applications were initiated in the Criminal Division of the Magistrates Court whilst 591 DVRO applications were initiated in the Family Division of the Magistrates Court. (FWRM, 2018, p. 19)

The graph in Figure 5.1 shows DVRO applications in both divisions of the Magistrate's Court in Fiji between the years 2012 and 2017. While a high

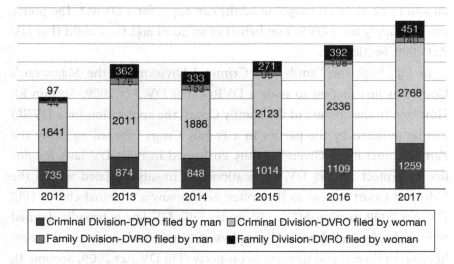

Figure 5.1 DVRO applications in the Family and Criminal Divisions of the Magistrate's Court. (Adapted from Fiji Women's Rights Movement, 2018, p. 22.)

percentage of DVRO applications are lodged in the Criminal Division of the Magistrate's Court in Fiji, no data are available on the outcomes of these applications (FWRM, 2018).

In terms of the outcomes from the Family Division of the Magistrate's Court, Figure 5.2 shows that a high number of applications for DVROs are not granted (FWRM, 2018, p. 22).

THE CRIMINALIZATION OF DV IN THE FIJIAN CONTEXT

In Fiji, a breach of a DVRO is a criminal offense, and offenses constituting the breach have the possibility of being charged as a criminal offense, such as assault. A criminal penalty is prescribed when the perpetrator is found guilty of a breach of a DVO; the penalty is a maximum fine of $1,000 and a term of imprisonment of 12 months [Fiji DV Act 2009, Section 77(1)].

Since the enactment of the DV legislation in Fiji, research showed an increasing interaction of women with the DV system through applications for DVROs (FWRM, 2018). According to data submitted by the Fiji

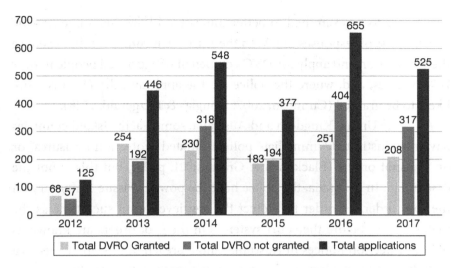

Figure 5.2 Outcome of the DVRO applications in the Family Division of the Magistrate's Court. (Adapted from Fiji Women's Rights Movement, 2018, p. 22.)

judiciary to the FWRM, a majority of DVRO applications were initiated in the Criminal Division of the Magistrate's Court. These applications were not initiated by the police or victims but by the court itself (FWRM, 2018, p. 19).

Following the enactment of the DV legislation, the trend in Fiji seems to be a reactive approach to DV whereby the police usually charge for a criminal offense in DV cases, and thereafter the court issues a DVRO when the case reaches the court system (FWRM, 2018). Section 26(1)(b) of the Fiji DV Act allows the court to make DVROs on its own motion to ensure the safety and well-being of a victim of DV (FWRM, 2018, p19). The court's application of this section in criminal cases where parties are in a domestic relationship accounts for the high number of DVRO applications initiated in the Criminal Division of the court (FWRM, 2018, p. 19).

Responses to DV by the police in Fiji are influenced by a range of factors. First, police in Fiji do not have the power to issue on the spot DVROs but are expected to apply for a DVRO (Fiji DV Act 2009, Section 14). This has the potential to influence how efficiently police respond to DV. The extent to which police in Fiji are able to carry out their duties under existing DV laws needs to be examined to better understand how this influences the effectiveness of responses to DV. In the Australian context, police exercise their discretion and apply for DVOs on behalf of aggrieved people in over 70% of cases, and, where the police are the applicant, the DVO is more likely to be granted (Cunneen, 2007; Douglas & Fitzgerald, 2018).

As in the United Kingdom and Australia, some Pacific Island countries have now instituted "immediate police-initiated protection measures" or on the spot orders (Blackburn & Graca, 2021, p. 33), but this is not the case in Fiji. In Australia, the police have the power to issue temporary on the spot orders in order to protect the aggrieved until such time as the matter comes before the court system. On the spot orders are known as police protection notices in Australia, and a breach of this order carries a hefty fine and a maximum of 3 years imprisonment. In both the Solomon Islands and Tonga, police are empowered to issue police safety notices in urgent circumstances requiring immediate protection from DV for victims (Solomon Islands Family Protection Act 2014, Section 12; Tonga Family Protection Act 2016, Section 22). Breaches of police safety notices in both the Solomon Islands and Tonga also carry hefty fines and a maximum imprisonment sentence of 3 years. While research is needed to assess the effectiveness of on-the-spot orders in the Pacific for those countries that have them, one can argue that they do empower the police to act in DV situations where the risk is high. On-the-spot orders can also be useful when victims of DV are unable to reach the court urgently given geographical location (i.e., those living in island or rural communities in the Pacific). While there are advantages in expanding police powers to effectively respond to DV, there remains the risk that increasing criminalization of DV may contribute to high incarceration rates. In essence, on-the-spot orders authorize police to exercise their discretion within the ambit of the law to address DV urgently, although temporarily. This option is missing in Fiji's DV legislation.

In Fiji, "each police officer has the duty to prevent the commission of DV offences, to detect and bring offenders to justice" (Fiji DV Act 2009, Section 12). In the absence of police powers for on-the-spot orders in Fiji's DV law, there is a tendency for police to charge for a criminal offense first in some DV cases before a DV order is issued in the Magistrate's Court

(*State v. Meniusi Veikila*, 2020). This may be the only available option taken by police given the absence of police powers to issue on-the-spot orders.

In some situations, police have charged substantive criminal offenses in place of breach of DVROs in cases involving serious offenses, letting the case run its course in the court system (*State v. Dinesh Chand*, 2020). Given this, it is unclear whether there is a correlation between the absence of police powers to issue on-the-spot DVROs and increased incarceration rates for DV offenses in Fiji since the introduction of DV laws in Fiji. In Australia and the United States, studies have shown increasing incarceration rates of Indigenous women as a result of their interaction with the DVO system. This has been attributed to how DV is policed as well as sentencing decisions for DV (Douglas & Fitzgerald, 2018). In the context of Fiji, the policing of DV orders is expected to be challenging given limited police powers, leading back to the instituting of criminal proceedings under criminal law as the first option taken by police. This is likely even more so given the existing colonial legal framework in Fiji, which is focused on utilizing the criminal law, which has the potential to influence how police respond to DV. Furthermore, the focus on the criminalization of DV through the DVPO system has been criticized in other countries as resulting in the imprisonment of Indigenous women rather than their protection. In Australia, for example, data reveal that nearly 50% of Indigenous women who died in DV situations were previously named as perpetrators in DV cases (Watego et al., 2021). This is an important consideration in the Fijian system as data reveal a growing number of applications for DVROs by men (FWRM, 2019), and cultural values and practices may likely influence responses to DV, especially within the criminal justice system (Rankine et al., 2017, p. 2783).

Given the above, one must assess whether the police revert to criminal proceedings or whether the police determine how they respond to DV situations and DVRO breaches depending on the circumstances. In the Australian context, Douglas and Fitzgerald (2018, p. 43) explained that police exercise their discretion regarding whether to investigate and charge a contravention of a DVO. In Fiji, the approach is likely to be similar. In Fiji, police would be responding in two main ways. The first is intervening in a DV situation if a DV report is lodged. The second is responding when there has been a breach of an existing DVRO. In both instances, there is the requirement for a complaint to be made or a report lodged to warrant police response and action. Police do not go about proactively enforcing orders and checking on respondents.

Stanko (1995, p. 33) highlighted the difficulty faced by police in dealing with DV: "Whilst from the police perspective this may be attributed to the challenge of the effective use of resources to address domestic violence, feminists view this as police allegiance to preserving the male order." Stanko attempted to reconcile these two perspectives but identified another assumption between policing and protection. Stanko highlighted that police protection and/or coercive protection does not exist when it comes to personal violence, and that police are more accustomed to their role of maintaining public order (Cretney et al., 1994; Stanko, 1995).

In Fiji, it is questionable whether police responses to DV have a deterrent effect. As it is, the law allows police in Fiji to arrest without a warrant only when a DVRO is already in place, meaning they can only arrest when there is an actual breach or likelihood of a breach of a DVRO in DV situations (Fiji DV Act 2009, Section 78) or alternatively charge a criminal offense.

CONCLUSION

There is a likelihood of an increasing rate of incarceration in Fiji as a result of the DVRO system. In Fiji, and more generally in the Pacific, existing colonial legal frameworks and colonial experiences of Pacific communities have implications for the application of DV laws. The increasing pressure for the criminalization of DV can be a form of colonization if Indigenous ways of addressing social problems and colonial experiences are not given sufficient consideration. Furthermore, the implementation of the DVRO system in the Pacific has mainly been underpinned by feminist and human rights approaches without any consideration of the colonial experiences of Indigenous people.

In Fiji, important players in the DVRO system are the police and the courts, with the courts exercising more power in the initiation of DVROs as compared to the police. The growing trend toward the criminalization of DV in Fiji is evident in the increasing DVRO applications lodged within the Criminal Division of the Magistrate's Court of Fiji. While understanding the number of breaches of DVROs and the penalties imposed for breaches would require further analysis, this chapter has highlighted the current practice in Fiji when it comes to legal responses to DV and the challenges faced by police in responding to DV.

A majority of DVROs are initiated in the Criminal Division of the Magistrate's Court following police institution of criminal charges for DV offenses. This is because the court has the power to initiate DVROs and has increasingly exercised this option under section 26(1)(b) of the Fiji DV Act, which allows the court to make orders on its own motion for the safety and well-being of a victim of DV (FWRM, 2019, p. 19). Given this, the court rather than the police are the main actors in initiating DVROs. Existing data demonstrates the high dismissal rate of DVROs in the Family Courts and the increasing number of DVROs issued in the Criminal Courts of Fiji. These statistics (see Figures 5.1 and 5.2) indicate a trend toward reliance on the criminal justice system in dealing with DV. As it is, police responses to DV in Fiji indicate that their first option in responding to DV is to charge for a criminal offense. This may be due to the limited police powers available to them. In grave DV situations when courts are not easily accessible or not open and police are required to act urgently, it is expected that police will respond by charging a criminal offense first. This is normally the first step in the process of initiating a DVRO application by the police before it comes to the courts in Fiji's case.

REFERENCES

Bates, L., & Hester, M. (2020). No longer a civil matter? The design and use of protection orders for domestic violence in England and Wales. *Journal of Social Welfare and Family Law, 42*(2), 133–153. https://doi.org/10.1080/09649069.2020.1751943

Blackburn, K., & Graca, S. (2020). A critical reflection on the use and effectiveness of DVPNs and DVPOs. *Police Practice and Research, 22*(1), 23–39. https://doi.org/10.1080/15614263.2020.1759059

Connell, R. (2014). The sociology of gender in Southern perspective. *Current Sociology, 62*(4), 550–567. https://doi.org/10.1177/0011392114524510

Connelly, C., & Cavanagh, K. (2007). Domestic abuse, civil protection orders and the "new criminologies": Is there any value in engaging with the law? *Feminist Legal Studies*, *15*, 259–287. https://doi.org/10.1007/s10691-007-9069-7

Corrin, J. (2017). Exploring the deep: Looking for deep legal pluralism in the South Pacific. *Victoria University of Wellington Law Review*, *48*(2), 305–322. https://doi.org/10.26686/vuwlr.v48i2.4738

Cretney, A., Davis, G., Clarkson, C., & Shepherd, J. (1994). Criminalizing assault: The failure of the "offence against society" model. *British Journal of Criminology*, *34*(1), 15–29.

Cunneen, C. (2007). Crime, justice and Indigenous people [UNSW Law research paper no. 2008-11]. In E. Barclay, J. Donnermeyer, J. Scott, & R. Hogg (Eds.), *Crime in rural Australia* (pp. 142–153). Federation Press.

Cunneen, C., & Tauri, J. (2016). *Indigenous criminology*. Policy Press. https://doi.org/10.51952/9781447321781

Dinnen, S. (2019). Security governance in Melanesia: Police, prisons and crime. In E. Hirsch & W. Rollason (Eds.), *The Melanesian world* (pp. 269–284). Routledge. https://doi.org/10.4324/9781315529691

Domestic Violence Act, Laws of Fiji, Section 8-77, Act No. 33 (2009). https://www.laws.gov.fj/Acts/DisplayAct/922

Douglas, H. (2008). The criminal law's response to domestic violence: What's going on? *Sydney Law Review*, *30*(3), 439–469.

Douglas, H., & Fitzgerald, R. (2018). The domestic violence protection order system as entry to the criminal justice system for Aboriginal and Torres Strait Islander people. *International Journal for Crime, Justice and Social Democracy*, *7*(3), 41–57. https://doi.org/10.5204/ijcjsd.v7i3.499

Etherington, E. (1996). The gendering of indirect rule: Criminal law and colonial Fiji, 1875–1900. *Journal of Pacific History*, *31*(1), 42–57.

Family Protection Act, Solomon Islands, Section 12, Act No. 15 (2014). https://solomons.gov.sb/wp-content/uploads/2020/02/Family-Protection-Act-2014.pdf

Family Protection Act, Kingdom of Tonga, Section 22, Chapter 17.25 (2016). https://ago.gov.to/cms/images/LEGISLATION/PRINCIPAL/2013/2013-0018/FamilyProtectionAct_2.pdf

Fiji Women's Crisis Centre (FWCC). (1998). *For the National Congress on Women*. http://www.fijiwomen.com/flare/discussion/for-the-national-congress-on-women/

Fiji Women's Crisis Centre (FWCC). (2013). *Somebody's life, everybody's business!: National research on women's health and life experiences in Fiji*. https://pacificwomen.org/wp-content/uploads/2017/09/FWCC-National-Research-on-Womens-Health-Fiji.pdf

Fiji Women's Crisis Centre (FWCC) and UN Women Fiji MCO. (2019, September 16). Engaging Pacific men to prevent violence against women and girls. https://asiapacific.unwomen.org/en/news-and-events/stories/2019/09/engaging-pacific-men-to-prevent-violence-against-women-and-girls

Fiji Women's Rights Movement. (2018). Data analysis—Family law and violence against women and children cases: Fiji courts. https://www.fwrm.org.fj/images/A2J/Court-Annex.pdf

George, N. (2016). "Lost in translation": Gender violence, human rights and women's capabilities in Fiji. In A. Biersack, M. Jolly, & M. Macintyre (Eds.), *Gender violence & human rights: Seeking justice in Fiji, Papua New Guinea and Vanuatu* (pp. 81–126). ANU Press. https://doi.org/10.22459/GVHR.12.2016

Jivan, V., & Forster, C. (2009). Challenging conventions: In pursuit of greater legislative compliance with CEDAW in the Pacific. *Melbourne Journal of International Law*, 10(2), 655.

Knox-Mawer, R. (1961). Native courts and customs in Fiji. *International and Comparative Law Quarterly*, 10(3), 642–647.

Office of the High Commissioner of Human Rights. (n.d.). United Nations Treaty Body database: Ratification status for Fiji. https://tbinternet.ohchr.org/_layouts/15/TreatyBodyExternal/Treaty.aspx?CountryID=60&Lang=EN

Rankine, J., Percival, T., Finau, E., Hope, L.-T., Kingi, P., Peteru, M. C., Powell, E., Robati-Mani, R., & Selu, E. (2017). Pacific peoples, violence, and the power and control wheel. *Journal of Interpersonal Violence*, 32(18), 2777–2803. https://doi.org/10.1177/0886260515596148

Secretariate of the Pacific Community. (2021, September 7). Vanuatu's experience: Implementation of domestic violence legislation. https://www.spc.int/updates/blog/2021/09/vanuatus-experience-implementation-of-domestic-violence-legislation

Stanko, E. A. (1995). Policing domestic violence: Dilemmas and contradictions. *Australian and New Zealand Journal of Criminology*, 28(1 Suppl.), 31–44. https://doi.org/10.1177/00048658950280S104

State v. Dinesh Chand, High Court of Fiji, Criminal Case No. 309 of 2020. http://www.paclii.org/cgi-bin/sinodisp/fj/cases/FJHC/2020/971.html?stem=&synonyms=&query=Dinesh%20Chand

State v. Meniusi Veikila, Magistrates Court of Fiji Criminal Case No. 50 of 2020. http://www.paclii.org/cgi-bin/sinodisp/fj/cases/FJMC/2021/16.html?stem=&synonyms=&query=Veikila

UN Committee on the Elimination of Discrimination Against Women (1992), *CEDAW General Recommendation No. 19: Violence against women*. https://www.refworld.org/docid/52d920c54.html

Watego, C., Macoun, A., Singh, D., & Strakosch, E. (May 25, 2021). Carceral feminism and coercive control: When Indigenous women aren't seen as ideal victims, witnesses or women. *The Conversation*. https://theconversation.com/carceral-feminism-and-coercive-control-when-indigenous-women-arent-seen-as-ideal-victims-witnesses-or-women-161091

PART 2

Criminalization, Criminal Justice Challenges, and Consequences

6

Sentencing Aboriginal Women Who Have Killed Their Partners

Do We Really Hear Them?

KYLLIE CRIPPS ■

INTRODUCTION

On September 26, 2019, the attorney general for Western Australia announced that Aboriginal woman Jody Gore would be released from prison just 4 years into a 12-year minimum sentence for the murder of her abusive ex-partner (Baird & Gleeson, 2019). In recognition of the substantial history of domestic violence experienced by Gore, the government had intervened with an exercise of the Royal Prerogative of Mercy acknowledging that this had caused, or at least significantly contributed to, the events of June 13, 2015, that resulted in the death of her ex-partner (Baird & Gleeson, 2019). It also spoke to appreciating more broadly Gore's story through the lens of "social entrapment" (Douglas et al., 2020), recognizing that the ongoing tactics of coercive control used by perpetrators have lasting impacts on victims. These tactics undermine their autonomy, "closing down her space for action," and this is compounded further by structural inequality that can entrap victims in a cycle of violence presenting very limited safety options in times of crisis (Douglas

Kyllie Cripps, *Sentencing Aboriginal Women Who Have Killed Their Partners* In: *The Criminalization of Violence Against Women*. Edited by: Heather Douglas, Kate Fitz-Gibbon, Leigh Goodmark, and Sandra Walklate, Oxford University Press. © Oxford University Press 2024. DOI: 10.1093/oso/9780197651841.003.0007 et al., 2020, p. 488). This case is one of many within our Australian criminal justice system that highlights that while our legal system has, over time, developed the capacity to understand and explain the nuance of these situations and introduced and developed a range of legal defenses that can also mitigate sentences for women who kill violent men, available evidence suggests that for some they can be ineffectual in practice.

Indeed, evidence clearly establishes that men and women's violence in the intimate sphere is characterized, justified, and/or excused differently based on gender (Douglas, 2012; Sheehy et al., 2012a). Research also established that the ways in which individuals conform with traditional notions of masculinity and femininity impact how their conduct is understood and whether it can be rationalized as "reasonable" and therefore deserving of acquittal or of reducing their culpability in the circumstances (Sheehy et al., 2014). In a legal sphere dominated by male perspectives, women's narratives of domestic violence can often be minimized or, worse, excluded in the practice of law. Gore's case is an example of this, but it is not an isolated example; this chapter examines 12 New South Wales (NSW) cases where Aboriginal women were prosecuted for the homicide of their partner or ex-partner (see Table 6.1). The cases span approximately 30 years (1989–2021). The focus on Aboriginal women's cases is in recognition of the overrepresentation of Aboriginal women as both victims and offenders in domestic and family violence–related matters, appreciating in particular how women's experiences of victimization can make them also vulnerable to criminalization (Kaiser-Derrick, 2019).

This chapter has five parts. The first reflects whether the practice of law really hears women's narratives of domestic violence. The second explores the available defenses to homicide in NSW. The third reviews how the practices of law and legal personnel hear or fail to hear women's narratives of abuse, making the defenses ineffectual. The fourth explores the outcomes for Aboriginal women when the law fails to hear their experiences of abuse. Finally, the chapter reflects current calls for law reform to address the inadequacies of current defenses. It is argued that it is not necessarily law reform that is needed but rather training and ongoing

Table 6.1 SAMPLE OF NSW HOMICIDE CASES WHERE ABORIGINAL WOMEN KILLED THEIR ABUSIVE PARTNER

R v. Blanks. [2016] NSWSC 707.
R v. Burke. [2000] NSWSC 356.
R v. Cavanough. [2007] NSWSC 561.
R v. Doolan. [2010] NSWSC 615.
R v. Kennedy. [2000] NSWSC 109.
R v. Melrose. [2001] NSWSC 847.
R v. Mercy. [2004] NSWSC 472 (19 April 2004).
R v. Parker. [2016] NSWSC 813.
R v. Roberts. [1989] BC8902940, NSW unreported judgment.
R v. Srsa. [2021] NSWSC 924 (30 July 2021)
R v. Wilson. [2017] NSWSC 1730.
R v. Duncan. [2010] NSWSC 1241.

practice evaluation to ensure that the practice of law responds appropriately to the social entrapment that is domestic violence.

THE PRACTICE OF LAW: DOES IT REALLY HEAR WOMEN'S NARRATIVES OF DOMESTIC VIOLENCE?

Police and public prosecutors have discretionary powers to charge, prosecute, and negotiate plea bargains in cases where women have killed a violent partner. The significance of these decisions is widely acknowledged, yet little is known about the "unchecked power of the decision makers" and what factors influence them in this work (Follingstad et al., 2015). It is recognized that the practices in this area have been widely inconsistent and divergent largely because of "society's ambivalent attitudes toward battered women, and the fact that the woman is usually the only witness to the events" (Follingstad et al., 2015, p. 861). There is evidence that, unlike men, in circumstances where women have killed their violent partners, women are quick to admit what happened and to accept the consequences of their actions, often before legal advice is given (Eades, 2015; Stubbs & Tolmie, 2008). Often women in these circumstances, not knowing how the law operates, falsely assume that their conduct was justified and reasonable, while also exhibiting intense feelings of regret and remorse (Douglas, 2012; Stubbs & Tolmie, 2008). How police and prosecutors interpret women's stories of abuse and apply the law in these circumstances will determine whether the women are charged with murder or the lesser offense of manslaughter. While this will be largely dependent on the facts of the case, the decisions of police and prosecutors in these circumstances will often turn on whether they believe the woman intended to kill or inflict grievous bodily harm; whether she was acting in self-defense; whether she believed on reasonable grounds that it was necessary to do what she did; and whether the force used was excessive given due regard to the danger she was presented with (*R v. Alpagut*, 1989; Roth & Blayden, 2012). In NSW, murder carries a maximum sentence of life imprisonment and a standard nonparole period of 20 years imprisonment. The state, if unable to prove the mens rea of the offense beyond reasonable doubt will be open to the lesser charge of manslaughter, for which there is no standard nonparole period.

In representing Aboriginal women for such serious offenses, in what are clearly sensitive contexts, the need for legal counsel to establish trust and rapport in these matters to enable the mutual sharing of information to support decision-making is essential. But, it is equally important to ensure that both legal counsel and client are speaking the same language with the same understanding: Sociolinguistics and cross-cultural miscommunications can have unfortunate consequences in cases such as these. The Australian case of Robyn Kina, an Aboriginal woman convicted of murdering her abusive de facto partner in 1988 and sentenced to life in prison is well known. In this case, as Eades (1996) so clearly articulated, Kina was visited by four different legal representatives before her trial for a total of 7 hours 25 minutes from February until September. The trial was one of the shortest in Queensland's history, with less than 3 hours of evidence, and only 50 minutes for the jury to return a verdict of guilty. It was not until Kina was interviewed by journalists in 1992 (ABC, 1992) and

1993 (ABC, 1993) that the telling of her story was enabled and the grave injustice that she had experienced was fully appreciated. This case is also a useful one for retrospectively applying a social entrapment lens of analysis because it also demonstrates that the lasting impacts of violence, in the wake of a threat and crisis, closes down a victim's opportunity for action or indeed advocacy for themselves. If legal counsels are not trained or experienced in identifying or digging for further information, through methods that foster trust and rapport, the result can be an entrenchment of the entrapment that victims like Kina experience (Eades, 1996).

It should also be noted that it is common practice to overcharge women in these circumstances, resulting in significant pressure being placed on women as victims of domestic violence to plead guilty to the more serious offense of murder or the lesser offense of manslaughter rather than proceeding to trial on the basis of self-defense (Legislative Council, 2013; Sheehy et al., 2014). In pleading guilty, there is no testing of the case; rather, there is an acceptance of specific facts relevant to the case (Sheehy et al., 2012b, 2014; Tolmie & Stubbs, 2008). The women's stories, however, are relevant in the deliberation of sentence imposed. The weight given to the women's stories in this process is at the discretion of the judge, and as discussed further in this chapter, the practice of this discretion can be equally inconsistent and divergent and relies heavily on the extent to which the judge and legal practitioners understand the gendered complexities of domestic violence.

AVAILABLE DEFENSES AND SENTENCING CONSIDERATIONS

The complete defense of self-defense is open to women in domestic violence situations, yet it is rarely successful due to its traditional association with a one-off spontaneous encounter between male strangers such as a pub brawl (Roth & Blayden, 2012). This defense holds that a person is not criminally responsible for an offense if the person carries out the conduct in self-defense [e.g., *Crimes Act 1900* (NSW), s418(1)]. This defense is only open if the person believes the conduct is necessary to defend herself [*Crimes Act 1900* (NSW), s418 (2)]. The conduct must be a *reasonable response* in the circumstances as she finds them, and the onus is on the prosecution to prove beyond reasonable doubt that the person did not act in self-defense [*Crimes Act 1900* (NSW), s419]. Two issues arise in respect to this. First, did the woman genuinely believe that self-defense was necessary? Second, was her response reasonable? There is much confusion about how juries and judges, in the case of a judge-alone trial, determine the second issue, and this is explored in further detail in the case analysis presented in the next section.

The partial defense of provocation, or extreme provocation as it is now known in NSW, and its application has had a contested history in the domestic violence sphere, largely as a consequence of the use of the defense by men to excuse their anger and jealousy (Coss, 2006; Legislative Council, 2013; Roth & Blayden, 2012). In NSW in 2014, following the public furor over the justice system's handling of the *Singh* case (*Singh v. R*, 2012), in which a jury accepted that the husband had been "provoked" by his wife's supposed threats of having him deported, the NSW Parliament amended in the Crimes Act, limiting the use of provocation (Crofts & Tyson, 2013). Under the current NSW law, the partial defense of extreme provocation reduces what would otherwise be a murder charge to manslaughter, which has a significant impact in sentencing as there is no mandatory nonparole period prescribed, meaning that the sentence can be at one end wholly suspended to a maximum sentence of 25 years. This defense is enlivened if

- The act of the accused that causes death was in response to the conduct of the deceased—this can be because of a single incident or the cumulative effect of multiple incidents,
- The conduct of the deceased was a serious indictable offence punishable by a term of 5 years imprisonment,
- The conduct of the deceased caused the accused to lose self-control, and
- The conduct of the deceased could have caused an ordinary person to lose self-control to the extent of intending to kill or inflict grievous bodily harm on the deceased. [*Crimes Act 1900* (NSW), s23(2)(a)-(d)]

Concern has been expressed that reforms to the provocation law in NSW have likely restricted its application to the point of redundancy (Fitz-Gibbon, 2017). The restriction of the application of the defense to provocative conduct on the part of the victim that can be characterized as a "serious indictable offense" punishable by imprisonment for at least 5 years produces a threshold that is often difficult to meet. This is particularly so for women, who neither report violence to the police nor keep records that might enable them to demonstrate the seriousness of the offenses that have been committed on them (Easteal, 1993; Stubbs & Tolmie, 2008). It also fails to recognize the breadth and depth of abuses perpetrated against the women as it essentially is only recognizing specific types of violence, mainly physical and sexual abuse, or stalking (Fitz-Gibbon, 2017). The emotional and psychological abuse, spiritual abuse, cultural abuse, or financial abuse that women also experience, which can be equally damaging, will not meet the burden required to enliven this defense.

There is also a partial defense of diminished responsibility, also referred to as substantial impairment by abnormality of the mind [*Crimes Act 1900* (NSW), s23A (1)]. To enliven this defense requires, first, that women establish that they suffered an "abnormality of the mind" that impacted their ability to understand events and to assess their actions as right or wrong; second, that it arose from a nontransitory, preexisting mental or physiological condition; and third that it substantially impaired their capacity to control themselves. There is evidence that this defense and provocation are sometimes raised together to reduce murder charges to manslaughter (Legislative Council, 2013).

The extent to which drugs and/or alcohol can be used as a defense in situations in which women kill violent men is rarely discussed in the literature, but based on the 12 cases reviewed for this chapter, it does play a significant role in the context of Indigenous intimate partner violence. The *Crimes Act 1900* (NSW), s428C, allows intoxication to be raised in murder cases but only in respect to its relevance to whether the accused possessed specific intent to meet the mens rea standard for the crime. It is, however, not to be considered in determining whether her response to the circumstances was reasonable (Whittle & Hall, 2018). In all 12 cases examined for this chapter, drug and/or alcohol abuse was a feature of not only the violent incident that resulted in the victim's death but also of the relationship, with both partners using drugs and/or alcohol. The extent to which judges understood the use of alcohol and/or drugs as a feature and function of the violence was variable. As discussed below, in this sample of cases some judges respected that women used alcohol to numb their pain, yet other judges perceived the use of alcohol and drugs as an aggravating feature of the relationship; consequently, any resulting violence was not to be regarded as domestic violence in its stereotypical form. For example, in *R v. Doolan*, Grove J asserted that "the reality is as described by your neighbours: you and Mr Green lived a life in an alcoholic haze, punctuated by the passage of verbal and physical abuse between you. I do not regard the history as a matter of significant weight in diminution of sentence" (*R v. Doolan*, 2010, [17]).

The above statement is in stark contrast to precedents and practices of Australian courts in responding to largely violent offenses committed by Aboriginal male offenders. For example, the High Court of Australia in *Bugmy v. R* (2013) recognized that an offender's sentence may be mitigated by their experience of being an Aboriginal "offender raised in a community surrounded by alcohol abuse and violence . . . because his or her moral culpability is likely to be less than the culpability of an offender whose formative years have not been marred in that way" (*Bugmy v. R*, 2013, [40]). Further:

> The experience of growing up in an environment surrounded by alcohol abuse and violence may leave its mark on a person throughout life. Among, other things, a background of that kind may compromise the person's capacity to mature and to learn from experience. It is a feature of a person's makeup and remains relevant to the determination of the appropriate sentence. (*Bugmy v. R*, 2013, [430])

This case relied on an older precedent set in *R v. Fernando* (1992). The facts of *R v. Fernando* (1992) were more directly relevant to this chapter as it involved a male offender maliciously wounding his de facto partner with a knife. In this case, similar to *Bugmy v. R* (2013), two important points were noted:

c) It is proper for the court to recognise that the problems of alcohol abuse and violence which to a very significant degree go hand in hand within Aboriginal communities are very real ones and their cure requires more subtle remedies than the criminal law can provide by way of imprisonment.

e) While drunkenness is not normally an excuse or mitigating factor, where the abuse of alcohol by the person standing for sentence reflects the socio-economic circumstances and environment in which the offender has grown up, that can and should be taken into account as a mitigating factor. This involves realistic recognition by the court of the endemic presence of alcohol within Aboriginal communities where poor self-image, absence of education and work opportunity and other demoralising factors have placed heavy stresses on them, reinforcing their resort to alcohol and compounding its worst effects (*R v. Fernando*, 1992, pp. 62–63).

The extent to which these precedents are utilized, and impact positively, in the sentencing of Indigenous women victims of domestic violence who ultimately kill their partners is unclear. This chapter discusses this further in relation to the sample of cases in the final section of this chapter.

ABORIGINAL WOMEN'S CASES IN NSW

In the 12 cases examined for this chapter, many of the judges acknowledged that the Aboriginal women lived in conditions characterized by frequent and severe emotional, physical, and sexual violence. This violence was escalating in severity at the time of the incident to the point where "all manner of cruelty" (*R v. Kennedy*, 2000, [5]) had been inflicted on them. The length of the relationship (4 years to 20 or more years) impacted significantly on the women's sense of helplessness and ability to change their situations, the latter directly impacting how the women perceived what was reasonable in the circumstances. For example, in *R v. Duncan*, Duncan explained being on autopilot that "he would just have to raise his voice and I would be looking for a somewhere to hide" (2010, [5]). Duncan also spoke about not wishing it to be known within her community that she lived in an abusive relationship as she felt that she was perceived as a role model and as she put it "I wouldn't be seen as a very good role model if I couldn't be seen handling my own situation, in trying to help other people get their lives together and support them" (*R v. Duncan*, 2010, [7]).

Judges also further acknowledged that these women were denied "anything even approaching the physical and psychological integrity and the human dignity to which every person should be entitled" (*R v. Roberts*, 1989, [10]), that "her life was not her own" (*R v. Kennedy*, 2000, [5]). The consequences of such violence resulted in many women resorting to alcohol abuse, as one judge described, using it to excess so that it was "easier to bear [the violence] and perhaps to help forget" (*R v. Kennedy*, 2000, [21]). The cases also highlighted, that for some women not only have they "existed in socially deprived circumstances . . . consigned to a lifestyle of poverty, deprivation and entrenched alcohol abuse in an atmosphere where she is the subject of violence [she is also] conditioned to violence as a social response" (*R v. Burke*, 2000, [43]). One judge observed that had she not acted as she did she "likely would have been on the receiving end of more violence" (*R v. Wilson*, 2017, [88]). Like the Gore case, mentioned at the start of this chapter, many of the circumstances these women confronted were ones of "kill or be killed" (Baird & Gleeson, 2019). The judges accepted in all cases that the women acted "impulsively and quickly" in the "heat of the moment" (*R v. Duncan*, 2010; *R v. Kennedy*, 2000, [42], [1], [27]).

While accepting the above circumstances within their lives and that abuse had occurred, there was still a reluctance on the part of judges (and two juries that found the women guilty) to accept that the women's conduct was a "reasonable response in the circumstances" as required by the defense of self-defense [*Crimes Act 1900* (NSW), s418]. This appears to have been largely because in all 12 cases the women used a weapon, a knife in most instances, to kill their partners, and this was viewed as "excessive." This categorization pays little regard to context, specifically that the knives used were everyday kitchen knives, "whatever was close at hand in an attempt in some way to make the deceased modify his behaviour" (*R v. Kennedy*, 2000, [36]). The women's continuing experience of fear and their belief in the imminence and potential seriousness of anticipated injury based on years of abuse was also dismissed (Tyson et al., 2017). The women in these cases were also aware that engaging in retaliatory action or "fighting back" was unlikely to stop the violence being perpetrated against them as they were physically unable to match the size and strength of their partners. In two examples, using retaliatory violence in the past had resulted in the women receiving a worse beating for doing so (*R v. Kennedy*, 2000; *R v. Wilson*, 2017).

In several of the cases there was also evidence suggestive that the women's choice of conduct was being questioned in light of an expectation that they would use the law to protect themselves and services to assist them to act on the relationship (see, e.g., *R v. Doolan*, 2010; *R v. Duncan*, 2010; *R v. Kennedy*, 2000; *R v. Melrose*, 2001; *R v. Roberts*, 1989; *R v. Wilson*, 2017). Where women had sought assistance prior to the offense, judges were more accepting of the narrative that the offense took place in the context of self-defense and provocation. Indeed, in *R v. Duncan* (2010), Hidden J. states:

> While the basis of manslaughter in her case is not excessive self defence or provocation, there are elements of both in her arming herself with the knife and striking as she did. She acted quickly and impulsively in the heat of a violent incident which, as Mr Stratton put it, was not of her choosing (2010, [27]).

The extent to which Aboriginal women were able to use the partial defense of diminished responsibility or abnormality of the mind varied. Seven cases involved lengthy conversations about the women being mentally impaired. The exact nature and source of the impairment related to the women having extensive trauma histories that had largely been undiagnosed and consequently untreated until this event. The trauma histories relating to domestic violence were often compounded by histories of child abuse, including child sexual abuse (e.g., *R v. Blanks*, 2016; *R v. Burke*, 2000; *R v. Cavanaugh*, 2007; *R v. Srsa*, 2021). Related histories of alcohol and substance abuse were common as the women turned to these widely accessible drugs to numb their pain (e.g., *R v. Blanks*, 2016; *R v. Kennedy*, 2000). There was also evidence of a further spiraling of the women's mental health as the women learned that their actions resulted in the death of their partners (e.g., *R v. Melrose*, 2001).

WHAT HAPPENS WHEN THE LAW DOESN'T HEAR?

This chapter has highlighted that the law selectively hears women's stories of victimization, and that the impact is significant in terms of how the justice system then manages their cases from charging, through to plea bargaining, through to conviction and sentencing. While there have been reforms, in both law and legal practice with respect to the experience of battered women since the 1970s, influenced to a large degree by the work of Lenore Walker (1979), the Australian legal arena still struggles to genuinely hear and to act with compassion in response to women's experiences of domestic violence, at the same time balancing how to hold women accountable for killing violent men (King et al., 2016; Sheehy et al., 2012a). Legal actors, in addition to the institution itself, struggle to embrace in practice the lens of social entrapment to fully appreciate the context in which domestic violence occurs and for which justice needs to be served.

There is evidence within both the cases examined and the literature discussed that legal actors in this area attempt to fit the facts and circumstances of these cases into the frames of the law, which are traditionally male derived and continue to be heavily influenced by male perspectives. The consequence for women is that rather than hearing their individual stories, their story becomes a stereotype, and they are variously labeled in ways that demean them (Buxton-Namisnyk & Butler, 2017; Weare, 2013). The law and its actors look for the authentic "victim" (see Chapter 7, this volume) derived from traditional understandings of femininity; when victims fail to conform, their label actively shifts to "mad" or "bad," and with it the emphasis on the reasonableness of the victim's actions moves to a focus on flaws within the individual that confirm gender stereotypes and silence the "victim's" experience of domestic violence (Weare, 2013).

In the cases examined for this chapter, four cases fit neatly into an authentic victim narrative; four cases fit a narrative of "mad," with a specific focus on the individual mental impairments of the women; and in two cases the women were labeled as "bad," suggesting in both cases that the domestic violence was "not all one sided," that the women were "angry" and that their alcohol and drug use contributed to the situation they found themselves in (e.g., *R v. Cavanough*, 2007; *R v. Doolan*, 2010).

In reducing the women's stories to labels or stereotypes, the legal system not only denies the women agency, but also hopes that they can choose a life free from violence now and in the future. It also neglects to turn the mirror back on the legal system's failings of these women such that the only option available to them was to act "defensively" in the heat of the moment.

LAW REFORM OR NOT?

It is not surprising when cases like Gore's (Baird & Gleeson, 2019) mentioned at the start of this chapter become public, that there are demands for law reform. But does the law need reforming, or rather is it the practice or practitioners of law who need reforming? I would argue it is the latter, but this is far from a new demand. The literature in this field is awash with recognition that legal practitioners, particularly police and public prosecutors, need training to understand not only domestic violence and its complexities but also its intersections with race, class, gender, sexuality, drug and alcohol abuse, and mental impairments. Extending the training to judicial officers also has the potential to improve directions on how reasonableness should be deduced in circumstances of domestic violence and may also increase their confidence in calling expert testimony to assist jurors in their comprehension and application of these concepts.

There is evidence within the Indigenous cases examined in this chapter of a narrowing or retreat generally from *Fernando* principles (*R v. Fernando*, 1992) and the more recent precedent set by *Bugmy v. R* (2013), as only 4 of the 12 cases acknowledged their relevance in the sentencing of Aboriginal women in the case sample. It could be argued that Aboriginal women who have killed their intimate partners may be affected by this narrowing and retreat more acutely. These principles clearly establish the interrelationship of past and present experiences with violence and alcohol to current offending. I would argue that given the practice of hearing expert evidence about the significance of domestic violence in determining reasonable conduct (Judicial Commission of New South Wales, 2021), we should extend this to also inviting expert evidence to speak to the *Fernando* principles (*R v. Fernando*, 1992) and their relevance for Aboriginal women who kill their violent partners. This would facilitate an intersectional, multidimensional engagement with their lived reality rather than assuming that their experience of violence closely resembles that of non-Indigenous women, or in the case of *Fernando* principles (*Bugmy v. R*, 2013; *R v. Fernando*, 1992)n=, that of Indigenous men rather than being uniquely different in their own right.

Should we tinker with the homicide defenses further and/or add new defenses specific to domestic violence? My view is that, as a separate or isolated action to the above, it may not achieve the desired objectives. The history of reforms in this space, which have intended defenses to be more inclusive, have in practice resulted in women being further excluded from using the defenses. Law reform does not always result in outcomes that appreciate the specific and nuanced context of women who kill in the response to prolonged histories of domestic violence.

CONCLUSION

The stories presented throughout this chapter speak to women being constrained in their choices—with no meaningful choice available to them in how to react to and contend with the ongoing domestic violence they have experienced. It speaks to Aboriginal women living in fear and "in the heat of the moment" acting defensively knowing instinctively, based on long histories of domestic violence, that the situation was escalating and in all likelihood it was a situation of "kill or be killed." While the law provides a range of defenses to women in these tragic circumstances, as this chapter has explained, the threshold for enlivening them is often out of their reach. There is a need to remedy this situation, but law reform on its own is not the answer; rather, legal actors need to be appropriately trained in domestic violence and its consequences so that the practice of law can more sensitively hear and act on the experiences shared by domestic violence victims who kill their violent partners.

REFERENCES

ABC. (1992). *Without consent*. Australian Broadcasting Commission.

ABC. (1993). *Excuse to murder*. Australian Broadcasting Commission.

Baird, J., & Gleeson, H. (2019, September 27). *Ladies who stab: Are we failing abused women who kill?* https://www.abc.net.au/news/2019-09-28/ladies-who-stab-abused-woman-who-kill/11553582

Bugmy v. R. (2013). 249 CLR 571 [2013] HCA 37.

Buxton-Namisnyk, E., & Butler, A. (2017). What's language got to do with it? Learning from discourse, language and stereotyping in domestic violence homicide cases. *Judicial Officers Bulletin, 29*(6) 499–452, 456.

Coss, G. (2006). The defence of provocation: An acrimonious divorce from reality. *Current Issues in Criminal Justice, 18*(1), 51–78. https://doi.org/10.1080/10345329.2006.12036378

Crimes Act 1900 NSW.

Crimes Amendment (Provocation) Act. (2014). NSW.

Crimes (Domestic and Personal Violence) Act. (2007). NSW.

Crimes and Other Legislation Amendment (Assault and Intoxication) Act. (2014). NSW.

Crofts, T., & Tyson, D. (2013). Homicide law reform in Australia: Improving access to defences for women who kill their abusers. *Monash University Law Review, 39*(3), 864–893.

Douglas, H., McGlade, H., Tarrant, S., & Tolmie, J. (2020). Facts seen and unseen: Improving justice responses by using a social entrapment lens for cases involving abused women (as offenders or victims). *Current Issues in Criminal Justice, 32*(4), 488–506. https://doi.org.10.1080/10345329.2020.1829779

Douglas, H. (2012). A consideration of the merits of specialised homicide offences and defences for battered women. *Australian New Zealand Journal of Criminology, 45*(3), 367–382. https://doi.org/10.1177/0004865812456851

Eades, D. (1996). Legal recognition of cultural differences in communication: The case of Robyn Kina. *Language and Communication, 16*(3), 215–227. https://doi.org/10.1016/0271-5309(96)00011-0

Eades, D. (2015). Judicial understandings of Aboriginality and language use in criminal cases. In P. Toner (Ed.), *Strings of connectedness: Essays in honour of Ian Keen* (pp. 27–51). ANU Press.

Easteal, P. (1993). *Killing the beloved: Homicide between adult sexual intimates*. Australian Institute of Criminology.

Fitz-Gibbon, K. (2017). Homicide law reform in New South Wales: Examining the merits of the partial defence of "extreme" provocation. *Melbourne University Law Review, 40*(3), 769–815.

Follingstad, D., Rogers, M. J., Welling, S., & Priesmeyer, F. J. (2015). Decisions to prosecute battered women's homicide cases: An exploratory study. *Journal of Family Violence, 30*(7), 859–874. https://doi.org/10.1007/s10896-015-9725-7

Kaiser-Derrick, E. (2019). *Implicating the system: Judicial discourses in the sentencing of Indigenous women*. University of Manitoba Press.

King, C., Bartels, L., Easteal, P., & Hopkins, A. (2016). Did defensive homicide in Victoria provide a safety net for battered women who kill? A case study analysis. *Monash University Law Review, 42*(1), 138–178.

Judicial Commission of New South Wales. (2021). *Handbook for judicial officers, 2021*. https://www.judcom.nsw.gov.au/publications/benchbks/judicial_officers/index.html

Legislative Council. (2013). *Select Committee on the Partial Defence of Provocation: The partial defence of provocation report*. Legislative Council.

R v. Alpagut unreported NSW 26 July 1989.

R v. Blanks [2016] NSWSC 707.

R v. Burke [2000] NSWSC 356.

R v. Cavanough [2007] NSWSC 561.

R v. Doolan [2010] NSWSC 615.

R v. Duncan [2010] NSWSC 1241.

R v. Fernando [1992] 76 A Crim R 58.

R v. Kennedy. [2000] NSWSC 109.

R v. Melrose. [2001] NSWSC 847.

R v. Mercy. [2004] NSWSC 472 (19 April 2004).

R v. Parker. [2016] NSWSC 813.

R v. Roberts. [1989] BC8902940, NSW unreported judgment.

R v. Srsa. [2021] NSWSC 924 (30 July 2021).

R v. Wilson. [2017] NSWSC 1730.

Roth, L., & Blayden, L. (2012). *Provocation and self-defence in intimate partner and sexual advance homicides* (NSW Parliamentary Research Service Briefing Paper No. 5/2012). NSW Government, Sydney.

Sheehy, E., Stubbs, J., & Tolmie, J. (2012a). Battered women charged with homicide in Australia, Canada and New Zealand: How do they fare? *Australian & New Zealand Journal of Criminology*, *45*(3), 383–399. https://doi.org/10.1177/0004865812456855

Sheehy, E., Stubbs, J., & Tolmie, J. (2012b). Defences to homicide for battered women: A comparative analysis of laws in Australia, Canada and New Zealand. *Sydney Law Review*, *34*(3), 467–492.

Sheehy, E., Stubbs, J., & Tolmie, J. (2014). Securing fair outcomes for battered women charged with homicide: Analysing defence lawyering in R v Falls. *Melbourne University Law Review*, *38*(2), 666–707.

Singh v R. [2012] NSWSC 637 (7 June 2012).

Stubbs, J., & Tolmie, J. (2008). Battered women charged with homicide: Advancing the interests of Indigenous women. *Australian & New Zealand Journal of Criminology*, *41*(1), 138–161. https://doi.org/10.1375/acri.41.1.138

Tyson, D., Kirkwood, D., & McKenzie, M. (2017). Family violence in domestic homicides: A case study of women who killed intimate partners post-legislative reform in Victoria, Australia. *Violence Against Women*, *23*(5), 559–583. https://doi.org/10.1177/1077801216647796

Walker, L. (1979). *The battered woman syndrome*. Springer Publishing.

Weare, S. (2013). "The mad," "the bad," "the victim": Gendered constructions of women who kill within the criminal justice system. *Laws*, *2*(3), 337–361. https://doi.org/10.3390/laws2030337

Whittle, M., & Hall, G. (2018). Intimate partner homicide: Themes in judges' sentencing remarks. *Psychiatry, Psychology and Law*, *25*(6), 922–943. https://doi.org/10.1080/13218719.2018.1482571

7

United States v. Maddesyn George

The Consequences of Criminalization for Native Women in the United States

LEIGH GOODMARK ■

INTRODUCTION

United States v. Maddesyn George can be described simply: On July 12, 2020, Maddesyn George shot and killed Kristopher Graber. She pled guilty and was sentenced to 6.5 years in federal prison. But beneath that simplified story lies a thicket of thorny issues: the criminalization of gender-based violence in the United States, historic tropes about Native women, the inability of tribes to hold white men accountable for the violence they do to Native women, the epidemic of missing and murdered Indigenous women in the United States, and the punishment of survivors of gender-based violence for acts of self-defense. This chapter explores those intersections, arguing that the punishment of Maddesyn George was the unjust but entirely predictable outcome of the confluence of these forces.

Leigh Goodmark, United States v. Maddesyn George In: *The Criminalization of Violence Against Women*. Edited by: Heather Douglas, Kate Fitz-Gibbon, Leigh Goodmark, and Sandra Walklate, Oxford University Press.
© Oxford University Press 2024. DOI: 10.1093/oso/9780197651841.003.0008

THE FACTS

Kristopher Graber was a familiar figure on the Colville Reservation. Graber, a white man, lived near the reservation in Omak, Washington. He helped people fix their cars. He dated Native women, including Maddesyn George's older sister. He was a meth dealer—George's meth dealer. And he was "known" for "beat[ing] the living shit out of a woman" (Criscione, 2021). On July 11, 2020, George was hanging out with Graber in his home in Omak when Graber began touching her without her consent. When George tried to leave, Graber pulled out his gun and told her that she wasn't going anywhere. Graber raped George with a vibrator, then fell asleep. George fled with money, drugs, and Graber's gun. The next day, Graber came to the reservation to find George. He went house to house with a shotgun looking for her. Graber found George sitting in a friend's car and reached for George through the open car window. George shot Graber with his gun, hitting him in the chest. Graber died from his injuries (Law, 2021).

Federal prosecutors initially charged George with a number of crimes, including second-degree murder, possession of a stolen firearm, possession with intent to distribute methamphetamine (the drugs George took from Graber's home), and robbery. George ultimately pled guilty to voluntary manslaughter and possession with intent to distribute methamphetamine. On November 17, 2021, U.S. District Court Judge Rosanna Peterson sentenced George to 6.5 years imprisonment—far less than the 17 years prosecutors requested and under the standard sentencing range of 9–11 years, but 6.5 years imprisonment nonetheless (Campaign to Free Maddesyn George, 2021).

GENDER-BASED VIOLENCE AGAINST NATIVE WOMEN IN THE UNITED STATES

Maddesyn George is one of the countless Native women victimized by white men in the United States, a history that started at colonization.

Colonizers from various European nations, including Spain and Great Britain, raped and sexually assaulted Native women. Law professor Sarah Deer wrote: "Columbus' arrival not only represents the destruction of indigenous culture, but also the beginning of rape of Native American women by European men" (Deer, 2005, p. 458).[1] Rape was used as a war tactic by the U.S. military, and, as Deer noted: "Some wars with Indian nations arose, in part, due to the failure of the United States to stop their soldiers from sexually abusing Native women" (Deer, 2017, p. 774).[2] In 1864, Native women were killed and sexually mutilated at Sand Creek, Colorado, by members of the U.S. Army, who "cut a woman's private parts out, and had them for exhibition on a stick" and "cut out the private parts of females, and stretched them over their saddle-bows and wore them over their hats" (Carroll, 1973, pp. 94–95). White men continued to abuse Native women throughout the westward expansion; sexual violence against Native women increased during the land rush in Oklahoma and California's gold rush (Deer, 2017). Such violence was common in Washington State as well. As urban planning professor Margo Hill explained, white settlers living on Spokane lands killed Native people who they accused of theft, but never investigated or prosecuted white men accused of raping Native women (Hill, 2021). More recently, the migration of workers in response to oil booms on or near Native lands has coincided with significant increases in rape and sexual assault of Native women in those areas (Bleir & Zoledziowski, 2018).

Native women continue to be subjected to gender-based violence at staggering rates across the United States. Of Native women, 56% experienced sexual violence over their lifetimes, 14% in the past year. And 55% reported being physically abused by an intimate partner, with 8% experiencing such violence in the past year (Rosay, 2016). Some sources dispute these numbers, arguing that they are too low. Deer explained:

> When I travel to Indian country, however, advocates tell me that the Justice Department statistics provide a very low estimate, and rates of sexual assault against Native American women are actually much higher. Many of the elders that I have spoken with in Indian country

tell me that they do not know any women in their community who have not experienced sexual violence. (Deer, 2005, pp. 455–457)

Similarly, Sunrise Black Bull, a project coordinator with White Buffalo Calf Women, which serves Lakota victims of gender-based violence living on the Rosebud Reservation in South Dakota, estimated that two thirds of the women on the reservation have been raped or sexually assaulted (Sood, 2020). In some U.S. counties, murder rates for Native women are more than 10 times the national average (Bachman et al., 2008). Studies have consistently shown that non-Native, and particularly white, men are responsible for this violence. A 2016 study found that 97% of Native women who reported experiencing violence have been abused by a non-Native person (Rosay, 2016). A 1998 report had similar findings; 88% of those who abused Native women were non-Native, and 70% were white (Bureau of Justice Statistics, 1998). The high rates of rape and sexual assault of Native women are tied to perceptions of them as rapeable. As gender studies professor Luana Ross noted in *Inventing the Savage: The Social Construction of Native American Criminality*, rape laws were intended to protect "respectable" white women; other women had to fend for themselves. Native women who conform to the stereotype of the virginal princess—as portrayed in the Disney movie *Pocahontas*, for example— "are too noble to ravage." But Native women perceived to be "squaws"— "savage, whorish"—can be raped with impunity (Ross, 1998, p. 168).

Native women experience rape and sexual assault in ways common to many women: They feel shame; suffer from physical and mental injury, including unwanted pregnancy and sexually transmitted diseases; and may self-medicate with illegal substances (Deer, 2017). And like other women of color, Native women face racism from service providers and others when they report (Deer, 2003/2004). But rape and sexual assault are particularly debilitating for Native women given the strong ties between rape and colonization. As Deer wrote:

> When speaking with Native American women who have survived rape, it is often difficult for them to separate the more immediate experience of their assault from the larger experience that their people

have experienced through forced removal, displacement, and destruction. (Deer, 2005, p. 459)

Deer concluded: "The survivor may experience a sexual assault as part of a larger policy to silence, dis-empower, and ultimately destroy her nation" (Deer, 2003/2004, p. 6).

THE LEGAL RESPONSE TO GENDER-BASED VIOLENCE ON NATIVE LAND

A typical criminal case in the United States involves an individual state enforcing state criminal law, unless there is some reason for the federal government to become involved (e.g., because the crime occurred on federal lands or because the crime involved interstate conduct in some way). Prior to 1817, tribal lands were viewed in the same way as states: as sovereign authorities responsible for enforcing the law in their jurisdiction. Tribal nations could and did hold both Native and non-Native people accountable for crimes committed on tribal lands. Tribal nations exercised jurisdiction over claims of rape and "most tribal communities had a strong response to sexual crimes against women, including corporal punishment and banishment" (Deer, 2003/2004, p. 14).

But in 1817, the United States significantly curtailed tribal nations' power to enforce their criminal laws by passing the General Crimes Act. The act granted the federal government jurisdiction over crimes committed by non-Natives against Natives on Native lands. That law was followed in 1885 by the Major Crimes Act, which restricted tribal courts to prosecuting Native people and capped incarceration for acts tried in tribal courts to 3 years. Most importantly, the Major Crimes Act conferred jurisdiction to prosecute all felonies on the federal government (although tribes may have concurrent jurisdiction over certain felony prosecutions when the defendant is Native) (Deer, 2003/2004).

By the 1950s, several states had regained the power to prosecute both Native and non-Native defendants for criminal acts, including sexual assault, committed on Native lands. Public Law 280, enacted in 1953, restored that power to Alaska, California, Minnesota, Nebraska, Oregon, and Wisconsin; state-specific laws like the Kansas Act, enacted in 1940, had a similar effect. But state police and prosecutors were unaware of or confused about their power to act on Native lands (Deer et al, 2007), a confusion exacerbated by the Supreme Court's 1978 decision in *Oliphant v. Suquamish Indian Tribe*, which held that Indian nations lacked criminal jurisdiction over non-Natives who committed crimes on reservations. That confusion will likely increase because of the Supreme Court's conflicting rulings on criminal jurisdiction on tribal lands in two recent decisions, *McGirt v. Oklahoma* and *Oklahoma v. Castro-Huerta*.

By the late 1980s and early 1990s, the United States had begun to rely heavily on the criminalization of gender-based violence as its primary response to that violence (Goodmark, 2018). Federal resources were disproportionately poured into policing and prosecution via the Violence Against Women Act (VAWA), the signature piece of federal legislation on gender-based violence in the United States. As of 2013, approximately 85% of VAWA funding supported the criminal legal system in some way (Messing et al., 2015). VAWA was also used to promote the policies undergirding criminalization, including mandatory and preferred arrest and aggressive prosecution policies. Ironically, policies like mandatory arrest led to a significant increase in the number of arrests of women, particularly women of color, not because women had become more violent, but because of the ways that police enforced those laws (Miller, 2005).

The focus on criminalization was problematic for Native victims of gender-based violence. Tribes often lacked jurisdiction over non-Natives who sexually and physically abused Native people. Even in cases where tribal courts issued civil protective orders to protect Native people from non-Native abusers, courts could not criminally enforce those orders (Leeds, 2011). In theory, the federal government could have prosecuted these claims. As Deer noted, however: "Granting federal officials the authority to prosecute major crimes does not mandate that they do so" (Deer, 2017, p. 776). A 2020 U.S. Department of Justice report found that federal prosecutors declined to pursue almost a third of the cases committed on reservations, including a substantial number of cases of gender-based violence (United States Department of Justice, 2020). Deer argued that its failure to prosecute these cases has made the federal government a "historical culpable bystander" to gender-based violence (Deer, 2017, p. 780).

In recent years, VAWA has restored tribal authority to prosecute certain kinds of gender-based violence inflicted on Native people by non-Native people on Native lands. VAWA's 2013 iteration conferred special domestic violence criminal jurisdiction on tribes, empowering tribes to prosecute cases of intimate partner violence involving Native victims and non-Native defendants as long as the non-Native defendant had "sufficient ties" to the tribe. Those ties include residing on tribal lands, being employed on tribal lands, or being a spouse, intimate partner, or dating partner of a Native person residing on tribal lands. The 2022 reauthorization of VAWA extended that special jurisdiction to include sexual violence and sex trafficking, among other crimes (Office on Violence Against Women, 2022). In the future, then, prosecution of gender-based violence on tribal lands may be more robust, although that prosecution is still restricted to non-Natives with some direct connection to the tribe. Until the impact of expanded jurisdiction becomes clear, Native women might continue to echo the words of Ojibwe survivor Lisa Brunner:

> We have always known that non-Indians can come onto our lands and they can beat, rape and murder us and there is nothing we can do about it.... Now, our tribal officers have jurisdiction for the first time to do something about certain crimes. But ... it is just the first sliver of the full moon that we need to protect us. (Horowitz, 2014)

WHAT DOES THIS HAVE TO DO WITH MADDESYN GEORGE?

The history of violence against Native women by white men in the United States is well documented. Nonetheless, the U.S. legal regime stripped jurisdiction from tribes to prosecute gender-based violence on their lands. And despite the focus in the United States on criminalization of gender-based violence, the federal government has largely failed to act to protect Native women in response to that violence. These factors created the context within which Maddesyn George acted to protect herself from Kristopher Graber.

Washington State, where the Colville Reservation is located, is not a Public Law 280 state. And VAWA's special domestic violence crime jurisdiction likely would not have extended to violence by Graber against George on the Colville Reservation. In 2020, that jurisdiction only applied to people in domestic or dating relationships, and, as George noted, she and Graber had never been romantically involved. George told reporter Victoria Law: "We never had a sexual relationship. . . . He was my drug dealer and that was it" (Law, 2021). Had Graber physically or sexually abused George during their confrontation the day after the rape, the Colville Tribe probably would not have had jurisdiction to prosecute Graber. The Colville Tribe would therefore have been reliant on the federal government to prosecute. Such a prosecution would have been unlikely, according to former Colville tribal court prosecutor Jonnie Bray: "I've never seen the United States prosecute a non-Indian on behalf of the Colville Tribes. And I've been working in the court system for 26 years" (Criscione, 2021).

The United States' focus on criminalization as the solution to gender-based violence obscures how difficult accessing the criminal legal system can be for many women, particularly Native women. Knowing that the government frequently declines to pursue these cases, especially when they involve non-Native defendants, Native women often do not report the gender-based violence they endure (Deer, 2017, 2003/2004). Maddesyn George was no different. She did not report that Graber had raped her until after she was arrested for killing Graber. In addition to the common understanding that reporting a rape by a white man was a futile endeavor, George had had previous unsatisfying experiences with reporting violence (Criscione, 2021). George also specifically had reason to fear the law enforcement officers who might have investigated the rape. Okanogan County Detective Isaiah Holloway had sexually harassed George in the past, sending unwanted messages, propositioning her, and sending her pictures of his genitals (Law, 2021; Reyna, 2021). George was so unnerved by Holloway's behavior that she moved to another town (Reyna, 2021). Sexual violence by law enforcement officers against women seeking assistance with gender-based violence is depressingly common (Ritchie, 2017), but, as lawyer, author, and organizer Andrea Ritchie noted: "The widespread, systemic, and almost routine nature of police sexual violence remains largely invisible to the public eye, though it chronically festers on the streets and in alleys, squad cars, and police lockups" (Ritchie, 2017, p. 109). Given how few deputies worked in the Okanogan County Sheriff's Office, Holloway might well have been responsible for investigating Graber's rape of George (Reyna, 2021), giving George little hope that she would find safety by reporting.

When George did report to both tribal and Okanogan County police that she had been raped, they did nothing with that information. They did not offer George a forensic examination (although the norm in many communities is to conduct a forensic examination within 72 hours of the rape). Had they ordered the rape kit, however, there was no guarantee that any further action would have been taken. Police did not bother to investigate George's claim; George "felt they didn't believe me" (Law, 2021). Had they done so, they might have learned that two women had previously sought protection orders against Graber as a result of his violence. One of the women wrote that Graber appeared to be "physically sexually aroused from beating me up and almost taking my life" (Defendant's Response to Government's Sentencing Memorandum, 2021). Investigators might also have found the handcuffs bolted to the wall next to a bed in Graber's home or taken statements from the people (not in law enforcement) to whom George did report the rape prior to the shooting.

There is no guarantee that earlier intervention by the criminal legal system would have stopped Graber's continued use of violence. There is much reason to believe, in fact, that the criminal legal system is ineffectual in decreasing or deterring gender-based violence and exacerbates the correlates of that violence (Goodmark, 2018). Indeed, Graber's own criminal history (Graber had been arrested several times for crimes of domestic violence and for violating protective orders and was on electronic home monitoring at the time of the shooting) makes it clear that intervention by the criminal system does not prevent recidivist violence (Criscione, 2021). But what is important here is George's belief that she would have to protect herself because she could not rely on law enforcement to protect her. As her attorney, Stephen Graham, wrote in response to the government's sentencing memorandum in George's case: "Indigenous women are forced to assess self-defense in the context of [a] system that does not come close to protecting them from men like Mr. Graber" (Defendant's Response to Government's Sentencing Memorandum, 2021).

Native women on the Colville Reservation might remember the 1972 case of Yvonne Wanrow when making those assessments. Wanrow's son was at the home of Wanrow's friend, Shirley Hooper, when he reported that a man had tried to abduct him. Hooper's neighbor, William Wesler, came to Hooper's porch shortly thereafter and said: "I didn't touch the boy." Hooper's daughter identified Wesler as having molested her 2 days earlier, and Hooper's landlord told Hooper that Wesler had previously tried to molest another child. Hooper called the police, but police said Hooper would have to come into the station to file a complaint before they were willing to arrest Wesler. Hooper then called Wanrow to come stay with her. Wanrow brought a gun. Later that evening, Wanrow's brother-in-law brought Wesler to Hooper's home. In the ensuing confusion after Wesler was told to leave and refused, Wanrow found herself standing next to Wesler. Wesler was intoxicated and was almost a foot taller than Wanrow, who was on crutches and in a cast. Wanrow shot and killed Wesler. Wanrow was convicted of second-degree murder, a conviction later overturned on appeal. One of the lessons of Wanrow's case, argued law professor Janet Halley, could be that assessing whether Wanrow's actions were reasonable would require determining whether Wanrow "could not rely on the State to provide meaningful protection for her and her child" because they were Native (Engle et al., 2003). Wanrow did not trust police and believed she had to protect herself because she did not expect the police to protect her (Schneider, 2000). Gender and sexuality studies professor Emily Thuma situated that lack of trust in the broader context of "virulent anti-Indian racism in eastern Washington" (Thuma,

2019, p. 42), a racism that, according to Native women, has not dissipated (Swaby, 2021). George shared Wanrow's belief that she had to protect herself, and Yvonne Wanrow, now Yvonne Swan, agreed with her assessment. Speaking to a rally in support of George, Swan said she believed that Graber would have killed George had she not defended herself—"and I am convinced he would have gotten away with it" (Ball, 2021).

And so Maddesyn George decided to defend herself. The problem for George, as for many women who act in self-defense, is that police, prosecutors, and courts approach the cases of these women with attitudes ranging from skepticism to hostility. This is particularly so when those women fail to adhere to perfect victim stereotypes: "The 'true' or 'worthy' victim loses some of her halo if her presentation falters" (Dunn, 2002, p. 83). Perfect victims are meek, passive, white, heterosexual, and well behaved. They are not tough, abrasive, argumentative, or aggressive. They conform to traditional gender roles. They do not use violence. They do not use drugs or alcohol (Goodmark, 2023).

Maddesyn George was an imperfect victim. George was addicted to methamphetamine, a fact that would certainly have caused police to doubt her story of rape. As Jonnie Bray, the former tribal prosecutor explained, if George had gone to police to report, they would have been "looking at her as an addict" and been more interested in determining whether she had outstanding warrants than whether she had been raped (Criscione, 2021). George had previously been convicted of drug possession and burglary (Law, 2021), and she took drugs, cash, and Graber's gun from Graber's home after the rape. George had a relationship with local police that could be described as problematic at best. And of course, George is Native, and Graber was white. George understood how being an imperfect victim undermined her credibility in the eyes of law enforcement: "I didn't feel they would listen because of the life I was living" (Law, 2021).

The same federal government that has repeatedly failed to protect Native women on tribal lands (Ball, 2021; Nagle & Lower, 2022), moved swiftly and harshly against George. George was charged with second-degree murder, assault with a dangerous weapon, discharging and using a firearm during and in relation to a crime of violence, robbery, and possession with intent to distribute methamphetamine. Prosecutors quickly made it clear that they did not believe that George had been raped and opposed George's motion to present evidence to support a claim of self-defense at trial. They also opposed George's attempts to introduce evidence of Graber's history of violence against women. The story prosecutors told was of a drug-addicted woman who robbed her drug dealer and bragged about it later. That prosecutors dismissed George's self-defense claims and questioned the sincerity of her fear of Graber was not surprising. When victims become defendants, prosecutors' ability to appreciate a criminal defendant's victimization disappears. To bring a case, prosecutors must have a good faith belief that they can prove their case beyond a reasonable doubt. Once they decide to take a case forward, prosecutors become committed to their theory of the case. They make the facts fit their argument. Prosecutors reject defendants' victimization claims and offer alternative explanations for defendants' actions (Goodmark, 2023). Consciously or not, prosecutors use stereotypes—like stereotypes about perfect victims, Native people, and substance abuse—to undermine the credibility of a defendant's assertion of self-defense. All of these forces were at play in Maddesyn George's case. As George's defense attorney argued in his sentencing memorandum: "Is it possible that Maddesyn George is both a flawed individual AND a victim of rape? The government has never made allowance for such a possibility. The defense would contend that both are true. But no amount of drug abuse or thievery from Walmart or juvenile court convictions forfeit a woman's right to bodily autonomy" (Defendant's Sentencing Memorandum, 2021, p. 5).

Facing a potential sentence of more than 40 years imprisonment, George pled guilty to possession with intent to distribute methamphetamine and voluntary manslaughter. As many as 95% of all criminal cases in the United States are resolved through plea bargains. Substantial numbers of criminalized survivors plead guilty in cases where they might otherwise have credible defenses. Many, like George, take pleas because they want to get home to their children as quickly as possible. And prosecutors incentivize plea bargaining by overcharging initially and threatening to add additional charges or seek longer sentences if the defendant declines the plea.

In their sentencing memorandum, prosecutors made it clear that they did not believe George's rape allegation. For prosecutors, this was a simple case of a "drug rip" carried out by someone with "a history of violence and drug dealing" and an "escalating criminal history" (United States' Sentencing Memorandum, 2021). Prosecutors included statements from several individuals who described Graber as kind and generous and who contended that he would never be "inappropriate" with a woman. Missing from the prosecution's memorandum: Graber's history of violence against women, the specific allegations contained in protective orders filed by women who had had relationships with Graber, and the failure of police to remove firearms from Graber's home despite the existence of these protective orders.

Ultimately, prosecutors requested a sentence of 17 years imprisonment; the defense asked that George be sentenced to 5 years in prison. At sentencing, Judge Peterson "made it unequivocally clear that she found Maddesyn's account of sexual assault to be credible" (Free Maddesyn George, 2021). She criticized prosecutors' failure to address Graber's history of violence against women and to prosecute Graber's violations of federal firearms laws. She cited the epidemic of missing and murdered Indigenous women in the United States in setting George's sentence and referred to laws passed specifically to address that crisis. Although George's defense attorney believed that "the judge expressed understanding for the plight of Indigenous women . . . . We finally felt heard and listened to and understood" (Reyna, 2021), Judge Peterson nonetheless sentenced George to 6.5 years imprisonment. The sentencing range for the charges to which George pled guilty is 9–11 years; for Judge Peterson to order a sentence below the guidelines required justification. Neither the evidence that she had been sexually assaulted nor the judge's willingness to credit that evidence changed the fact that Maddesyn George would spend a substantial portion of her life in prison for Kristopher Graber's death. Prosecutors had won their case as soon as George pled guilty.

CONCLUSION

The case of Maddesyn George is not nearly as simple as it seems. When Maddesyn George shot Kristopher Graber, she acted against a backdrop of epidemic levels of violence against Native women by non-Native men and the historical failure of the U.S. legal system to keep them safe.

Criminalization of gender-based violence in the United States has failed women, both because it has not curbed the epidemic of violence against them and because it has increased the number of women punished by the criminal legal system. The reliance on criminalization to address gender-based violence in the United States created an expectation that women would turn to law enforcement for assistance. The criminal system's response has been inconsistent at best, particularly for Native women, who encounter both legal hurdles and harmful stereotypes when they seek help from law enforcement.

At the same time, the United States, like a number of other countries, faces a crisis of missing and murdered Indigenous women. Native women are murdered at almost three times the rate of white women in the United States (Petrosky et al., 2017). According to the Urban Indian Health Institute: "Murder is the third leading cause of death for Native women" (2018). In a 2018 report, the institute identified 506 missing and murdered Indigenous women in the United States, a figure that it believes to be an undercount given the lack of data on this phenomenon. Washington State had the second highest number of missing and murdered women, with 71. According to journalist Luna Reyna: "Data from the Sovereign Bodies Institute showed that Okanogan County, the county George lives in, has had the fourth highest per capita rate of incidents of missing and murdered Indigenous women in the state since 2010" (Reyna, 2021). But despite the scores of missing and murdered Native women in the United States, police and prosecutors still don't find Native women's claims about violence credible, and when women act to protect themselves, they face punishment. As a result, Native women are faced with an impossible choice: Do you act in self-defense, knowing that the same system that has failed to protect you from violence is likely to react harshly against you when you do? That's the choice that Maddesyn George faced. It's a choice no victim of gender-based violence should ever have to make.

NOTES

1. Although Columbus was born in Genoa, now part of Italy, he colonized Native peoples in the Americas on behalf of Spain.
2. This chapter relies significantly on the work of Sarah Deer, the foremost U.S. scholar on Native women, violence, and the U.S. legal system.

REFERENCES

Bachman, R., Zaykowski, H., Kallmyer, R., Poteyeva, M., & Lanier, C. (2008). *Violence against American Indian and Alaska Native Women and the criminal justice response: What is known*. U.S. Department of Justice. https://www.ojp.gov/pdffiles1/nij/grants/223691.pdf

Ball, E. (2021, November 8). Open wounds: The case of Maddesyn George and the legal legacies of colonialism. *Range*.

Bleir, G., & Zoledziowski, A. (2018). Murdered and missing Native American women challenge police and courts. Center for Public Integrity. https://publicintegrity.org/politics/murdered-and-missing-native-american-women-challenge-police-and-courts/

Bureau of Justice Statistics. (1998). *American Indians and crime*. United States Department of Justice.

Campaign to Free Maddesyn George. (2021). Defense committee statement on sentencing. https://www.freemaddesyn.com/sentencing

Carroll, J. (1973). *The Sand Creek massacre: A documentary history*. Sol Lewis.

Criscione, W. (2021, February 25). A Native American says she shot her alleged rapist in self-defense. Federal prosecutors charged her with murder. *Inlander*. https://www.inlander.com/spokane/a-native-american-says-she-shot-her-alleged-rapist-in-self-defense-federal-prosecutors-charged-her-with-murder/Content?oid=21192760

Deer, S. (2003/2004). Expanding the network of safety: Tribal protection orders for survivors of sexual assault. *Tribal Law Journal*, 4, 3–23. https://digitalrepository.unm.edu/tlj/vol4/iss1/3

Deer, S. (2005). Sovereignty of the soul: Exploring the intersection of rape law reform and federal Indian law. *Suffolk University Law Review*, 38(2), 455–466. https://ssrn.com/abstract=987702

Deer, S. (2017). Bystander No More? Improving the Federal Response to Sexual Violence in Indian Country. *Utah Law Review*, 7(4), 771–800. https://dc.law.utah.edu/ulr/vol2017/iss4/7

Deer, S., Goldberg, C., Singleton, H. V., & White Eagle, M. (2007). *Final report: Focus group on Public Law 280 and the sexual assault of Native women*. Tribal Law and Policy Institute.

Defendant's Response to Government's Sentencing Memorandum (2021). United States v. Madelyn Danielle George, Case Number 2:20-CR-153-RMP.

Defendant's Sentencing Memorandum (2021). United States v. Maddesyn Danielle George, Case No. 2:20-CR-00153-RMP-1.

Dunn, J. L. (2002). *Courting Disaster: Intimate Stalking, Culture, and Criminal Justice*. New York: Transaction Publishers.

Engle, K., Schneider, E. M., Schultz, V., Berman, N., Davis, A., & Halley, J. (2003). Round table discussion: Subversive legal moments? *Texas Journal of Women and the Law, 12*, 197–246.

General Crimes Act, 18 U.S.C. s 1152 (1817).

Goodmark, L. (2023). *Imperfect victims: Criminalized survivors and the promise of abolition feminism*. University of California Press.

Goodmark, L. (2018). *Decriminalizing domestic violence: A balanced policy approach to intimate partner violence*. University of California Press.

Hill, M. (2021). No honor in genocide: A case study of street renaming and community organizing in the wake of national decolonization efforts. *Journal of Hate Studies, 17*(1), 85–107. https://doi.org/10.33972/jhs.200

Horowitz, S. (2014). New law offers protection to abused Native American women. *Washington Post*. https://www.washingtonpost.com/world/national-security/new-law-offers-a-sliver-of-protection-to-abused-native-american-women/2014/02/08/0466d1ae-8f73-11e3-84e1-27626c5ef5fb_story.html

Kansas Act, 18 U.S.C. s 3243 (1948).

Law, V. (2021). Maddesyn George killed her alleged rapist. Prosecutors blocked her self defense claims. *The Intercept*. https://theintercept.com/2021/10/08/maddesyn-george-self-defense-rape/

Leeds, S. L. (2011). A tribal court domestic violence case: The story of an unknown victim, an unreported decision, and the all too common injustice. In E. M. Schneider & S. M. Wildman (Eds.), *Women and the law stories* (pp. 453–463). Foundation Press.

Major Crimes Act, 18 U.S.C. s 1153 (1885).

Messing, J. T., Ward-Lasher, A., Thaller, J., & Bagwell Gray, M. E. (2015). The state of intimate partner violence intervention: Progress and continuing challenges, *Social Work, 60*(4), 305–313. https://doi.org/10.1093/sw/swv027

Miller, S. (2005). *Victims as offenders: The paradox of women's violence in relationships*. Rutgers University Press.

Nagle, M. K., & Lower, E. (2022). What will it take to end violence against Native women? *Boston Review*. https://bostonreview.net/articles/what-will-it-take-to-end-violence-against-native-women/

Office on Violence Against Women, United States Department of Justice. (2022). *Implementation of VAWA 2022's tribal jurisdiction reimbursement program*. https://www.ovwtjreimbursement.org/#:~:text=VAWA%202022%20requires%20that%20the,exercising%20special%20Tribal%20criminal%20jurisdiction

Oliphant v. Suquamish Indian Tribe, 435 U.S. 191 (1978).

Petrosky, E., Blair, J. M., Betz, C. J., Fowler, K. A., Jack, S. P. D., & Lyons, B. H. (2017). Racial and ethnic differences in homicides of adult women and the role of intimate partner violence—United States, 2003–2014. *Morbidity and Mortality Weekly Report*, 66(28), 741–746. https://doi.org/10.15585/mmwr.mm6628a1

Public Law 83-280 (1953).

Reyna, L. (2021, December 7). Colville mother's conviction raises justice issues facing Native women, *Crosscut*. https://crosscut.com/equity/2021/12/colville-mothers-conviction-raises-justice-issues-facing-native-women#:~:text=Equity-,Colville%20mother's%20conviction%20raises%20justice%20issues%20facing%20Native%20women,advocating%20for%20incarcerated%20Native%20women

Ritchie, A. (2017). *Invisible no more: Police violence against Black women and women of Color*. Beacon Press.

Rosay, A. B. (2016). Violence against American Indian and Alaska Native women and men. *NIJ Journal*, 277, 38–45.

Ross, L. (1998). *Inventing the savage: The social construction of Native American criminality*. University of Texas Press.

Schneider, E. M. (2000). *Battered women and feminist lawmaking*. Yale University Press.

Sood, R. (2020). Repairing the jurisdictional "patchwork" enabling sexual assault on Indian reservations. *University of Maryland Law Journal of Race, Religion, Gender, and Class*, 20(2), 230–262.

Swaby, N. (2021). Poor data, racism fueling crisis of missing and murdered indigenous people, activists say. *KING5*. https://www.king5.com/article/news/community/facing-race/washington-missing-murdered-indigenous-people-awareness-action/281-1e7c2fff-10a1-4829-8835-6d766b7e5920

Thuma, E. (2019). *All our trials: Prisons, policing, and the feminist fight to end violence*. University of Illinois Press.

United States Department of Justice. (2020). *Indian country investigations and prosecutions 2019*.

United States' Sentencing Memorandum. (2021). United States v. Maddesyn Danielle George, Case No. 2:20-CR-00153-RMP-1.

Urban Indian Health Institute. (2018). *Missing and murdered Indigenous women and girls*.

Violence Against Women Act, P.L. 103-322 (1994).

8

Prosecuting Intimate Partner Sexual Violence

Reforming Trial Process by Reimagining the Judicial Role

ELISABETH MCDONALD

INTRODUCTION

Rape as a form of family violence has limited public visibility and low reporting rates (McOrmond-Plummer et al., 2017) even though the rate of sexual harm within intimate relationships is high (Fanslow et al., 2021; Jeffrey & Barata, 2021; McMullan, 2021; Wilson et al., 2019), and such offending is one of the red flags of lethality (Cox, 2015; Tarrant et al., 2019). Despite the removal of the marital rape immunity in the majority of common law jurisdictions by the early 1990s, this reform of itself has not delivered an effective criminal justice response as many had predicted (Featherstone & Winn, 2019). Low reporting rates also reflect the concern that the trial process will adversely affect the well-being of the complainant. It is well documented that those within the criminal justice system—judges, lawyers, police officers—would not recommend to a family member that they should report sexual offending. Complainants in the Aotearoa New Zealand (NZ) rape trial process studies, which formed the basis of this chapter (McDonald, 2020, 2022, 2023), expressed such concerns in a variety of ways while giving their evidence (case names and names of the complainant are pseudonyms):

> When I reported to the police, I just want him stop coming to my place but I did not want him to be imprisoned, and I didn't want to hurt anybody but now I have been hurt so badly. I am very hurt and in front of all these people, like being unstripped, I didn't think I would be stripped off like this. Can I please leave. I don't want to lose myself in front of all these people here. (*Quinn*, 2010, cross-examination)
>
> I think it's horrific given how much I've had to go through to get here and how many times I've been forced to relive what had happened to me. . . . I definitely did not want this to ever happen to me and to have my family and my friends have to go through this traumatic event as well, no I, I definitely—the accusation that I would have made this up is outrageous. (*Lowrie*, 2018, reexamination)

> PROSECUTOR (P): Did it occur to you to go to the police at this time?
> COMPLAINANT (C): Not at this time, I definitely didn't think that I would be believed or taken seriously. I had heard very bad things about how these cases are handled, I definitely didn't want to go to the police and I was extremely embarrassed. (*Tutaia*, 2018, examination-in-chief)

Reform of the trial process, aimed at improving the in-court experience of complainants, should ideally result in not only a reduction in the retraumatization of an individual but also a change to the public perception of the impact of a trial (see Chapter 4, this volume). Concern about participating in the criminal justice system should not be one of the reasons for low reporting rates. The following discussion is situated in the context of an ongoing reliance on the historical form of the adversarial trial model as the primary mechanism of the state's response to sexual offending. However, even if less primacy is given in the future to a judicially led in-court resolution process, any such process should still ensure a fair trial experience for complainants who choose to participate in this form of state response.

For this chapter, I drew on the analysis of 20 intimate partner rape trials (15 heard by a jury and 5 by a judge sitting alone) held in various courts across Aotearoa New Zealand from June 2010 to June 2020 (McDonald, 2023). In all cases, both the complainant and defendant were adults at the time of the alleged rape; they had been or were in a relationship, and the issue at trial was consent and/or belief in consent (not identification or penetration). Due to the definition of the offense of rape in Section 128 of the Crimes Act 1961 (NZ), a defendant must have a penis and a complainant must have female genitalia. Based on the material available, all of the complainants and defendants in these cases were cisgender.

In 3 of the 20 cases, the complainant and the defendant were married at the time of the alleged rape. In 11 cases, they were in a relationship in the nature of marriage, and in 6 cases they were not living together but were having a sexual relationship. The original form of the marital rape immunity only applied to defendants who were legally married to the complainant; however, this research made no distinction between the nature of the relationship.

Rarely available access to the audio of the complainant's evidence allowed researchers to annotate the Notes of Evidence (trial transcript) by adding judicial interactions, counsel objections, legal argument, and observations about the tone and emotionality of the complainant and questioning counsel. None of these matters form part of the evidence at trial, so they are not transcribed for the purposes of the proceeding. Access was also permitted to the closing arguments of counsel and the summing-up by the judge in the jury trials and to any closing submissions and reasons for verdict in the judge-alone trials, as well as to any pretrial decisions that impacted complainant experience, such as admission of sexual history evidence or directions about how the complainant was to give evidence (by video-recorded interview, while screened from the defendant, or via closed-circuit television [CCTV] or video link).

Access to, and consideration of, these materials allowed us to pay particular attention to the role of the judge in intimate partner rape cases. Matters examined that impacted complainant experience included the nature and content of personal judicial interaction with the complainant; the extent to which the judge controlled inappropriate questioning, including that which relied on misconceptions about complainant behavior; and whether and how the judge rejected forensic use of myths and misconceptions when directing the jury or reaching a verdict in a judge-alone trial. It is suggested that a uniformly changed approach to all these aspects of the judicial role will result in an improved experience for complainants in intimate partner rape trials.

COMPLAINANT VULNERABILITIES AT TRIAL

Research has highlighted the relatively high proportion of victims of sexual assault who suffer some form of mental, physical, or social vulnerability (Tidmarsh & Hamilton, 2020). Those who experience family harm are also very likely to be impacted by other vulnerabilities (Douglas, 2021). In the 20 intimate partner rape trials, 3 of the women had cognitive or learning challenges that were mentioned, or became apparent, during trial. One of these women was described by the defendant as "retarded," and a further one was referred to by the defendant as a "dopey bitch," with the judge noting (in a discussion with counsel):

> I have no idea what it was that was difficult in the first place but she seemed to not be clear about basic questions and not understand things. Either nerves or hostility or issues of cognition, I don't know what the cognitive issues are, it could be a whole lot of things.

One complainant was dependent on the defendant for secure immigration status, and she required translation assistance at the trial. Two other complainants also had access to an interpreter. Four complainants disclosed diagnoses of post-traumatic stress disorder (PTSD) or bipolar disorder. During questioning, eight complainants (40%) disclosed current or past struggles with types of mood disorders, including depression, anxiety, self-harming behavior, and suicidal ideation or attempts. Three other complainants attempted suicide close in time to the alleged offending. Two reported having drug or alcohol addiction issues and had been in residential treatment programs. Fourteen complainants (70%) gave evidence of being strangled or unable to breathe for periods of time during the alleged assaults or rapes (see Douglas & Fitzgerald, Chapter 11, this volume). Loss of oxygen to the brain can cause traumatic brain injury, which has implications for cognitive difficulties (Ayton et al., 2021; Rajaram et al., 2021; Toccalino et al., 2022). Therefore, of the 20 complainants, only 3 reported an *absence* of brain injury or mental health issues—in other words, 85% of complainants had conditions that may have affected their cognitive abilities at trial.

Six complainants gave all their evidence in an alternative way—either by pre-recorded evidential video interview (or EVI) as part their evidence in chief, with the rest of the questions from behind a screen or via video link or CCTV. Twelve complainants gave all of their evidence from behind a screen or at a distance (no EVI played). One complainant gave evidence in court with no special accommodation, while for another their EVI was played as their evidence in chief, but the other questioning took place in open court. Fourteen of the 20 complainants had a support person near them while they gave evidence, which is an entitlement under Section 79 of the Evidence Act 2006 (NZ).

In no case was communication assistance (Section 80) provided for a complainant (except for translation), and in only one case was any mention made in the reasons for verdict or directions to the jury about how the physical effects of the abuse may have impacted the complainant's accuracy and reliability in recounting events. In *Farrell*, the complainant gave evidence of being referred to a neurologist due to regular and severe headaches and of presenting at the emergency department of the hospital 4 years later with concussion. At trial, she described the ongoing impact of her injuries:

My eyes I still get a bit blurred vision in one and my pupils, one of the black bit in my eye is like pop, popped it's not round it's kinda like how an egg yolk breaks and it's got a little and I got, yeah like get headaches still quite a lot. I got this like I don't you can see it but you can feel a caved in a bit on my skull up there and just yeah, and my hearing.

Given the extent of complainant vulnerabilities in these cases, even leaving aside the nature of the evidence they needed to give, it was important for the prosecutor and the judge to provide the best possible support and assistance before and during the trial. While the judge in most cases relies on the prosecutor to advise of any particular witness needs, this does not, and should not, exempt the judge from providing relevant accommodations and applying rules with the vulnerabilities of the complainant firmly in mind. Such practices are consistent with the underlying principles of the Evidence Act 2006, which specifically mentions fairness to witnesses. Accommodations that assist a complainant (as witness) to give their best evidence are also entirely consistent with the aims of a fair trial process under the New Zealand Bill of Rights Act 1990.

The following sections outline the extent to which the judge in the 20 intimate partner rape trials assisted the complainants when they gave evidence, and acknowledged their difficulties, counterintuitive behavior, and presentation at court when directing the jury or reaching a verdict.

JUDICIAL INTERACTION WITH COMPLAINANTS: CARE AND COMPASSION OR DISTANCE AND DISENGAGEMENT?

In Aotearoa New Zealand, complainants in sexual violence cases should be provided with the opportunity of a pretrial courtroom orientation visit (Crown Law, 2014, 2019). However, even where such visits are undertaken, they are usually carried out in an empty courtroom, and the experience is an abstract one. Those who give evidence via CCTV at the trial will likely not have "seen" the courtroom through that medium with the lawyers and judge present. Entering the courtroom, whether physically or via CCTV, while it is in session and seeing the jury and defense counsel for the first time may be confronting. A welcome and some explanatory orientation from the judge when the complainant first enters the courtroom may help to humanize the courtroom and settle complainants in what is likely to be an unfamiliar environment (Holder, 2015). Complainants have reported that just having one courtroom orientation is not enough to "take it all in" or remember the processes that will impact them (Boyer et al., 2018). On the day, reminders and direct and respectful communication may therefore contribute to clearer and better evidence from the complainant.

In the 20 intimate partner rape trials, the amount and manner of communication from the judge to the complainant fell along a spectrum of three broad groups. In eight (40%) cases, there was minimal (or no) communication and assistance. There were six (30%) cases in the middle band, featuring more judicial interaction with the complainant, but mostly for the purposes of communicating information or giving instructions. At the other end of the spectrum were six (30%) cases where judges were active in their engagement with the complainant and more apparently attentive to her needs and well-being.

The extent of personalized judicial interaction with the complainant was a matter of the style of the individual judge. There was no evidence in the case files (although not all physical files in this sample were able to be examined) or in the electronically available material to indicate that any judges met with the complainant out of the courtroom before the start of their evidence. However, there were six cases of judges introducing themselves, in two instances before the complainant had been sworn in, explaining the trial process and being alert to potential complainant difficulties.

The best practice example noted in the 20 cases was *Connors*, in which the judge talked to the complainant (giving evidence via EVI and CCTV) at every break and at the start of her evidence (a total of 15 occasions), in which the judge began the interaction with the complainant by taking her affirmation:

JUDGE (J): OK. Thank you for being here today, and I understand you might have been present over the previous couple of days in the background, so thank you for that too. So, we're just going to have you sworn either to, on the bible or to make an affirmation that's a promise to tell the truth. Do you have a preference between those two?

COMPLAINANT (C): Yes, affirmation.

J: An affirmation, alright. [Reads out affirmation.]

C: Yes.

J: Thank you very much. I'll now ask [Crown counsel] to lead your evidence initially and that will be followed shortly by us seeing the DVD interview [EVI].

J: Good morning Hana; how are you today?

C: Good.

J: Good? I'm just going to re-swear you, so I'll give you another affirmation, since we're starting court again, so same as yesterday.

J: Thank you very much. And we'll continue with the questions from [defense counsel], OK?

C: OK [*sounds small and scared.*]

J: And if you need a break at any stage, just sing out and we can stop, there's no problem with that.

C: Yeah, thank you.

J: Thank you. Thanks.

P. Sir, I'm moving on to a new topic. I'm happy to continue?

J: Are you happy to continue at this stage, or would you like a morning tea break Hana?

C: Morning tea break please.

J: Ok, that's fine. Alright, well look we'll take 15 minutes, we'll resume after that. Thank you very much. Thank you.

J: Yes, I have no more questions for you Hana. I know it's been a long session for you over the last couple of days. Thank you very much for coming to give evidence and you're free to go now.

C: Thank you [*voice very small, sniffs*].

J: Thank you. Goodbye.

C: Bye.

Importantly in this series of interactions, the judge is focusing on what will work best for the complainant. The judge seems to know the importance of reminding the complainant about the process and that she can ask for breaks. At the end of her evidence, the judge also acknowledges it has been difficult for her and thanks her, using her first name (which the judge has previously asked permission to use). While judges have commented to the author that this type of interaction with a rape complainant is unexceptional and appropriate, this research reiterates that guidance, responsiveness, and acknowledgment to complainants is relatively infrequent.

JUDICIAL INTERVENTION DURING QUESTIONING: OPPORTUNITIES TO REDUCE HEIGHTENED EMOTIONALITY

In this part of the chapter, consideration is given to the times in the intimate partner rape trials when the complainant expressed "heightened emotionality" and the extent to which judges intervened to prevent these occurrences. Lack of expressed emotionality does not mean, of course, that a complainant was not experiencing emotional difficulty. Flat affect is also associated with traumatic experiences and may in fact be a symptom of PTSD.

Heightened emotionality was coded by the researchers when there were long pauses; crying; asking for a break; struggling to give a complete answer; failure to answer a question or giving an answer that could hardly be heard; and/or where the judge or counsel suggested an unscheduled break following one of these occurrences. Such impacts tended to be a consequence of challenges to credibility based on misconceptions; challenges to credibility based on inconsistencies or gaps; having to describe body parts or penetration and having to recount (and repeat) distressing details related to the alleged offending.

Judges in Aotearoa New Zealand can rely on their inherent jurisdiction to control court proceedings and also on Section 85 of the Evidence Act 2006. At the time these 20 cases were heard, the section provided that a judge may prevent an "unacceptable" question being asked or a witness answering a question if the judge considered it to be "improper, unfair, misleading, needlessly repetitive, or expressed in language that is too complicated for the witness to understand." To determine which questions are unacceptable, the judge may (among other matters) have regard to "any physical, intellectual, psychological, or psychiatric impairment of the witness" and "the nature of the proceeding." The 2021 amendments added "vulnerability" to this list and also that the judge should pay attention to the way in which a question is asked (manner and tone) and to the cumulative impact of the questions.

Complainants in the intimate partner rape cases studied experienced high levels of emotional impact—with all complainants experiencing at least two episodes, with three experiencing 42 or more during their evidence. There were, however, low levels of judicial intervention in reliance on Section 85, with judges in 11 of 20 intimate partner rape cases not intervening on this basis at all. Further, when judges did intervene, it was only for the purpose of clarification and sometimes to note repetition, not to prevent unacceptable questions based on manner and tone or when the complainant was being challenged on the basis of myths or misconceptions.

Expectations about complainant behavior, or "real" victims of rape, were apparent in these intimate partner rape cases. For example, challenges based on delay were targeted at the failure to report the alleged rape when first seeking any help in relation to physical violence. Challenges about having ongoing contact with the defendant after the alleged rape were particularly focused on the unlikelihood that a real victim of rape would subsequently have consensual sex with her rapist. Not only was a counternarrative or explanation not provided or reinforced by the judge, as is discussed in the next section, but repetitive and unnecessarily distressing cross-examination on these points was permitted to occur without objection (Kendall, 2021).

Challenges to complainant credibility and reliability due to their memory for the details of the events (regarding gaps and inconsistencies) had a significant impact in these cases—given the particular context of the offending (often historical) and the neurodisabilities of the complainants. *Farrell* provides a striking example. Even though undisputed evidence was offered about Sophie's (the complainant's) traumatic brain injuries, the judge did not intervene when she was repeatedly asked to recall dates, chronological order, times and the ages of various people which often caused Sophie distress, embarrassment or annoyance. For example:

DEFENCE COUNSEL (D): How old was your son at the time you moved?
COMPLAINANT (C): I can't remember how old he was [*sounds resistant*].
D: Well—
C: Like I said I can't remember dates off the top of my head. I, he was young [*sounds resistant and irritated*].
D: Well if it's 2002 when you moved how old was he?
C: [*Heavy exhale*] I'm not gonna do figures in my head [defence counsel]. I, I can't remember how old he was [*sounds resistant*].

It is suggested that this level of detail (age of her son at a particular time) was not necessary to ask of her, given that whether she could remember his age at that time was not relevant to what happened. While much cross-examination of rape complainants focuses on how well they remember details, it is unhelpful to keep asking someone with a documented history of brain injury about pinpointed dates and times.

In *Connors*, in which the judge comments to counsel that the complainant, Katie Smart, is struggling with comprehension, Katie also gave evidence of being strangled as part of the alleged rape. Despite this, she is asked to remember minute details of the surrounding context, and there was no intervention from the judge, despite the following interaction:

DEFENCE COUNSEL (D): I'm putting to you that when you went to bed that night, the Thursday night which is what you call the day before the incident, that you had sexual intercourse with Ronin and that during that sexual intercourse he bit you, do you recall that?
COMPLAINANT (C): On the night of the incident, yes.
D: I'm talking about the night, the day that [friend] came around and you went to bed, you had sexual intercourse with Ronin?
C: No, he bit me on the incident.

Judges control the courtroom and should ensure that witnesses are supported and their needs are accommodated—even if their particular vulnerabilities are not apparent until the trial. While the provision of alternative ways of giving evidence assists complainants to cope with the presence of the defendant and the unfamiliar environment, the nature and content of questioning at trial must be more effectively managed by the judge. Although the limited defense disclosure regime means that the issues at trial will not always be clear, in rape cases consent and credibility will invariably be the focus in almost all trials, and experienced judges should be able to appropriately control cross-examination. This can be done in the absence of the jury and following a pretrial reminder of the now mandatory (since 2021) judge's obligation to prevent unacceptable questions. The scope of those questions should include those that rely on contestable assumptions, which should also be resisted in jury directions and reasons for verdict, as discussed in the next part.

JUDICIAL DISRUPTION OF MYTHS AND MISCONCEPTIONS ABOUT INTIMATE PARTNER RAPE

In only 1 of the 20 trials was expert counterintuitive evidence offered, and in 1 other case the judge "self-directed" on such material. These were both judge-alone trials. In none of the 15 jury trials was the jury given any help to evaluate the forensic value of complainant behavior, and there was no reference to any counterintuitive material in the other three trials, except reference to Section 127 of the Evidence Act 2006 (regarding time taken to complain). In particular, no information was given to the jury or referred to by the judge with regard to the meaning to be made of ongoing consensual sex—despite such occurrences being argued in defense closings to have significant importance. In *O'Connell* the defense counsel stated:

> [Ms. Dowd] says she resumes consensual sex a couple of days later and that consensual sex lasts right through till [month]. This is consensual sex, remember, with your rapist. Not with someone who has

given you a slap or domestic violence, this is your rapist. Consensual sex, "Enthusiastic consensual sex," were the words she used. Does that fly in the face of common sense?

In this case, the prosecutor tried to explain how victims might behave, which may be contrary to juror expectations. However, the judge directed the jury to ignore that submission and instead to use their common sense to assess her behavior:

> As to the delay in complaining, the Crown said to you that victims of domestic abuse behave in a certain way. [Defense counsel] submitted to you in his closing address that [the Crown] had stated that there was evidence before you. [Defense counsel] is correct that there is no evidence before you as to how victims of domestic abuse do behave or what is typical. So, if you were confused to think there was some evidential basis for those submissions there is no evidential basis for them but of course you can use your common sense in assessing how a person in Ms. Dowd's situation might behave.

The difficulty with suggesting that jurors revert to using their common sense is the risk that the behavior of a victim of rape, especially within a relationship, may not behave in a "common sense" way. While there may be increased understanding about the range of reasons women may stay in a situation in which they are subject to violence or coercive control, arguably less is known about the behavior of women who are raped by their partner.

The only content of the expert evidence that can be commented on, given researchers did not have access to the transcripts of other witnesses, was that found in the summary in the prosecutor's closing submission:

> [The psychologist] covered the domestic and intimate partner violence reporting rates and part of that evidence or the reason that domestic violence by intimate partners is the least frequently reported crime is a fear of retaliation by the offender, a fear of

retribution. . . . [The psychologist] also gave evidence about why victims stay with abusive partners and why do they return to them and she referred to the research suggesting that the majority of domestic violence victims stay with an abusive partner for a prolonged period of time after the beginning of the violence. Many report previous attempts to terminate the relationship but they usually return to the abusive partner on one or more occasion. [The psychologist] also talked about the sexual assault and rape in the context of intimate partner violence and the delays in reporting and of course this evidence is the very common counter-intuitive evidence given in cases of this type and again they include a fear of retaliation, a denial and suppression, fear of the criminal justice system and matters of that kind.

This summary does not include reference to the specific types of misconceptions deployed by the defense in intimate partner rape cases—such as the incremental nature of the reporting and that staying with a partner can include consensual sex. Further, in no trials was expert evidence offered about the impact of traumatic brain injury on accuracy and reliability. In *Farrell* the judge accepted (as part of the reasons for a verdict) that a degree of confusion by the complainant, Sophie Poite, given her multiple head injuries was not surprising:

> Given the complainant's evidence of receiving multiple punches to the head during her relationship with Mr. Farrell (some of which are admitted and are the subject of previous convictions, see for example [para] below) a degree of confusion when looking at 20-year-old medical records is not entirely surprising. While unfortunate, I am not persuaded that this is evidence of deliberate dishonesty, or even gross carelessness with the truth.

However, despite this acknowledgment, the judge still took into account Sophie's "poor recall" when assessing her reliability:

In conclusion, I found the complainant to be an honest and credible witness. She did, however, have poor recall of some matters, or appeared to be genuinely mistaken in relation to them, which affected the reliability of her evidence on those particular issues. I will highlight any specific reliability concerns I have when I address each specific charge.

In *Lincoln* the judge noted counsel had agreed that expert evidence was not necessary, and that they would take into account the appellate authority on counterintuitive evidence when making their decision. Defense counsel, however, argued that such evidence did not assist in the particular case as the complainant's behavior (in continuing contact and not reporting) "beggared belief," given the context of the offending.

In the verdict the judge explained why he took judicial notice of the social science research regarding victim behavior and concluded that in the particular context the fact of delay and continuing to have contact did not "degrade the credibility of the complainant":

As a judge, I have heard the evidence of hundreds of victims. I have heard many experts give evidence about counter intuitive behaviour and I have attended educational seminars on the same. I adopt the appellate principles . . . on counter-intuitive evidence which supports the existence, indeed the preponderance, of such behaviour. As I have noted above, there is no prescription or script for how individuals will react. Victims do stay with their attackers. They also allow their attackers to return and return. There is an irrebuttable inference in this case that [the defendant] had a strong emotional and psychological hold over [the complainant]. There is nothing unusual in counter-intuitive complainant behaviour in such circumstances. It is trite that victims do not complain out of fear, shame or a multitude of other reasons. In this particular case, lack of avoidant behaviour does not degrade the credibility of the complainant.

While it is significant that the judge included this context, in the absence of expert evidence, to support the verdict choice, their knowledge about complainant behavior did not result in any limiting of the extensive and repetitive cross-examination on delay and ongoing contact.

This analysis of intimate partner rape cases confirms the validity of the concerns expressed by Louise Ellison: "Unless complainant behaviours are placed in context, a danger arises that jurors will make assessments clouded by misperceptions and faulty logic, leading to unjust conclusions" (Ellison, 2019, p. 272). The almost uniform lack of guidance provided for jurors in such cases supports the recommendation for mandatory directions on the dynamics of family violence. However, self-direction by a judge sitting alone has been upheld by the New Zealand Court of Appeal in *R v. Keats* (2022):

> It is now generally accepted that juries can be instructed about counter-intuitive principles without calling an expert witness on that topic. It is axiomatic that, if juries can be properly directed on counter-intuitive principles, then there is even less need for evidence on those principles when the trial is being conducted by a judge sitting without a jury.

The absence of specific legislation should not therefore deter judges directing juries on the dynamics of family violence, including challenging misconceptions regarding intimate partner rape.

REIMAGINING THE JUDICIAL ROLE: CONCLUDING THOUGHTS

In the current absence of alternatives to the adversarial trial process in most common law jurisdictions, it remains imperative to improve the trial experience of adult rape complainants. The judge in an adversarial model has control over the courtroom, including the implementation of law, practices, and procedures. After examining the role of the judge in 20 intimate partner rape trials, it is apparent there is more that could be done to support and accommodate vulnerable complainants without the need for further legislative reform.

Judges can, and do, interact with the complainant while they are giving evidence in a respectful, personal, and compassionate way without such communication undermining the fair trial rights of a defendant. Judges need to remember how overwhelming and unfamiliar the court environment is for complainants and can help reduce the feeling of alienation and fear by gentle reminders of the process, addressing complainants by their preferred name and thanking them at the conclusion of their evidence.

To further assist complainants to give their best evidence, judges should be more vigilant about ensuring the appropriate nature and content of questioning, especially during cross-examination. While it can be difficult to control the scope of cross-examination until the issues at trial are apparent, experienced judges must be able to prevent needless repetition, mocking and belittling manner and tone, and questions that are unfair given the particular vulnerabilities of the complainant.

Finally, judges must put their knowledge and training into effect when directing juries or reaching a verdict in intimate partner rape trials. The relative wealth of social science research now available to judges, and endorsed at appellate level, must be reflected in what juries are told about the dynamics of family violence and in a judge's verdict when sitting as fact-finder.

The unexceptional and incontestable nature of these suggestions is of concern. Judges should not need to have their role reimagined for such cases. The role they should be playing is clearly apparent, and good practices already exist. Uniform and consistent judicial conduct is what is required and should change not only complainant experience but also public perception of what fair trial process looks like in adult rape cases.

REFERENCES

Ayton, D., Pritchard, E., & Tsindos T. (2021). Acquired brain injury in the context of family violence: A systematic scoping review of incidence, prevalence, and contributing Factors. *Trauma, Violence & Abuse*, *22*(1), 3–17. https://doi.org/10.1177/1524838018821951

Boyer, T., Allison S., & Creagh, H. (2018). *Improving the justice response to victims of sexual violence: Victims' experiences*. Gravitas Research and Strategy Ltd/Ministry of Justice.

Cox, P. (2015). *Sexual assault and domestic violence in the context of co-occurrence and re-victimisation: State of knowledge paper*. ANROWS.

Crimes Act, New Zealand §128 (1961) www.legislation.govt.nz

Crown Law. (2014). *Victims of crime—Guidance for prosecutors*.

Crown Law. (2019). *Solicitor-general's guidelines for prosecuting sexual violence*.

Douglas, H. (2021). *Women, intimate partner violence, and the law*. Oxford University Press.

Ellison, L. (2019). Credibility in context: Jury education and intimate partner rape. *International Journal of Evidence & Proof*, *23*(3), 263–281. https://doi.org/10.1177/1365712718807225

Evidence Act, New Zealand §79 (2006) www.legislation.govt.nz

Evidence Act, New Zealand §80 (2006) www.legislation.govt.nz

Evidence Act, New Zealand §85 (2006) www.legislation.govt.nz

Evidence Act, New Zealand §127 (2006) www.legislation.govt.nz

Fanslow, J., Hasmani, L., Gulliver, P., & McIntosh, T. (2021). A century of sexual abuse victimisation: A birth cohort analysis. *Social Science & Medicine*, *270*, 113574. https://doi.org/10.1016/j.socscimed.2020.113574

Featherstone, L., & Winn, A. G. (2019). Marital rape and the marital rapist: The 1976 South Australian rape law reforms. *Feminist Legal Studies*, *27*(1), 57–78. https://doi.org/10.1007/s10691-018-9382-3

https://doi.org/Holder, R. (2015). Satisfied? Exploring victims' justice judgments. In D. Wilson & S. Ross (Eds.), *Crime, victims and policy: International contexts, local experiences* (pp. 184–213). Palgrave Macmillan.

Jeffrey, N. K., & Barata, P. C. (2021). Intimate partner sexual violence among Canadian university students: Incidence, context, and perpetrators' perceptions. *Archives of Sexual Behaviour*, *50*, 2123–2138. https://doi.org/10.1007/s10508-021-02006-8

Kendall, S. (2021). Reconceptualising reforms to cross-examination: Extending the reliability revolution beyond the forensic sciences. *Canberra Law Review*, *19*(1), 36–59.

McDonald, E. (2020). *Rape myths as barriers to fair trial process*. Canterbury University Press.

McDonald, E. (2022). *In the absence of a jury*. Canterbury University Press.

McDonald, E. (2023). *Prosecuting intimate partner rape*. Canterbury University Press.

McMullan, S. (2021). Exploring intimate partner sexual violence: A practitioner's perspective. In R. Kellean, E. Dowds, & A. McAlinden (Eds.), *Sexual violence on trial: Local and comparative perspectives* (pp. 122–132). Routledge.

McOrmond-Plummer, L., Levy-Peck, J. Y., & Easteal, P. (Eds.). (2017). *Perpetrators of intimate partner sexual violence: A multidisciplinary approach to prevention, recognition, and intervention*. Routledge.
New Zealand Bill of Rights Act (1990) www.legislation.govt.nz
R v. Keats [2022] NZCA 149.
Rajaram, S. S., Reisher, P., Garlinghouse, M., Chiou, K. S., Higgins, K. D., New-Aaron, M., Ojha, T., & Smith, L. M. (2021). Intimate partner violence and brain injury screening. *Violence Against Women, 27*(10), 1548–1565. https://doi.org/10.1177/10778 01220947164
Tarrant, S., Tolmie, J., & Giudice, G. (2019). *Transforming legal understandings of intimate partner violence: Research report 03/2019*. ANROWS.
Tidmarsh, P., & Hamilton, G. (2020). *Misconceptions of sexual crimes against adult victims: Barriers* to justice [Trends & Issues No. 611]. Australian Institute of Criminology.
Toccalino, D., Haag, H., Estrella, M. J., Cowle, S., Fuselli, P., Ellis, M. J., Gargaro, J., & Colantonio, A. (2022). The intersection of intimate partner violence and traumatic brain injury: Findings from an emergency summit addressing system-level changes to better support women survivors. *Journal of Head Trauma Rehabilitation, 37*(1), E20–E29. https://doi.org/10.1097/HTR.0000000000000743
Wilson, D., Mikahere-Hall, A., Sherwood, J., Cootes, K., & Jackson, D. (2019). *E Tū Wāhine, E Tū Whānau: Wāhine Māori keeping safe in unsafe relationships*. Taupua Waiora Maori Research Centre.

9

"If It's Good for the Goose, It's Good for the Gander"

Perceptions of Police Family Violence Policy Adherence in Victoria, Australia

ELLEN REEVES ■

INTRODUCTION

The misidentification of women victim-survivors as "predominant aggressors" is a significant shortcoming of policing responses to domestic and family violence (DFV) in a number of Western jurisdictions (Hester, 2012; Larance & Miller, 2017; Tolmie et al., 2018). In the last decade, it has received notable attention in Australia (Nancarrow et al., 2020; Reeves, 2020, 2021; Ulbrick & Jago, 2018). Policing culture, practice, and policy have come under scrutiny, with misidentification largely framed as a consequence of poor policing. The Australian state of Victoria has undergone significant shifts in its DFV response, primarily in the wake of the landmark Royal Commission Into Family Violence (RCFV; 2016) and the 227 recommendations borne out of it. Recommendation 41 advised Victoria Police to embed guidelines for identifying the predominant aggressor into their DFV policy, a recommendation that has since been implemented.

However, in the 6 years since the RCFV, there is no evidence to suggest that misidentification has abated (Family Violence Reform Implementation Monitor, 2021).

Police officers in Victoria, as with police services across the globe, are facing unprecedented pressure to respond appropriately to DFV, pressure resulting from a series of high-profile DFV deaths, and a growing awareness of DFV in the community. While this pressure is a positive shift, research has suggested that it might increase reliance on risk-averse practices, with police taking a "better-safe-than-sorry" approach to DFV (Meyer & Reeves, 2021) rather than relying on thorough investigation, which can result in victim-survivors incorrectly identified as perpetrators. In this chapter, I consider the issue of misidentification through the lens of Black and Lumsden's (2020) concept of "precautionary policing," qualitatively drawing on interviews with 21 DFV legal system actors. While the findings suggested that police may misidentify a victim-survivor when they adhere too rigidly to policy, our findings also suggest that in the Victorian context, where policies are designed to reduce risk-averse practices, police officers may be bypassing policy and relying on external factors to determine risk. This appears to equally contribute to misidentification.

LITERATURE REVIEW

Since the 1980s, coinciding with the growing shift toward DFV criminalization in Western countries, ever-increasing pressure has been placed on police services to improve their responses to DFV. Criminal law, civil law, and policy reform have attempted to redefine police roles, encouraging a move beyond law-and-order responses toward a more victim-centric, therapeutic, and safety-oriented approach in order to better respond to a crime that is stark in its differences from "traditional" crimes. Despite efforts to encourage this shift, policing responses have remained problematic. Across jurisdictions, research has extensively documented poor responses often characterized by victim-blaming attitudes, a reluctance or unwillingness to enforce appropriate laws and sanctions, and the criminalization of women victim-survivors (Diemer et al., 2017; Gezinski, 2020; Goodman-Delahunty & Corbo Crehan, 2016; Hester, 2012). Poor policing responses are often exacerbated for women from multiple marginalized backgrounds, such as women of color, Aboriginal women, women with disability, migrant and refugee women, and nonheterosexual and/or gender diverse women (Maher et al., 2018; Nancarrow, 2019; Nancarrow et al., 2020; Richie, 2012).

There is a significant emphasis on training and education as key tools to improve police responses to DFV. However, the literature is conflicted about the ability of training to have a notable impact on police responses (for discussion, see Brennan et al., 2021). Early in the efforts to improve police responses to DFV, skepticism about training resulted in an increased reliance on policy (Pence & McDonnell, 1999). The most useful example of policy reform in this space is the use of pro and mandatory arrest policies, which mandate or strongly encourage police officers to arrest persons whom they believe have committed DFV. The policies have, however, poorly translated into practice, with officers then and now showing resistance to their utilization (Hirschel & Deveau, 2017; Miller, 2005). In Australia, Segrave et al. (2018) demonstrated that police may be frustrated by rigid DFV policies, which often require them to take action and spend significant time filling out paperwork, even where they do not believe that action is necessary; this may result in resistance to policy (see also Black & Lumsden, 2020). There are also broader factors at play concerning whether policy change will be effective—factors that go beyond police officer attitudes about DFV (see Barlow & Walklate, 2020). Robinson (2000), speaking of the impact of pro and mandatory arrest policies on police schemata, highlighted that the impact was minimal, attributing this to police perceptions of the change as "politically driven," that the policies are inflexible, and that the information informing the change, and the required police behaviors, is conflicting.

Another key development in DFV policing policy is the use of risk assessment tools, which serve to identify high- and low-risk behaviors or attributes of perpetrators and victim-survivors, thus informing what action should be taken by police. Research has suggested that while police officers consider a broad range of risks associated with DFV to inform their response, they tend to focus primarily on a few: the threat of or use of weapons, strangulation, and physical assault (Robinson et al., 2018). Thus, despite the range of nonphysical forms of abuse outlined in risk assessment tools, which can sometimes be more telling about the severity of abuse and risks to victim-survivors (Stark, 2012), police tend to focus on physical violence; this focus may be closely tied to whether the abuse is prosecutable. Police officers may also focus on extralegal factors, such as "personal preferences, the interaction between the parties, or the interaction between the offender and the police" (Perez Trujillo & Ross, 2008, p. 466). Research has documented a resistance to risk assessment tools, with officers—particularly general duties officers—often treating them as a "form-filling process," rather than an important step in understanding the abuse experienced by a victim-survivor and taking action accordingly (Diemer et al., 2017; Segrave et al., 2018).

Precautionary Policing

Risk assessment tools, alongside broader police DFV policy, work to limit police discretion. This, in theory, counters the role that personal and institutional biases can play in the police response to DFV. However, rigid policies may have unintended consequences. As Pence and McDonnell (1999, p. 54) argued: "Policies should not turn practitioners into robots, mechanically applying a few predetermined actions to a case." Research has suggested that rigid policies, coupled with increased pressure on police to appropriately respond to DFV, have resulted in risk-averse practice that is more closely aligned with risk to the *police* than risk to *victim-survivors*. Police may use policies as a way to "cover their backs" for fear that no action will result in professional retribution (Diemer et al., 2017; Meyer & Reeves, 2021; Myhill & Johnson, 2016; Segrave et al., 2018).

Black and Lumsden (2020) referred to "precautionary policing" to highlight the ways in which precautionary risk—borne out of events such as the September 11 terrorist attacks and the subsequent emergence of "unmanageable risks"—has come to inform policing, including DFV policing. The authors emphasized that whereas *prevention* is often based on knowable risks, *precaution* operates on the premise of uncertainty and unknowable risks. In their study, which explored the ways in which risk is governed in a police control room, rigid policy minimized police decision-making and ultimately reinforced "their awareness and practices of risk-aversion," predominantly through a policy that saw all domestic abuse calls to be categorized as high risk, requiring an immediate or priority response (Black & Lumsden, 2020, p. 74). Within this context, police staff and officers engage in precautionary policing in order to avoid the worst-case scenario—thus undermining "risk artifacts" such as risk assessment tools that are designed to allow police to make informed decisions about DFV risk. Similarly, Meyer and Reeves (2021, p. 1175) found that some officers attributed risk-averse practice to "the unpredictability of risk." This concept of precautionary policing proves useful in understanding the misidentification of women as predominant aggressors. Inherently, precautionary policing renders risk artifacts irrelevant, as it operates in a way that presumes DFV risk is unknowable, thus action is based on what *could* happen rather than what risk assessment processes suggest is *likely* to happen (Black & Lumsden, 2020; Meyer & Reeves, 2021). Looking to Australia, misidentification commonly occurs within the civil protection order (CPO) context (called "family violence intervention orders" [FVIOs] in Victoria), and this is largely due to Australia's unique policy context whereby police initiate approximately 75% of CPOs (Crime Statistics Agency, 2021), and the breach of a CPO is a criminal offense, rendering the police gatekeepers of this system. Research suggests that police may apply for CPOs against women victim-survivors for a number of reasons (Nancarrow et al., 2020; Reeves, 2020), one of which is the increased pressure to take action in *all* cases that appear to involve DFV. However, understandings of what DFV is may be narrow, and police may misinterpret the presentation or actions of women victim-survivors for indicators of their being the predominant aggressor, resulting in misidentification (Nancarrow et al., 2020). This chapter explores some of the links between precautionary policing, policy adherence, and misidentification.

METHODOLOGY

This chapter draws on data collected for a larger study on the misidentification of victim-survivors as predominant aggressors in Victoria, Australia.[1] Twenty-one DFV legal system actors, including legal practitioners ($n = 18$) and magistrates ($n = 3$) were interviewed for the project. Legal system actors are a key source of knowledge in criminological research, given their ability to provide insight into the inner workings of the system that may not be available to researchers through secondary data sources, and due to their extensive experience, in the context of this study, with victim-survivors of DFV (Kaye et al., 2003). Participants were contacted and recruited via their publicly available contact information. In three instances, where more than one member of an organization wished to participate, focus groups were conducted. Participants were asked about their broad views on misidentification (e.g., why it happens and how the system responds to it) and about their experiences with victim-survivors who have been misidentified.

Given the nature of the DFV system, participants frequently spoke about their interactions with Victoria Police. Thus, while the absence of police voices from the study is a limitation, the experiences of these stakeholders with police provide valuable insight in their own right. These stakeholders interact with police every day in their work. For example, magistrates make decisions in FVIO cases based on the evidence provided to them in court by police. Similarly, legal practitioners may face challenges in having misidentification rectified because police refuse to withdraw FVIO applications against victim-survivors. Their views thus provide insight into policing responses and practice and the ways in which police decision-making impacts how misidentification progresses through the DFV system.

Data analysis was conducted using the qualitative data management program NVivo. Grounded theory allowed for the use of an inductive approach; however, themes largely aligned with specific interview questions. Policing responses emerged in the larger study as a dominant theme, given the prominent role that police play in the misidentification of predominant aggressors (Nancarrow et al., 2020; RCFV, 2016; Ulbrick & Jago, 2018).

FINDINGS

Adherence to Policy

Following Recommendation 41 of the RCFV (2016), the Victoria Police Code of Practice now advises officers that to identify the predominant aggressor they should look for "respective injuries; likelihood or capacity of each party to inflict further injury; whether either party has defensive injuries; which party is more fearful; and patterns of coercion, intimidation and/or violence by either party" (Victoria Police, 2019, p. 23). If officers remain uncertain, they should determine the predominant aggressor based on who appears most "fearful." It is also important that police take steps to ensure that both parties can communicate their account without interference from each other (e.g., police must interview parties separately, seek interpreters where appropriate, and have specialist DFV officers attend the scene if deemed necessary) (Victoria Police, 2019). Participants in this study were specifically asked by the interviewer about their views on police adherence to the code, and a number were of the view that adherence is minimal:

> I know of a number of occasions in my personal work... where I know that the Victoria Police manual and the [Code] isn't followed.... The manual simply isn't followed. They don't know it. I say, "have you read the manual?" "No, no, I haven't read it." And it's systematic across the board. (Legal Practitioner 15)

> People in the family violence command are not even familiar with the Code of Practice. (Legal Practitioner 1)

> It doesn't really matter to them. (Legal Practitioner 3)

Some participants were of the view that officers believe that because they have undergone DFV training they do not need to rely on the code—as if the two are mutually exclusive, and the code exists only for those officers who have not yet undergone training. Participants found this concerning given that, at the time of the study, improvements borne out of increased training were yet to become apparent:

> We're not encouraged by what we're seeing coming out of the [Centre of Learning][2] in terms of making sure that the police are ready to do that risk assessment to properly identify the predominant aggressor. (Legal Practitioner 1)

Legal Practitioner 1 was of the view that the code reflects best practice and is an extremely useful risk artifact, and were it adhered to, misidentification would be prevented. They believed, however, that policy and the use of risk artifacts are often trumped by individual and institutional biases:

> In the absence of really utilising that policy, we're kind of thrown back on existing culture, existing unconscious bias, existing conscious bias, existing quite profound problems in VicPol around attitudes towards women, and attitudes to minorities, around attitudes towards anyone who doesn't hold that kind of position of power, that police do. (Legal Practitioner 1)

A key example provided by participants of police not adhering to the code was the use of cross applications. The code states: "Only one primary aggressor should be identified. Do not make cross applications for intervention orders" (Victoria Police, 2019, p. 28). However, participants were of the view that police-initiated cross applications still occur in Victoria. Wangmann (2009) argued that the use of cross applications can sometimes reflect lazy police work, and this is captured in a case described by Legal Practitioner 15. They spoke of a case where the police attended an incident between two parties—the woman in the relationship was from a non-English-speaking background and was apparently experiencing acute abuse from her male partner. When the police attended, after minimal investigation, they determined that it was a case of mutual abuse and applied for orders against both parties. Later, the pair were seen by police again—this time, the woman was hitting the man with her handbag, which Legal Practitioner 15 suggested was done in retaliation. She was charged with breaching the order and placed on remand. Legal Practitioner 15 was of the view that the police used cross applications in lieu of a meaningful investigation into the relationship and the nature of the violence.

Contrarily, some participants suggested that policies against the use of cross applications may have negative unintended consequences, highlighting that adherence to the policy means that if the perpetrator "gets in first" in obtaining an order and police later realize that the other party also needs protection, they may refuse to initiate an application:

> We see a lot of pregnant women throughout our case work and that's a big frustration of mine where there might be an [FVIO] where the woman is the respondent and then she's about to give birth and he's making threats, "I'll come to the hospital." ... Police then won't intervene because as I said previously, they say well "she's the respondent, we don't do cross apps" and I'm like "but yeah, how about this fresh incident and what we know about the risk factors around pregnancy and childbirth?" (Legal Practitioner 5)

Magistrate 3 also suggested that there may be a place for cross applications, arguing that it can be a useful way to "keep the parties apart." However, their colleague Magistrate 2 expressed caution, stating: "The mutual order scenario has certainly given rise to a lot of charges often in my view, involving accused persons who are not the predominant aggressor."

Where official policy was viewed as being minimally adhered to, others spoke about officer reliance on *informal* policy, and these informal policies were often described as being extremely risk averse, such as refusing to withdraw FVIO applications in court and prosecuting all breaches:

It's not written anywhere but it's a mandate from someone high up and it filters down and unfortunately it's often a blanket mandate and you're having to fight against this policy that's not written down anywhere and perhaps in this case there's a policy at the moment that's saying . . . "alright, we're prosecuting any breaches of [FVIOs] regardless of the circumstances" and as I say, I think, perhaps most of the time that's not necessarily a bad thing but the problem is it captures scenarios like this where there is misidentification. (Legal Practitioner 6)

Again, here we see the bypassing of risk artifacts, such as existing policy, toward a reliance on approaches to DFV that sit outside of formal documentation and direction. As highlighted by Legal Practitioner 6, informal policies may not be problematic in theory (e.g., police have long been criticized for not prosecuting breaches), but it does demonstrate the view of some police that they value their role as risk experts in a way that renders risk artifacts void.

Perceptions of Risk

There was a perception among a handful of participants that police practice in response to DFV has improved in the wake of the RCFV (2016), and this was often framed around an increased focus on risk and accountability. For example, Magistrate 3 stated: "The police are doing a pretty good job compared to practices of the past. . . . They know that it's a major risk to their organisation." However, for others, improvements to policing responses have been minimal. Speaking specifically of misidentification, Legal Practitioner 18 stated: "Nothing's changed despite being a couple of years on now from the Royal Commission." A number of participants acknowledged the increased awareness of risk and accountability cited above, but framed this as a double-edged sword and as something that actively contributes to the issue of misidentification. Concern was expressed that due to increased pressure on police to take DFV seriously, police officers are becoming much more risk averse, often taking "any" action instead of the "right" action. Legal Practitioner 1 cited an experience at a stakeholder training session, where a police officer stated: "If it's good for the goose, it's good for the gander. If she's using violence, we've got to arrest her." These comments suggest a lack of nuance about the ways in which victimized women use force against abusers (see Larance & Miller, 2017). Elaborating on such practice, Legal Practitioner 10 commented:

> My perception is that the police don't want to be held responsible for not reporting family violence. So there's a lot of pressure to just report and to make a safety notice on everything that in their mind is perceived as family violence. I don't think there's much training around identifying [the] primary victim and primary aggressor.... It depends on who gets first dibs on reporting to the police.

Legal Practitioner 15 echoed these concerns, arguing that Victoria Police officers fear "getting roasted for not having protected someone." They went on to state: "The risk isn't really risk of harm to the victim. It's reputational harm to Victoria Police." The views of DFV system actors highlighted that risk aversity in itself is not a negative shift; however, where there is a disjunction between what is considered "risk" to victim-survivors in training, formal policy, and risk assessment forms and "risk" as conceptualized by officers (e.g., organizational risk), the issue of misidentification may be exacerbated, with officers less inclined to look at the context of violence and instead focus on "who hit who." As highlighted by Legal Practitioner 17:

> I understand that police must act protectively, however, their "one size fits all" approach—ascertain who the aggressor is and get them out of the house—is not working. Particularly if the aggressor is misidentified.

Participants suggested that some police officers view it as their job to choose a predominant aggressor and then rely on the courts to "sort it out"—to rectify any mistakes that may have been made. Magistrate 3 expressed concern about this practice and the ways in which it places increased pressure on a court system already struggling under significant caseloads:

> An intervention order at this stage in the hands of police can be quite a blunt instrument. . . . You have a senior sergeant who simply says, "well if there's an injury, you take action." That's how we end up with so many in the [family violence] list.

As I have discussed elsewhere (Reeves, 2023), the reliance on the courts to provide redress for misidentified victim-survivors is problematic, both because this system is not designed to recognize and respond to misidentification and also because police prosecutors are reluctant to withdraw FVIO applications at first mention hearings—thus undermining their own unwritten policies of "letting the courts sort it out."

Conceptualizing the Role of Police

Participants reflected broadly on the role of police in responding to DFV. As highlighted above, police officers may be inclined to issue FVIO applications for the purpose of keeping parties apart, rather than to accurately identify the predominant aggressor—instead leaving it to the courts to decide. Legal Practitioner 1 reflected on the logic behind this approach:

> They also have this view that if there's any confusion, they say "we'll just put an intervention order on one of them and we'll keep them safe, we'll separate" and it doesn't really matter who's got the intervention order, as long as they're kept separate, that's the safe situation, and that's kind of an incident-based response to family violence.

This approach to policing DFV reflects the view that it is the role of the police to provide immediate protection to victim-survivors, aligning with traditional law and order responses. Participants, however, held mixed views on whether this is an appropriate response. Some, such as Legal Practitioner 11, emphasized the importance of police taking time and care in identifying the predominant aggressor, as the court cannot be relied on the rectify errors:

> It's really up to police to decide, "do I believe this person who has told me that she's mentally unwell and he needs protection from her? or do I go up and investigate? . . . And police are so time poor that they don't do that and the flow on effects, in a legal system, are big because once a police Sergeant decides "yeah there's enough here to go for a safety notice or intervention order" it's setting up a process that's very difficult to halt.

Participants critiqued the police response for lacking "nuance" and approaching DFV as a tick-a-box exercise (see also Segrave et al., 2018). Legal Practitioner 8 was adamant that the predominant aggressor should be determined before an FVIO application is made, and this determination should be made via thorough risk assessment processes. They did, however, acknowledge the difficult balancing act expected of police officers:

> It's that balance between, you know, acting with a sense of urgency and because of risk in some situations, and the balance between making sure there's a proper investigation and assessment done and about in fact, a) there is a risk, b) who needs the order and c) what the terms of that order are going to be and I think sometimes the balance goes one way or the other. (Legal Practitioner 8)

A number of participants empathized with the challenges faced by police officers. Legal Practitioner 9 stated: "With respect, it's a tough gig, to show up at an event and to figure out who the offender is in any given situation." Magistrate 1 questioned the responsibility and expectations placed on police officers in their response to DFV: "Maybe I think we have to be careful not to expect too much of the system at that point." Magistrate 1 held the view that emphasis should not be placed solely on police practice and policy, but should be directed toward ensuring that the DFV system is holistic and operates in a way that serves as a safety net for women who are misidentified as predominant aggressors.

DISCUSSION AND CONCLUSION

The misidentification of women victim-survivors as predominant aggressors is a key issue plaguing DFV policing in Australia, and Victoria serves as an important research context given recent efforts by Victoria Police to reduce its occurrence through policy reform. This study sought to better understand key DFV system actors' views on the role of police in misidentification and ultimately found varied and contradictory views on police adherence to DFV policy. Whereas some participants were adamant that police officers are unfamiliar with the code or actively ignore it, others suggested that officers, in adhering too rigidly to the code, minimize the importance of human judgment and therefore overlook clear signs indicating who is the person most in need of protection. In both circumstances, according to participants, these practices are to the detriment of victim-survivor safety and increase the risk of misidentification.

For those who adhere rigidly to policy, it may be that risk is conceptualized as risk of organizational harm rather than victim-survivor harm—as was the view of some participants. However, Meyer and Reeves (2021) observed that police officers in their Queensland-based study demonstrated risk-averse practices due to genuine concerns for victim-survivor safety, in addition to "covering their backs" (see also Black & Lumsden, 2020). Victoria Police were not interviewed for this research, and if they were, it may be that they would have expressed similar concerns for victim-survivor safety. Regardless of the justification, risk aversity through rigid policy adherence was seen as a key contributor to misidentification, with police applying for CPOs against all people who appeared to have committed DFV, regardless of the context (e.g., self-defense) (see also Miller, 2005; Nancarrow et al., 2020).

The lack of adherence to policy observed by a significant number of participants represents an important finding. Black and Lumsden (2020), in their study, clearly highlighted that precautionary policing emerged within the context of a specific policy that overwrote and undermined risk artifacts, requiring officers to treat all DFV incidents as high risk. Similarly, and as discussed above, other studies on risk aversity have highlighted its manifestation in a rigid adherence to policy (Meyer & Reeves, 2021; Myhill & Johnson, 2016; Segrave et al., 2018). However, in the current study, many participants seemed to have observed a precautionary policing that bypassed policy, instead observing officers who did not understand the importance of or adhere to police DFV policy and/or relied on *informal* policies. In Meyer and Reeves's (2021) study, officers viewed strict policy adherence as antithetical to the informed decisions that police made in the past when they had more discretion, which helps us make sense of why police may circumvent policy. The use of cross applications was discussed as a key example of a failure to adhere to policy, and the fact that Victoria Police has engrained in policy the barring of cross applications is important (Victoria Police, 2019). Victoria Police, in adopting an anti–cross application policy, are actively attempting to minimize risk-averse practices by officers—taking away the option to determine both parties as predominant aggressors and then defer it to the courts to decide who needs protection (see also Gezinski, 2020). However, the continued occurrence of police-initiated cross applications suggests that officers may view policy as undermining their role as risk experts. This is an important finding as it suggests that policy that seeks to restrict risk aversity may not be effective and may lead to resistance. Officers who resist policy may be the ones that draw on personal biases and stereotypes, particularly about women from marginalized backgrounds, thus valuing their own judgment over that of the risk artifacts.

Participants also shared their views on the role of the police moving forward. There was a consensus that the police response needs to improve, and that police need to understand the gravity of the decision that they make on the scene about who is the predominant aggressor (see Reeves, 2021); however, there was also an acknowledgment of the challenges faced by police in making this decision. Some suggested that expectations of the police are too high and emphasized the importance of strengthening other system responses to ensure a safety net for women who have been misidentified as the predominant aggressor. This is an important reflection in the Victorian context. Whereas the RCFV (2016) focused on preventing misidentification through reforms to police policy and training, the more recent evaluation of Victoria's progress in responding to misidentification shifted the reform focus to strengthening the "safety net." The Family Violence Reform Implementation Monitor (2021) made a number of recommendations that reflected the view that targeting police training and education alone is insufficient (see also Brennan et al., 2021), instead emphasizing the need for whole-of-system responses and the establishment of mechanisms designed to provide avenues of rectification in cases of misidentification. Concurrently, police responses do require improvement. There are elements of DFV risk that truly are unknowable—risk assessments tools are not foolproof. However, they, alongside key policy documents, have nevertheless been developed based on decades of empirical research. They are important tools, and it is critical that police officers both understand their importance and feel empowered by their organization to use them in ways that place victim-survivor safety at the fore.

NOTES

1. This study received approval from the Monash University Human Research Ethics Committee in April 2019, project no. 17743.
2. The Victoria Police Centre of Learning for Family Violence was established in response to Recommendation 42 of the RCFV and offers specific training on how to correctly identify the predominant aggressor.

REFERENCES

Barlow, C., & Walklate, S. (2020). Policing intimate partner violence: The "golden thread" of discretion. *Policing: A Journal of Policy and Practice*, 14(2), 404–413. https://doi.org/10.1093/police/pay001

Black, A., & Lumsden, K. (2020). Precautionary policing and dispositives of risk in a police force control room in domestic abuse incidents: An ethnography of call handlers, dispatchers and response officers. *Policing & Society, 30*(1), 65–80. https://doi.org/10.1080/10439463.2019.1568428

Brennan, I., Myhill, A., Tagliaferri, G., & Tapley, J. (2021). Policing a new domestic abuse crime: Effects of force-wide training on arrests for coercive control. *Policing & Society, 31*(10), 1153–1167. https://doi.org/10.1080/10439463.2020.1862838

Crime Statistics Agency. (2021). *Family violence data portal.* State of Victoria. https://www.crimestatistics.vic.gov.au/family-violence-data-portal

Diemer, K., Ross, S., Humphreys, C., & Healey, L. (2017). A "double edged sword": Discretion and compulsion in policing domestic violence. *Police Practice and Research, 18*(4), 339–351. https://doi.org/10.1080/15614263.2016.1230853

Gezinski, L. B. (2020). "It's kind of hit and miss with them": A qualitative investigation of police response to intimate partner violence in a mandatory arrest state. *Journal of Family Violence, 37*(1), 99–111. https://doi.org/10.1007/s10896-020-00227-4

Goodman-Delahunty, J., & Corbo Crehan, A. (2016). Enhancing police responses to domestic violence incidents: Reports from client advocates in New South Wales. *Violence Against Women, 22*(8), 1007–1026. https://doi.org/10.1177/1077801215613854

Hester, M. (2012). Portrayal of women as intimate partner domestic violence perpetrators. *Violence Against Women, 18*(9), 1067–1082. https://doi.org/10.1177/1077801212461428

Hirschel, D., & Deveau, L. (2017). The impact of primary aggressor laws on single versus dual arrest in incidents of intimate partner violence. *Violence Against Women, 23*(10), 1155–1176. https://doi.org/10.1177/1077801216657898

Kaye, M., Stubbs, J., & Tolmie, J. (2003). Domestic violence and child contact arrangements. (Australia). *Australian Journal of Family Law, 17*(2), 93–133.

Larance, L. Y., & Miller, S. L. (2017). In her own words: Women describe their use of force resulting in court-ordered intervention. *Violence Against Women, 23*(12), 1536–1559. https://doi.org/10.1177/1077801216662340

Maher, J., Spivakovsky, C., McCulloch, J., McGowan, J., Beavis, K., Lea, M., Cadwallader, J., & Sands, T. (2018). *Women, disability and violence: Barriers to accessing justice: Final report* (ANROWS Horizons, 02/2018). ANROWS.

Meyer, S., & Reeves, E. (2021). Policies, procedures and risk aversity: Police decision-making in domestic violence matters in an Australian jurisdiction. *Policing and Society, 31*(10), 1168–1182. https://doi.org/10.1080/10439463.2020.1869234

Miller, S. (2005). *Victims as offenders: The paradox of women's violence in relationships.* Rutgers University Press.

Myhill, A., & Johnson, K. (2016). Police use of discretion in response to domestic violence. *Criminology & Criminal Justice, 16*(1), 3–20. https://doi.org/10.1177/1748895815590202

Nancarrow, H. (2019). *Unintended consequences of domestic violence law gendered aspirations and racialised realities.* Palgrave Macmillan.

Nancarrow, H., Thomas, K., Ringwald, V., & Modini, T. (2020). *Accurately identifying the "person most in need of protection" in domestic and family violence law* (Research report, 23/2020). ANROWS.

Pence, E., & McDonnell, C. (1999). Developing policies and protocols. In M. Shepard & E. Pence (Eds.), *Coordinating community response to domestic violence: Lessons from Duluth and beyond* (pp. 41–62). Sage.

Perez Trujillo, M., & Ross, S. (2008). Police response to domestic violence: Making decisions about risk and risk management. *Journal of Interpersonal Violence, 23*(4), 454–473. https://doi.org/10.1177/0886260507312943

Reeves, E. (2020). Family violence, protection orders and systems abuse: Views of legal practitioners. *Current Issues in Criminal Justice, 32*(1), 91–110. https://doi.org/10.1080/10345329.2019.1665816

Reeves, E. (2021). "'I'm not at all protected and I think other women should know that, that they're not protected either": Victim-survivors' experiences of "misidentification" in Victoria's family violence system. *International Journal of Crime, Justice and Social Democracy, 10*(4), 39–51.

Reeves, E. (2023). A culture of consent: Legal practitioners' experiences of representing women who have been misidentified as predominant aggressors on family violence intervention orders in Victoria, Australia. *Feminist Legal Studies* (In press). https://doi.org/10.1007/s10691-022-09506-5

Richie, B. (2012). *Arrested justice: Black women, violence, and America's prison nation*. New York University Press.

Robinson, A. L. (2000). The effect of a domestic violence policy change on police officers' schemata. *Criminal Justice and Behaviour, 27*(5), 600–624. https://doi.org/10.1177/0093854800027005004

Robinson, A. L., Pinchevsky, G. M., & Guthrie, J. A. (2018). A small constellation: Risk factors informing police perceptions of domestic abuse. *Policing & Society, 28*(2), 189–204. https://doi.org/10.1080/10439463.2016.1151881

Royal Commission Into Family Violence (RCFV). (2016). *Royal commission into family violence: Report and recommendations* (Parl Paper No. 132). Victorian Government.

Segrave, M., Wilson, D., & Fitz-Gibbon, K. (2018). Policing intimate partner violence in Victoria (Australia): Examining police attitudes and the potential of specialisation. *Australian & New Zealand Journal of Criminology, 51*(1), 99–116. https://doi.org/10.1177/0004865816679686

Stark, E. (2012). Looking beyond domestic violence: Policing coercive control. *Journal of Police Crisis Negotiations, 12*(2), 199–217. https://doi.org/10.1080/15332586.2012.725016

Tolmie, J., Smith, R., Short, J., Wilson, D., & Sach, J. (2018). Social entrapment: A realistic understanding of the criminal offending of primary victims of intimate partner violence. *New Zealand Law Review, 2*, 181–217.

Ulbrick, M., & Jago, M. (2018). *Policy paper 1: "Officer she's psychotic and I need protection": Police misidentification of the "primary aggressor" in family violence incidents in Victoria*. Women's Legal Service Victoria.

Victoria Police. (2019). *Code of practice for the investigation of family violence*. Victoria Police.

Victorian Family Violence Reform Implementation Monitor. (2021). *Monitoring Victoria's family violence reforms: Accurate identification of the predominant aggressor*. Victorian Government.

Wangmann, J. (2009). *"She said..." "He said...": Cross applications in NSW apprehended domestic violence order proceedings* [Doctoral thesis]. University of Sydney.

10

Operationalizing Coercive Control

Early Insights on the Policing of the Domestic Abuse (Scotland) Act 2018

MICHELE BURMAN, OONA BROOKS-HAY, AND RUTH FRISKNEY ■

BACKGROUND

Scotland's Approach to Domestic Abuse

For 25 years, Scotland has pursued an ambitious approach to tackle domestic abuse (DA). Significant developments include the early adoption of a policy definition of DA that draws closely on the *1993 Declaration on the Elimination of Violence Against Women* and that recognizes a broad range of harms (physical, sexual, mental, emotional, and financial); the acknowledgment that abuse is overwhelmingly perpetrated by men against women; and a gendered understanding of DA as a cause and consequence of gender inequalities. This resulted in the Scottish approach being acknowledged as an international leader for embedding a distinctly feminist agenda at the heart of its policy response to DA (Brooks-Hay et al., 2018; Coy et al., 2007; McKie & Hearn, 2004).

There have also been notable efforts to improve aspects of the criminal justice response (Brooks et al., 2018; Mackay, 2010), including the establishment of a National DA Task Force, a National DA Co-ordination Unit with specialist DA units in every local policing division, and police-led multiagency tasking and coordination groups set up to target serious and serial perpetrators. Scotland's prosecution service, the Crown Office and Procurator Fiscal Service (COPFS) introduced a Victim Information and Advice (VIA) service and specialist training and guidance for prosecutors, alongside the creation of a lead national prosecutor for DA to oversee cases, provide guidance, and review policy and training. DA courts were established in 2004, with national training strategies for police, health workers, social workers, as well as the judiciary and court administration staff (Scott, 2018). The current government strategy *Equally Safe* builds on the partnership approach and sets out priorities to ensure the safety of women and girls, with an emphasis on criminal justice interventions and a more "robust" response to perpetrators (Scottish Government, 2014, 2015b), reflecting the growing commitment to a vigorous legal approach to violence against women and girls and a continuing reliance on "traditional" criminal justice.

The Domestic Abuse (Scotland) Act 2018

Building on these developments, the Domestic Abuse (Scotland) Act 2018 [DA(S)A], introduced in April 2019, created a new statutory offense of DA to cover the range of conduct that can make up a pattern of abusive behavior within an intimate relationship. Heralded as a "gold standard" in DA legislation (Brooks, 2018, Scott, 2018; Scott & Ritch, 2021) and characterized as a radical attempt to align the criminal justice response with a contemporary feminist conceptual understanding of DA (Burman & Brooks-Hay, 2018; Stark & Hester, 2019), DA(S)A intends to reflect what women and children say about their experiences of abuse. Although the term itself does not appear anywhere in DA(S)A, it draws centrally on "coercive control" (Stark, 2007, 2009), which emphasizes the importance of power and control in relationships characterized by DA and the cumulative subjugation that isolates and "entraps" women in relationships with men by making them constantly fearful (Stark, 2007).

The stated intentions of DA(S)A are to better reflect the experience of victims in its recognition of the impact and consequences of all types of abusive behavior and to ensure more effective investigation and prosecution (Scottish Government, 2015a, 2015b, 2017). The main argument for the creation of a distinct offense of DA in Scotland was that existing incident-focused, temporally bound criminal offenses did not adequately capture ongoing abuse, which has a cumulative impact. DA(S)A, like many other criminalizing efforts worldwide, aimed to address the "disjuncture" (Douglas, 2015) between what is known about the nature and characteristics of DA with its dynamics of control, power, and gender inequality and the limitations of existing criminal law with its "limited conception of harm" (Tuerkheimer, 2004). In its criminalization of a *course* of violent, threatening, or intimidating behavior that is abusive toward a partner or ex-partner, the new offense recognizes that DA is experienced as a continuum rather than a discrete incident. For the offense to have been committed, two conditions must be met: The behavior needs to be such that a reasonable person would consider it likely to cause the victim physical or psychological harm and the accused either intended to cause physical or psychological harm or else has been reckless as to whether their behavior would cause such harm. This effectively shifts the focus of prosecution to the behavior of the alleged perpetrator rather than relying on the victim's evidence that they were injured, harmed, or distressed by the abuse. DA(S)A also introduced an aggravator in relation to children, recognizing the ways in which children experience DA with the adult victim, although concerns have been raised about this taking the form of an aggravator rather than recognizing children as victims (Cairns & Callandar, 2022).

Unlike the offense of "controlling or coercive behavior" enacted in England and Wales (*Serious Crime Act 2015*, s. 76), DA(S)A is focused on partners and ex-partners and does not extend to other familial relationships. The restricted scope is, however, congruent with existing policy definitions of DA in Scotland (Scott, 2018) and has been justified on the basis that abuse of partners and ex-partners has a "different dynamic" than other forms of abuse within families (Scottish Government, 2015b).

The DA(S)A passage to enactment was marked by a relative absence of critical voices. Responses to a government consultation on whether a specific offense would improve the criminal justice response to DA reflected strong agreement that current laws were inadequate and that a specific offense would be an improvement (Scottish Government, 2015a). There was vocal support for a specific offense from the women's sector, victim's advocates, survivor groups, and COPFS (Scott, 2018), although some opposition was raised by the Law Society of Scotland regarding the creation of a distinct offense where that abusive behavior can already be prosecuted under existing legislation. Writing prior to DA(S)A's implementation, Burman and Brooks-Hay (2018) identified potential challenges of implementation, specifically in terms of shortcomings in police and legal professional understanding of DA; the necessity of a quantum leap in police investigations and evidence gathering; the ability of the legislation alone to benefit victims; and the potential adverse consequences that may arise, including the possibility that more women could be drawn into the criminal justice system as perpetrators and increased pressure on already overstretched police and court resources, resulting in further delays for those caught up within the system.

Section 14 of DA(S)A includes a 3-year reporting requirement to assess its effectiveness. This includes an obligation to report on information about the experience of witnesses at court. In January 2023, the government produced an interim report on the operation of DA(S)A presenting data from 1st March to April 2022 (Scottish Government, 2023). This shows an increase both in the numbers convicted of the offense (from 212 in 2019–20 to 383 in 2020–21) and in the use of the statutory sentencing aggravation intended to reflect the harm caused to children by DA (from 39 in 2019–2020 to 90 in 2020–2021). Citing findings from three small-scale research studies, that is, an online survey of women's experiences (Lombard et al.), a survey of men's experiences (Scottish Government, 2022a) and qualitative interviews with women and children (Houghton et al., 2022), the government report acknowledges the continued existence of negative experiences of survivors including long delays, and lack of communication, involvement or understanding of procedures, but situates these as existing issues rather than new issues specific to or resulting from the act, concluding that it was not yet possible to draw any substantive conclusions about the impact of DA(S)A on witness experience (Scottish Government, 2023).

The police response to DA is a strategic priority for Police Scotland and a key site of criticism by proponents of the legislation. Yet, there have been few studies of the police approach to DA in Scotland. In this chapter, we contribute to the building of an evidence base about the operation of DA(S)A by critically reflecting on police "perspectives and practices" (Reiner, 2010, p. 115) to determine the implications for the policing of DA. We focus on what police consider to be the benefits and challenges of DA(S)A and the ways that they consider it to have affected police practice and, by extension, the survivor experience. Before discussing the research findings, we provide some context on the use of the new offense.

Data About the Use of DA(S)A

Police and court data indicate that DA(S)A has been used relatively infrequently since its introduction. In 2019–2020, the first year of DA(S)A's operation, Police Scotland recorded 62,907 DA charges (Scottish Government, 2021a). In 2020–2021, this increased to 65,251 (Scottish Government, 2021b). However, these increases were part of a longer term trend; 2020–2021 was the fifth year in a row that this figure increased and therefore cannot be attributed to DA(S)A. In 2019–2020, only 1,065 of these charges were reported using the new offense, accounting for just 3.5% of all DA charges reported (COPFS, 2021); this increased to 1,581 in 2020–2021, accounting for 4.7% of all DA charges reported (COPFS, 2022). By 2021–2022, 5.5% of DA charges were recorded using the new offense. While the use of the new offense is steadily increasing, as detailed in the government's interim report on the operation of DA(S)A referred to above (Scottish Government, 2023), most charges of DA in Scotland continue to be a statutory aggravator under the Abusive Behaviour and Sexual Harm (Scotland) Act 2016, used with other statutory or common law charges (e.g., if an incident of assault committed in the context of DA is prosecuted).

Although the number of charges using the new offense is relatively low, comparison of data relating to gender of the accused between the new offense and DA incidents as a whole indicates interesting differences. The former have a higher proportion of males accused (96%) than other charges reported with a DA identifier (87%) (COPFS, 2022). This difference may reflect the aims of DA(S)A to effectively capture the experience of DA as a gendered course of conduct and merits further exploration going forward.

Like other DA charges, DA(S)A cases have a high likelihood of being prosecuted; in 2021–2022 court, proceedings were commenced in 94% of DA(S)A charges (COPFS, 2022). While the majority of DA(S)A cases are dealt with at the sheriff summary level, where the maximum penalty that can be imposed is 12 months imprisonment or a £5,000 fine, the proportion of cases prosecuted at the sheriff solemn level with a maximum penalty of 5 years imprisonment has more than doubled from 18% in 2019–2020 to 39% in 2021–2022 (COPFS, 2022). This marked rise in solemn procedure cases suggests an increase in seriousness, possibly due to the course of conduct requirement.

As the new offense requires a course of conduct, and only applies to behaviors since April 1, 2019, data for criminal convictions are at a very early stage. However, there were 383 convictions under DA(S)A in 2020–2021 (Scottish Government, 2022b). Of those convicted, 56% received a community penalty (a decrease from 61% in 2019–2020). The average custodial sentence for the new offense was 438 days (increasing by 21% from 363 days in 2019–2020).

METHODOLOGY

This chapter draws on work carried out for a wider study, Improving Frontline Responses to Domestic Violence (IMPRODOVA), funded by the European Union (under Horizon 2020, Grant Agreement No. 787054). This was a 4 year (2018–2021), eight-country study to improve individual agency responses and cooperation among police and other front-line services responding to DA (Branko et al., 2021).

Table 10.1 Number of Interviewees by Policing Tier and Interview Sweep

Sweep 1: 2019			Sweep 2: 2021		
Tier 1: Response	Tier 2: Divisional	Tier 3: National	Tier 1: Response	Tier 2: Divisional	Tier 3: National
12	9	4	9	8	4

As part of exploring police responses to DA in Scotland, two sweeps of qualitative interviews were carried out with police participants in spring/summer 2019 ($n = 25$) and spring/summer 2021 ($n = 21$). The first sweep was carried out as DA(S)A was coming into force and as most interviewees were undertaking specialist *Domestic Abuse Matters Scotland* training (rolled out across Police Scotland as part of their preparation for the new legislation). The second sweep took place after DA(S)A had been in force for 2 years.

Participants were purposively sampled to ensure the inclusion of officers from the "three tiers" of Police Scotland's DA response: Tier1 (T1), local response; Tier 2 (T2), divisional DA specialists; and Tier 3 (T3), national DA specialists. Where possible, interviewees that had taken part in the first sweep of interviews were reinterviewed at the second time point (September 2021) (Table 10.1).

The interviews included questions on police views and interpretation of DA(S)A and the new offense. We are aware that in asking for general views we risked eliciting "a sometimes distorted picture" (Hoyle, 1998, p. 34), but we were unable to ask officers about their response to specific cases or analyze case files.

FINDINGS

The Benefits and Challenges of DA(S)A From a Policing Perspective

In some contrast to proclamations about the value, uniqueness, and groundbreaking nature of DA(S)A, it received a more muted reception from T1 response officers, describing it as "just another piece of legislation" that they have to get used to and "another tool" that they can use (714, T1, second sweep)) as an extension of policing powers.

> It's still a domestic. You're still doing the basics of what you do on any domestic job. You're collating the information. You're, you know, ensuring the welfare of the victims, etc. . . . so this is just an extra bit of power, it's an extra crime that we can utilise. (712, T1, first sweep)

For front-line response officers in particular, DA(S)A was expected to bring a burdensome increase in their investigative work within the context of already overstretched resources and considerable amounts of paperwork associated with responding to reports of DA:

> I think from a response cop's kind of point of view, domestics are a pain in the arse basically, if I'm totally honest. . . . It's not like I don't think it's a thing or anything like that. I do support it and I do realise it makes people's life hell, like, but as a cop, there's so much paperwork that goes with it. . . . It's just frustrating and it's time consuming and it's time that you don't have and it's just really quite hard. (710, T1, second sweep)

That DA investigations require a lot of police work is well established (Hoyle, 1998; Myhill & Johnson, 2016). Response officers spoke of the frustrations and time-consuming nature of report writing and database logging involved in DA investigations and their concerns that DA(S)A would exacerbate this:

> Domestics aren't getting any easier and now with this coercive behaviour coming in, it's basically more things that you will be contacted on and requested to advise on as to whether . . . in order to try and determine whether or not it's a crime. Because that's something that's very difficult to prove, controlling behaviour. . . . To be

able to prove it, prove a crime's actually committed. . . . But it's just got to be dealt with and it's become a lot of Facebook enquiries, a lots of WhatsApp enquiries, it's literally, you know, you're trying your very best but it's trying to hold back the tide with your hands. (720, T1, first sweep)

Similar concerns were also voiced by a small number of T2 divisional specialists:

When we heard the legislation was coming out, we thought, we're going to be inundated with domestic crimes, how are we going to cope? How are we possibly going to record all these, investigate them, report them, because it seemed a piece of legislation that was going to identify crimes that had never been . . . well, incidents that had never been crimed before. (704, T2, second sweep)

Tier 2 (divisional specialist) officers typically viewed DA(S)A more positively, considering that its acknowledgment of the harm arising from a range of abusive behaviors moved these from the status of "background information" to recognized criminal behavior and gave them opportunities to recognize broader aspects of the survivor's experience as a crime:

Prior to the legislation, as you know, coercive control, mental, emotional abuse was something that the police could note as background information leading up to any criminality for domestic abuse, but it was never recognised as a crime, and the courts could never sort of do anything about that. So, I think it's made a huge difference. (704, T2, second sweep)

It's just given us a lot more options and we're maybe able to get evidence that maybe before we couldn't use. (737, T2, second sweep)

Tier 3 (national specialist) officers were the most enthusiastic about the value of DA(S)A for enabling recognition of a range of abusive behaviors that were largely overlooked in police investigations, perceiving it as an assistive tool for operational policing:

> It's been a great piece of legislation. It should have come about years ago ... because, you know, obviously there's like the financial abuse, the psychological abuse, that's probably actually worse to a victim than the physical side of it, I certainly feel and it's such a big an impact on them. It's things like, if you now wrote on a statement up here, that all means something ... the name calling, the controlling behaviour, looking through their phone, that all now means something whereas before this legislation, it was only a background. It was "no crime" when you know it should be a crime. (731, T3, second sweep)

For both T2 and T3 specialist officers, there was a clear sense that DA(S)A better reflected the coercive and controlling behavior that they had become familiar with during their investigations, and that these behaviors were "more evident for us in [T3] than it would be for the response officers" (700, T3, first sweep). When responding to call-outs, officers are required to interpret the meaning and applicability of DA(S)A, in particular the presence of a course of conduct. In the first sweep, it was evident that some front-line response officers lacked a nuanced understanding of the dynamics of an abusive course of conduct that would enable a consistent and effective response, echoing some of the concerns raised prior to DA(S)A's introduction (Burman & Brooks-Hay, 2018). Skepticism was also voiced by officers across all tiers about the ability of response officers to surmount the challenge of recognizing more subtle, nonphysical forms of abuse, but by the time of the second sweep these concerns were less evident. Some officers reported feeling more confident about using DA(S)A, and some second sweep interviews also revealed a depth of understanding of the dynamics of DA, moving beyond descriptions of acts of violence and threatening behavior to recognize other, more insidious, forms of controlling behavior, such as control of finances, destruction of personal property, and removal of mobile phones. It was apparent that DA(S)A offenses, relating to coercive and controlling behaviors, were also being identified through existing risk assessment practices such as the Domestic Abuse Questionnaire (DAQ). In addition, some officers spoke of looking for signs, such as excessive numbers of locks on doors, when on a call-out and attributed this to the specialist training that they had received.

In the intervening period between the first and second sweeps, the awareness-raising and cultural change training program *Domestic Abuse Matters (Scotland)* had been rolled out, with 18,500 officers and civilian staff completing the e-learning component, of which 14,000 attended face-to-face training (SafeLives, 2020). While the scale of this rollout is impressive and officers were generally positive about the training, specialist officers indicated that they prompt response officers to revisit cases and "no crime" files in order to identify connections between different incidents, suggesting that decision-making in relation to DA(S)A is variable. Not situating "incidents" of DA in a wider context is a feature noted by others (Barlow et al., 2020), yet while response officers are still likely to adhere to an incident-based approach, proactive case reviews by specialist officers can lead to further investigation, reflecting the Scottish requirements for a more robust policing approach:

> For example we've maybe got just a crime file for an assault but then they've answered the DAQ, that "oh yeah I was strangled last year. He's been taking my money." But none of that's actually in the crime file that they're dealing with. . . . We would then send back to them and say "look, she's said all these things, so you need to go back and get a further statement." . . . There's been this assault, that assault, over the last year there's been several assaults, but they've only recorded the one incident that they're out at that time. . . . We get the "no crime" VPDs [Vulnerable Persons Database] as well, they get reviewed by our unit. So, a lot of the time Sergeant will look at that and they will then send it back to the cops to say, I know you've said this is "no crime," there's no incident, but having reviewed all the previous VPDs, they would then say you need to go back and do a DA(S)A. (705, T2, second sweep)

Police Reflections on DA(S)A and the Victim-Survivor's Experience

From the upbeat perspective of the police, DA(S)A is going some way to achieving its aim of enabling the criminal justice system to recognize more fully the victim-survivor's experience of DA. They also considered that it might prompt some survivors to recognize their experiences of abuse as a crime and encourage them to report:

> I think, it's given a channel for victims to come through and say, well, actually, no, I need to report things that are happening. I might not be getting punched to the face, but I'm getting like controlled and there's a, sort of, course of behaviour the past, you know, x amount of years that I don't think is right. (730, T1, second sweep)

Police descriptions of the information coming from survivors now being "of use" or that it "all now means something" because it can be included under the new offense signals the importance of the interaction between the police and the survivor. Specialist officers at divisional and national levels identified aspects of their practice in terms of their interactions with survivors that they thought were beneficial, such as having the time to take statements around the survivor's work or caring commitments and being able to build up rapport and being able to offer the victim-survivor a specific name of someone who would keep them updated on progress, resonating with survivors who reported being treated respectfully and compassionately as important (Brooks-Hay et al., 2019; Forbes, 2021). Yet, this requires time and effort, and specialist officers contrasted their ability to manage interactions with survivors in these positive ways with the time pressures on response officers, who may deal with several call-outs on any one night. While DA(S)A might enhance the ability of response officers to interact more positively with survivors as it allows them to "see the bigger picture" (732, T1, second sweep), a more realistic view is that, with current resources, it is not possible for them to develop a more expansive role as they are "slave to the radio". (735, T1, second sweep) and as such unable to "dedicate the time to that crime file and that only" (730, T1, second sweep).

While DA(S)A was described by several interviewees as enabling them to encompass more of the survivors' experience within a criminal offense, there was also recognition that this came at costs, such as the time taken over a longer investigation.

> Things are more protracted, the statements will be a lot longer, there will be more statements because you are looking at the background of family, friends, you are tracking down a lot more witnesses for different incidents. Then the report itself will be a lot longer but... I don't think it is a bad thing. I think the reason it is more protracted is because there is a lot more work going into it for the benefit of the victim and the courts. (734, T1, second sweep)

While for this interviewee longer investigations were thought to be of overall benefit, to both the investigation and the courts, this may not be the same for the survivor. First, the focus on the victim in order to determine harm is somewhat at odds with the stated intention of the legislation that the focus of prosecution should be on the behavior of the alleged perpetrator rather than relying on the victim's evidence that they were in fact injured, harmed, or distressed. Second, research with survivors of DA and sexual violence (Brooks-Hay et al., 2019; Burman & Brooks-Hay, 2021; Forbes, 2021) suggested that the time taken for criminal offenses to progress through the courts has significant material and emotional negative impacts on them, contributing to a lack of confidence in the criminal justice system. This may be compounded as police interviews suggest that a DA(S)A investigation engages with wider parts of the victim-survivor's life, for example, obtaining statements from a broader range of people and investigation of social media with related issues such as the seizure and retention of survivors' mobile devices for long periods (Browning, 2011). DA(S)A may conceivably increase the time taken for cases to progress, against a background of delays and other pressures, including

Covid-induced court backlogs and the boycotting of DA(S)A summary cases by Scots defense lawyers due the perceived complexity and time-consuming nature of such cases and the inadequacy of legal aid to cover costs. It is not clear, therefore, particularly at the current time, whether the benefits of DA(S)A to the survivor in terms of encompassing more of her experience would balance against potential negative consequences around a longer police investigation and a longer criminal justice experience overall.

This resonates with wider literature indicating that survivors often just want the abuse to stop rather than pursue the prosecution of their partner (Hoyle & Sanders, 2000) and the observation that safety is not always easily achieved in the criminal justice system (Decker et al., 2022). Within the context of limited resources, one possible risk of DA(S)A is that it focuses policing on responding to an expanded range of behaviors as crimes, and progress that has been made around wider justice needs of survivors, such as through safety planning, might receive less attention.

CONCLUSION

The introduction of DA(S)A, and in particular the creation of a new statutory offense of DA, was accompanied by widespread media coverage, a round of applause in the Scottish Parliament, vocal support from Police Scotland and COPFS, and jubilance from specialist support organizations. Yet, all laws require interpretation and application. Our data indicate disparities in police views on the introduction of DA(S)A, with some warmly welcoming its rollout, while others viewed it as "just another piece of legislation" or a potentially time-consuming burden. Four years after inception, the new offense has been used relatively infrequently, accounting for only 1 in 20 DA charges reported to Scotland's prosecution service. While the number of DA(S)A charges as a proportion of all DA charges has increased over the past 4 years, its limited use points to complexities in the nature of the offense and challenges in its implementation, within the context of an overstretched criminal justice system that is traditionally incident focused.

The operation and effectiveness of this distinctive legislation is heavily dependent on police and broader criminal justice interpretation and implementation. The ability of the police to identify coercive and controlling behavior and elicit information on an interrelated series of abusive behaviors is crucial. As many have pointed out, this requires a quantum leap from an incident-focused police approach to recognition of a series of nuanced and sometimes subtle forms of coercive control that may not include physical violence (e.g., Barlow et al., 2020; Burman & Brooks-Hay, 2018; Robinson et al., 2016, 2018; Walklate et al., 2018). The shift in approach required by DA(S)A is most challenging for response officers, and this challenge is compounded by resourcing constraints alongside concerns about the onerous nature of gathering evidence in DA(S)A cases. Within this constrained context, it is possible that officers exercise their discretion to continue to treat cases as incidents, rather than seeking course-of-conduct evidence. This may go some way to explaining the limited use of DA(S)A to date.

While there are limitations in relying on general views, there are some positive indicators in our data of a broader understanding among response officers of DA as a course of conduct rather than a one-off incident, reflecting survivors' lived experiences of abuse as continuous. It is unclear, however, how much of any change in understanding and approach can be attributed to the new legislation per se and how much it is underpinned by the training that accompanied its introduction. Benefits derived from the introductory training will require an ongoing program of development and support if they are to be sustained. For specialist officers, the new legislation better reflected their understanding of DA, enhanced evidence-gathering opportunities, and facilitated the criminalization of behaviors they previously recognized as abusive. Despite early concerns about the complexity of evidencing coercive control, by the second sweep of interviews, officers were more confident about their ability to collect evidence and corroborate DA(S)A offenses in terms of a range of perpetrators' behaviors, enabling the range of survivors' experiences to be presented to the criminal justice system.

This does not appear to be without consequences for survivors, however, with police contacting potentially a very wide range of the survivors' contacts (family, friends, work colleagues) for statements; the criminal justice investigation is thereby potentially becoming more lengthy and invasive and contradicting the legislative intent of reducing the evidential burden on survivors. Interviewees also described the way that investigations are more protracted; for them, a more protracted process was worthwhile because it resulted in a more robust case being put before the courts. From the perspective of survivors, however, a more protracted process is a significant concern within the context of a criminal justice system that is already characterized by traumatizing delays. Questions also remain about whether a more robust case going before the courts is really the desired outcome for survivors, many of whom may simply want the abuse to stop or require prompt action to ensure their safety.

REFERENCES

Abusive Behaviour and Sexual Harm (Scotland) Act 2016. https://www.legislation.gov.uk/asp/2016/22/contents/enacted

Barlow, C., Johnson, K., Walklate, S., & Humphreys, L. (2020). Putting coercive control into practice: Problems and possibilities. *British Journal of Criminology, 60*(1), 160–79. https://doi.org/10.1093/bjc/azz041

Branko, L., Vogt, C., & Kersten, J. (Eds.). (2021). *Improving responses to domestic violence in Europe.* University of Maribor Press.

Brooks, L. (2018). Scotland set to pass "gold standard" domestic abuse law. *The Guardian.* https://www.theguardian.com/society/2018/feb/01/scotland-set-to-pass-gold-standard-domestic-abuse-law

Brooks-Hay, O., Burman, M., & Bradley, L. (2019). *Justice journeys: Informing policy and practice through lived experience of victim-survivors of rape and serious sexual assault* [Project report]. Scottish Centre for Crime & Justice Research.

Brooks-Hay, O., Burman, M., & McFeely, C. (Eds.). (2018). *Domestic abuse: Contemporary perspectives and innovative practices.* Dunedin Academic Press.

Browning, J. G. (2011). Digging for the digital dirt: Discovery and use of evidence from social media sites. *SMU Science and Technology Law Review 14,* 465–496. https://scho

lar.smu.edu/scitech/vol14/iss3/8/?utm_source=scholar.smu.edu%2Fscitech%2Fvo l14%2Fiss3%2F8&utm_medium=PDF&utm_campaign=PDFCoverPages

Burman, M., & Brooks-Hay, O. (2018). Aligning policy and law? The creation of a domestic abuse offense incorporating coercive control. *Criminology & Criminal Justice*, *18*(1), 67–83. https://doi.org/10.1177/1748895817752223

Burman, M., & Brooks-Hay, O. (2021, December). Delays in trials: The implications for victim-survivors of rape and serious sexual assault: An update. SCCJR Briefing, Scottish Centre for Crime and Justice Research https://www.sccjr.ac.uk/wp-content/uploads/2022/03/Delays-in-Serious-Sexual-Offence-Cases.-Dec-2021.pdf

Cairns, I., & Callander, I. (2022). "Gold standard" legislation for adults only: Reconceptualising children as "adjoined victims" under the Domestic Abuse (Scotland) Act 2018. *Social & Legal Studies*, *31*(6), 914–940. https://doi.org/10.1177/09646639221089252

Coy, M., Kelly, L., & Foord, J. (2007). Map of gaps: The postcode lottery of violence against women support services in the UK. End Violence Against Women Coalition. https://www.endviolenceagainstwomen.org.uk/wp-content/uploads/map_of_gaps1.pdf

Crown Office and Procurator Fiscal Service (COPFS). (2021). Domestic abuse and stalking charges in Scotland 2020–21. https://www.copfs.gov.uk/about-copfs/news/domestic-abuse-and-stalking-charges-in-scotland-2020-21/

Crown Office and Procurator Fiscal Service (COPFS). (2022). Domestic abuse and stalking charges in Scotland 2021–22. https://www.copfs.gov.uk/about-copfs/reports-and-statistics/domestic-abuse-and-stalking-charges-in-scotland-2021-2022/

Decker, M. R., Holliday, C. N., Hameeduddin, Z., Shah, R., Miller, J., Dantzler, J., & Goodmark, L. (2022). Defining justice: Restorative and retributive justice goals among intimate partner violence survivors. *Journal of Interpersonal Violence*, *37*(5–6), NP2844–NP2867. https://doi.org/10.1177/0886260520943728

Declaration on the Elimination of Violence against Women. Adopted 20th Dec 1993 by General Assembly resolution 48/104. https://www.ohchr.org/en/instruments-mechanisms/instruments/declaration-elimination-violence-against-women.

Domestic Abuse (Scotland) Act 2018. https://www.legislation.gov.uk/asp/2018/5/contents/enacted

Douglas, H. (2015). Do we need a specific domestic violence offense? *Melbourne University Law Review*, *39*(2), 435–471. https://law.unimelb.edu.au/__data/assets/pdf_file/0011/1774550/02-Douglas.pdf

Forbes, E. (2021). *Victims' experiences of the criminal justice response to domestic abuse: Beyond glass walls*. Emerald Publishing.

Houghton C., Morrison, F., Warrington C., & Tisdall, E. K. M. (2022). *Domestic Abuse Court Experiences Research: The perspectives of victims and witnesses in Scotland*. Scottish Government. https://www.gov.scot/publications/domestic-abuse-court-experiences-research-perspectives-victims-witnesses-scotland/

Hoyle, C. (1998). *Negotiating domestic violence: Police, criminal justice and victims*. Clarendon Press.

Hoyle, C., & Sanders, A. (2000). Police response to domestic violence; from victim choice to victim empowerment? *British Journal of Criminology, 40*(1), 14–36. https://www.jstor.org/stable/23638528

Lombard, N., Proctor, K., & Whiting, N. (2022, January). *Domestic Abuse (Scotland) Act 2018 and the criminal justice system: Women's experiences two years in; emerging findings*. Scottish Centre for Crime and Justice Research Report. https://www.sccjr.ac.uk/wp-content/uploads/2022/08/Domestic-Abuse-Scotland-Act-2018-and-the-Criminal-Justice-System.pdf

Mackay, F. (2010). Gendering constitutional change and policy outcomes: Substantive representation and domestic violence policy in Scotland. *Policy & Politics, 38*(3), 369–388. https://doi.org/10.1332/030557310X521062

McKie, L., & Hearn, J. (2004). Gender neutrality and gender equality: Comparing and contrasting policy responses to "domestic violence" in Finland and Scotland. *Scottish Affairs, 48*(1), 85–107. https://doi.org/10.3366/scot.2004.0043

Myhill, A., & Johnson, K. (2016). Police use of discretion in response to domestic violence. *Criminology and Criminal Justice, 16*(1), 3–20. https://doi.org/10.1177/1748895815590202

Reiner, R. (2010). *The politics of the police*. Oxford University Press.

Robinson, A. L., Myhill, A., & Wire, J. (2018). Practitioner (mis)understandings of coercive control in England and Wales. *Criminology & Criminal Justice, 18*, 29–49. https://doi.org/10.1177/1748895817728381

Robinson, A. L., Gillian, M., Pinchevsky, G., & Guthrie, J. (2016). A small constellation: Risk factors informing police perceptions of domestic abuse. *Policing and Society, 40*(3), 195–208. https://doi.org/10.1080/10439463.2016.1151881

SafeLives. (2020). *Police Scotland domestic abuse matters Scotland evaluation report*.

Scott, M. (2018). The making of the new "gold standard": The Domestic Abuse (Scotland) Act 2018. In M. McMahon & P. McGorrery (Eds.), *Criminalising coercive control* (pp. 177–194). Springer.

Scott, M., & Ritch, E. (2021). Gender justice advocates and the making of the Domestic Abuse (Scotland) Act 2018. In J. Delaney, C. Bradbury-Jones, R. J. Macy, C. Overlein, & S. Hol (Eds.), *The Routledge handbook of domestic violence and abuse* (pp. 590–604). Routledge. https://doi.org/10.4324/9780429331053

Scottish Government. (2014). *Equally safe: Scotland's strategy for preventing and eradicating violence against women and girls*.

Scottish Government. (2015a, December). *A criminal offense of domestic abuse* [A Scottish Government consultation paper]. https://webarchive.nrscotland.gov.uk/3000/https:/www.gov.scot/Publications/2015/12/6973/downloads

Scottish Government. (2015b). *Equally safe: Reforming the criminal law to address domestic abuse and sexual offenses*. https://webarchive.nrscotland.gov.uk/3000/https:/www.gov.scot/Publications/2015/03/4845/downloads

Scottish Government. (2017). *Domestic Abuse (Scotland) Bill (SP Bill 8). Policy memorandum*. https://www.parliament.scot/-/media/files/legislation/bills/previous-bills/domestic-abuse-bill/introduced/policy-memorandum-domestic-abuse-scotland-bill.pdf

Scottish Government. (2021a). *Domestic abuse recorded by the police in Scotland, 2019–20.* https://www.gov.scot/publications/domestic-abuse-statistics-recorded-police-scotland-2019-20/

Scottish Government. (2021b). *Domestic abuse recorded by the police in Scotland, 2020–21.* https://www.gov.scot/publications/domestic-abuse-recorded-police-scotland-2020-21/

Scottish Government (2022a). Domestic Abuse (Scotland) Act 2018—male victims' experiences of the criminal justice system: emerging findings. https://www.gov.scot/publications/domestic-abuse-scotland-act-2018-emerging-findings-male-victims-experiences-criminal-justice-system/

Scottish Government. (2022b). *Criminal proceedings in Scotland, 2020–21.* https://www.gov.scot/publications/criminal-proceedings-scotland-2020-21/

Scottish Government (2023). Domestic Abuse (Scotland) Act 2018: interim reporting requirement. https://www.gov.scot/publications/domestic-abuse-scotland-act-2018-interim-reporting-requirement/pages/1/

Serious Crime Act 2015. https://www.legislation.gov.uk/ukpga/2015/9/section/76

Stark, E. (2007). *Coercive control: How men entrap women in personal life.* Oxford University Press.

Stark, E. (2009). Rethinking coercive control. *Violence Against Women, 15*(12), 1509–1525. https://doi.org/10.1177/1077801209347452

Stark, E., & Hester, M. (2019). Coercive control: Update and review. *Violence Against Women, 25*(1), 81–104. https://doi.org/10.1177/1077801218816191

Tuerkheimer, D. (2004). Recognizing and remedying the harm of battering: A call to criminalize domestic violence. *Journal of Criminal Law and Criminology, 94*(4), 959–1031. https://doi.org/10.2307/3491414

Walklate, S., Fitz-Gibbon, K., & McCulloch, J. (2018). Is more law the answer? Seeking justice for victims of intimate partner violence through the reform of legal categories. *Criminology & Criminal Justice, 18*(1), 115–131. https://doi.org/10.1177/1748895817728561

11

The Consequences of Criminalizing Domestic Violence

A Case Study of the Nonfatal Strangulation Offense in Queensland, Australia

HEATHER DOUGLAS AND ROBIN FITZGERALD ■

INTRODUCTION

Nonfatal strangulation (NFS), understood as applying pressure to the neck that hinders breathing, is recognized as extremely dangerous because of the serious, but often invisible, injuries it can cause and the high risk of future harm and death associated with it, especially when carried out in the context of domestic violence (DV) (Strack et al., 2001; Strack & Gwinn, 2011). Research has identified that NFS is commonly experienced as a form of "coercive control" within intimate partner relationships (Stansfield & Williams, 2021), and it is highly gendered, with women most often the victims of NFS perpetrated by a male partner or ex-partner (Sorenson et al., 2014, e57). However, despite its seriousness, the behavior was often missed or undercharged by police (Strack et al., 2001). Scholars also identified limits of existing criminal offenses (Gombru et al., 2016). While common assault charges were available, some suggested they failed

Heather Douglas and Robin Fitzgerald, *The Consequences of Criminalizing Domestic Violence* In: *The Criminalization of Violence Against Women*. Edited by: Heather Douglas, Kate Fitz-Gibbon, Leigh Goodmark, and Sandra Walklate, Oxford University Press. © Oxford University Press 2024. DOI: 10.1093/oso/9780197651841.003.0012 to reflect the seriousness of the behavior. Moreover, serious assault offenses were difficult to prove because of the lack of visible injury; it was often difficult to prove the intent element associated with attempted murder, and criminal records did not record the behavior accurately.

In response to the observation that NFS was sometimes overlooked or undercharged, nearly every American state established discrete offenses of NFS throughout the 2000s (Pritchard et al., 2017). Most Australian jurisdictions, England and Wales, Canada, and New Zealand have subsequently followed their lead (Edwards & Douglas, 2021). In this chapter, we explore the implementation of the Queensland NFS offense and identify several troubling, albeit predictable, consequences associated with it. The next section overviews the context of the Queensland offense, before exploring the consequences of criminalization in the following section. The final section considers how to move forward, ultimately concluding that it is necessary to decenter the law (Smart, 1989) as a response to DV and more specifically to decenter incarceration as the penalty response.

THE QUEENSLAND CONTEXT

In 2014, the Queensland government established a task force to "make recommendations to inform the development of a long-term vision and strategy for Government and the community, and to rid" Queensland of DV (Special Taskforce on Domestic Violence [the taskforce], 2015, p. 6). Based on many submissions, including 185 from victim-survivors of DV, the taskforce (2015) made 121 wide-ranging recommendations around data collection, service provision, prevention programs, and law reform. Of particular interest in this chapter is that the taskforce found there was a "gap" in the criminal law and recommended the introduction of a "dedicated [NFS] offense" with "an appropriate penalty" as "perpetrators must be held to account" (2015, p. 15). The only submission to the taskforce that unambiguously objected to the introduction of an NFS offense was from the state's barristers' association, which argued the behavior was already covered in existing offenses, and it would be difficult to prove (Special Taskforce on Domestic Violence, 2015, p. 303).

An offense of NFS limited to the context of DV and titled "Choking, suffocation or strangulation in a domestic setting" was introduced into Queensland law in 2016 [*Queensland Criminal Code 1899* (Qld) (QCC)] s. 315A). The explanatory notes accompanying the introduction of the offense stated: It "would allow for better recording of domestic and family violence incidents leading to better risk assessment and increased protection of victims," and it would also denounce and deter the behavior of NFS (*R v. HBZ*, 2020, [35]; [37]). The new offense has a 7-year maximum prison penalty. A subsequent Queensland development in 2017 included the introduction of a presumption against bail in cases involving certain DV-related offenses, including NFS, and the allowance of tracking devices to be fitted to accused people who receive bail [*Bail Act 1980*, ss. 16(3)(g); 11].

IMPLEMENTATION OF THE NONFATAL STRANGULATION OFFENSE

Overview

Analysis of Queensland administrative courts data showed that since the introduction of the offense in mid-2016 to mid-2020, there were 1,229 NFS charges laid, and, of these, 929 NFS offenses were ultimately sentenced (Sharman, 2022, p. 6). Analysis also showed that the number of NFS charges laid, as well as the number of NFS offenses sentenced, rose each year since the introduction of the offense (Sharman et al., 2022, p. 8). Highlighting the gendered nature of NFS, information from files held by the Queensland Office of Department of Public Prosecutions (ODPP) (Fitzgerald et al., 2022, p. 8) showed that almost all (88%) of those charged with NFS were men, and almost all (90%) complainants were women. While we focus below on the troubling consequences of NFS criminalization, it is important to note that over 40% of complainants try to withdraw from the prosecution (Fitzgerald et al., 2022, p. 22). Furthermore, when

NFS charges are prosecuted, in most cases (91%) they are based on a plea of guilty (Fitzgerald et al., 2022, p. 15), so there is no need for the complainant to testify.

Imprisonment, Remand, and Bail Refusal

Queensland administrative court data showed that the most common penalty for NFS is imprisonment, that the number of immediate (unsuspended) imprisonment sentences for NFS have risen sharply since the offense was first introduced (see Figure 11.1), and that the length of imprisonment for NFS appears to have increased over time, such that by 2019–2020 the median sentence length was 2.5 years, ranging from 2 months to 6.5 years (Sharman et al., 2022, p. 8).

Reported judgments have emphasized the aims of specific and general deterrence, rather than rehabilitation, in sentencing NFS on the basis that

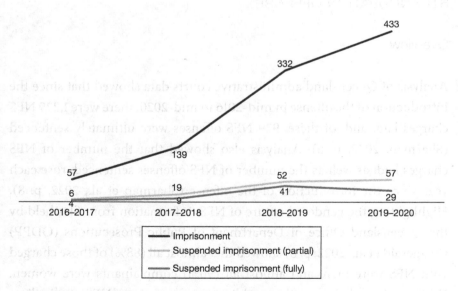

Figure 11.1 Imprisonment compared with suspended (partial or wholly) imprisonment sentences for the offense of nonfatal strangulation in Queensland one time. (Reprinted with permission from Sharman et al., 2022, p.7.)

the offense is viewed as a precursor to more serious offending with "much greater consequences for victims" (*R v. HBZ*, 2020, [72]).

Notably because the NFS offense is associated with a 7-year maximum jail penalty, it can only be dealt with in the higher courts, where cases typically take much longer to be finalized (Payne, 2007, p. viii). This results in considerable time, on average 9 months, between a person being charged with NFS and finalization of the case (Fitzgerald et al., 2022, p. 11). The implications of this extended time frame inevitably include prolonged engagement with the legal system and later closure for offenders and complainants alike, as well as heightened system costs.

Given the future risks to complainants associated with NFS and the fact that NFS is subject to a presumption against bail [Bail Act, 1980, s. 16(3)(g)] accused people charged with NFS are unlikely to be bailed. Queensland research suggested that less than 50% of those who are charged with NFS receive bail (Sharman et al., 2022, p. 8; Fitzgerald et al., 2022, p. 14). Furthermore, given the likelihood that those convicted will be sentenced to terms of imprisonment, many defendants may not seek bail. The result is that more than half of all accused people spend an average of 9 months as an unsentenced prisoner on remand waiting for their matter to be finalized. As defendants have usually not entered a plea at that stage, they are unlikely to be provided with access to rehabilitative programs, such as men's behavior change programs, literacy, employment, mental health, or drug and alcohol programs, while on remand (Productivity Commission, 2021, p. 19; Sofronoff, 2016, p. 430). Some NFS offenders are sentenced and released based on time served on remand, meaning following release they are unlikely to access prison-based rehabilitative intervention and will also have limited access to other education and vocational opportunities available to sentenced prisoners that have been shown to reduce reoffending (Cale et al., 2019).

Even if those convicted do receive a prison sentence postremand, the period they spend in prison (on the analysis reported above: less than 10 months) is unlikely to be sufficient time to allow access to prison-based support and rehabilitative programs, ensuring a "low-quality experience" of prison and higher rates of recidivism (Armstrong & Weaver,

2013, p. 292), but also serves to disconnect individuals from communities and support networks, which is particularly problematic for First Nations people (Productivity Commission, 2021, p. 38).

In the face of an almost inevitable prison sentence, many people charged with NFS offenses are likely to seek to negotiate a plea to an alternative offense, such as assault or assault causing bodily harm, both of are less likely to attract a prison sentence (New South Wales Bureau of Crime Statistics and Research, 2021). Research suggested that the guilty plea rate where alternative charges are negotiated is very high. Among a sample of NFS cases committed to prosecution from 2016 to 2020, over one quarter (26%) proceeded with an alternative charge, and nearly all (98%) of these cases were resolved by a plea of guilty (Fitzgerald et al., 2022, p. 16). In some cases, the alternative charge may be justified based on lack of evidence of NFS. However, in many cases where NFS occurred but is negotiated to an assault, the result is that the NFS behavior is not captured on the criminal record, which was one of the key reasons underpinning the introduction of the offense (R v. HBZ, 2020, [35]; [37]).

The Overrepresentation of First Nations People

Less than 5% of the Queensland general population are First Nations people (Queensland Government, 2021). First Nations people are significantly overrepresented at all stages of the criminal justice process, including bail refusal, conviction, and custodial sentences associated with NFS charges (Sharman, 2022). In an analysis of ODPP files where the accused was charged with NFS, First Nations people accounted for one in five (21%) defendants and one in four (26%) complainants (Fitzgerald et al., 2022, p. 11). In those matters where the accused was convicted of NFS, First Nations people accounted for an even higher proportion of cases, with First Nations people accounting for 26% of defendants and 38% of complainants (Fitzgerald et al., 2022, p. 10). The overrepresentation of First Nations people is particularly stark among young people sentenced for NFS, where First Nations people account for just under one half (47%) of those sentenced under 18 years of age (Sharman, 2022, p. 9). Many studies have identified the disproportionate imprisonment of First Nations people and highlighted the increased odds of imprisonment for DV-related offenses perpetrated by First Nations people compared to non-Indigenous people, irrespective of other factors related to sentencing (Fitzgerald et al., 2021; Thorburn & Weatherburn, 2018).

Consequences for Complainants

Lawyers who have been involved with the prosecution of NFS in Queensland have highlighted the lack of availability of third-party witnesses in most NFS cases (Douglas & Fitzgerald, 2021, p. 359). While this is common in DV-related prosecutions generally (Epstein & Goodman, 2018), in cases like NFS, where there is often no evidence of visible injury (Strack & Gwinn, 2011) and no available third-party witnesses, there may be heightened pressure placed on the complainant to testify even if she does not want to. In this context, complainants may be used as "an instrument" of the state (Wechsler, 2022) to fulfill prosecution goals without consideration of the underlying reason for complainants' withdrawal and their agency in the process.

If there are witnesses to the NFS, Queensland lawyers have suggested they are likely to be the complainant's children (Douglas & Fitzgerald, 2021, p. 359), and the complainant may also be, or feel, pressured by prosecutors to engage them in the process. This can be doubly traumatizing, not only exacerbating the complainant's own sense of secondary trauma through the criminal process but also, potentially, that of her children. As one lawyer stated: "I must say, a lot of the time, my clients are unwilling to force the children to become involved. And that often becomes a basis to try and resolve things. Because they don't want the children to have to give evidence" (Lawyer 6—Defendant, cited in Douglas & Fitzgerald, 2021, p. 359).

Some lawyers have suggested that complainants are more likely to withdraw their support for NFS prosecutions as compared to other DV-related offenses because the accused may be imprisoned (Douglas & Fitzgerald, 2021, p. 361). For example, one Queensland lawyer said: "We get a lot of victims or would-be victims who tell the police there's been a choking, not realising that that means that their partner's not coming home, and then retract the statement pretty quickly" (Lawyer 16 Prosecution, cited in Douglas & Fitzgerald, 2021, p. 362). The length of time between charge and finalization of the charge might also contribute to the complainant's wish to withdraw from the prosecution because the process, including discussions with prosecutors and court dates, is stressful and time consuming (Douglas & Fitzgerald, 2021, p. 362).

Queensland research suggested that among prosecutions that were completely discontinued and cases where an alternative charge proceeded, over three quarters (76%) of complainants withdrew from the prosecution, either communicating that position to the ODPP or becoming uncontactable (Fitzgerald et al., 2022, p. 22). In cases where the prosecution was discontinued, there was evidence that most (90%) complainants had withdrawn, while in cases where alternative charges were pursued—usually lower level charges—59% of complainants withdrew their support for the prosecution (Fitzgerald et al., 2022, p. 22). Some lawyers have reported they have to be careful not to get the complainant "offside" by pressuring her to stay engaged: "You don't want to be in a position where your complainant is reluctant or you're essentially causing them trauma by you continuing with the prosecution. But, on the other hand, you don't want to give sanction to an offender [who] just says, can you drop it, and they do" (Lawyer 15 Prosecution, cited in Douglas & Fitzgerald, 2021, p. 363).

A risk identified by lawyers regarding how far they should go in pressuring complainants to support the prosecution was that complainants facing pressure to engage with prosecution may recount a different version of events to protect the accused (Douglas & Fitzgerald, 2021, p. 363). This has potential negative implications for complainants. At worst, they could be charged (e.g., with perjury; Wechsler, 2022, p. 118), although we have heard no reports of this in Queensland regarding NFS prosecutions. The more likely risk is that the complainant's inconsistent statements may be subpoenaed by the accused to demonstrate the complainant's lack of credibility in subsequent criminal prosecutions or other forums (e.g., family court). As one lawyer reportedly said:

> We have the vexed issue that if we push forward and they then go on the stand and swear to the fact that they've lied, who's going to believe them next time they make a complaint? And we're in The Boy Who Cried Wolf territory. (Lawyer 16 Prosecution, cited in Douglas & Fitzgerald, 2021, p. 363)

In those cases where complainants become uncontactable, there is a real risk that they may disconnect, not just from prosecution services and police, but also other services that may be able to assist them with material and other safety and support needs.

Finally, there is a real question about whether individual victims of NFS are safer, in the longer term, when their abusive partner is incarcerated. Given that many people convicted of NFS will serve a majority of their "sentence" on remand with no access to programs, their mental health and drug misuse issues may be exacerbated while on remand and, if they had employment before being remanded, they are likely to lose that employment (Goodmark, 2018, p. 27). Periods of remand and incarceration may intensify social exclusion (Wakefield & Andersen, 2020), and the offender may leave detention feeling like he has nothing more to lose. There are many cases where obsessed abusers take revenge on the person who reported them to the police postrelease from prison (e.g., *R v. Ragg*, 2020). Thus, incarceration may heighten a complainant's risk and through the loss of her partner's income heighten her poverty as well.

THE ROLE OF THE CRIMINAL LAW IN RESPONDING TO NONFATAL STRANGULATION

A central aim of the introduction of the discrete NFS offense in Queensland was to address the seriousness of the offense, holding perpetrators to account with "an appropriate penalty" (Special Taskforce on Domestic Violence, 2015, p. 15). Our investigation of the operation and outcomes of the NFS offense in Queensland demonstrated that the response has veered toward punitiveness because imprisonment is the most likely outcome for those charged with the offense—and more recently, there have been calls to extend the 7-year sentence maximum to 14 years (Queensland Legislative Assembly, 2020, p. 985). While there have been benefits to some victim-survivors, and arguably, an increased system, if not public, awareness of the dangers of NFS, we also identified limitations arising from the criminalization of the offense. Whether and for what reasons DV harms should be criminalized is at the center of long-running feminist debates about the use of criminal law to address violence against women (Goodmark, 2018; Gruber, 2020; McGlynn, 2022; Smart, 1989; and others). Recently the debate has been pitched in an adversarial style, with one side "anticarceral" feminism (Goodmark, 2018; Gruber, 2020; Kim, 2018) positioned against the other side, "carceral feminism"—a term now used broadly to critique arguments in favor of criminal law responses to violence against women. In full circle, there is a growing third position that critiques what it argues is the binary, all-or-nothing, arguments from both camps, instead suggesting that a more nuanced "continuum" of approaches is required (McGlynn, 2022).

Considering the NFS offense within the framework of this debate, we suggest that there are at least three ways to approach the NFS offense and DV offenses more generally. The first is no change or "business as usual," and a second is to pursue a decriminalization (or an abolition) agenda in relation to the offense. While both approaches have merits, we suggest that a third hybrid approach that seeks to decouple criminalization from incarceration while at the same time marking the seriousness of the offense is the most appropriate/effective (interim) strategy. We discuss these ideas in turn.

Business as Usual

The "business-as-usual" case—or continuing to prosecute NFS and responding almost inevitably with penalties of imprisonment—may be argued on several fronts. NFS is one of the most dangerous and risky forms of DV and is strongly associated with the future risk of death. However, in part because in most cases there are minor or no visible injuries associated with NFS, evidence shows that without a specific offense of NFS, incidents are typically charged as minor assaults (Strack & Gwinn, 2011). It is argued that minor assault charges fail to reflect the seriousness of the behavior (Gombru et al., 2016). Further, because of this "undercharging," associated penalties are unlikely to reflect the seriousness and risk associated with NFS, meaning that the behavior is not appropriately denounced by the criminal justice system, and it appears as minimized by the criminal law system (McGlynn, 2022, p. 6). The business-as-usual approach might be argued to address these concerns.

Furthermore, the offense could be argued to address the gendered nature of NFS victimization. NFS is strongly associated with coercive control in domestic relationships, which is overwhelmingly experienced by women (Stansfield & Williams, 2021). Thus, it might be argued that the NFS offense and the strong sentencing response associated with it ensures that women's experiences of men's violence are acknowledged by the state, and that the sentencing response reflects women's harms (McGlynn, 2022, p. 5).

It is also arguable that the offense of NFS and its associated sentencing response in Queensland was introduced because of deliberative and consultative processes (Special Taskforce on Domestic Violence, 2015). McNamara and colleagues (2021, p. 398) observed, in the context of DV, that among members of the public and politicians: "There is a widely recognised need for a more appropriate and effective use of the criminal law, even if there is disagreement about how best to proceed." Therefore, another argument for maintaining the status quo might be that in a democratic system, public debate and deliberation should underpin criminal justice responses (Kleinfeld, 2017, p. 1457; Pettit & Braithwaite, 1994, p. 324). Notably, Kleinfeld (2017, pp. 1479–1480) would say that there is a need to balance criminalization with what he described as an expectation of "prosocial" punishment. We discuss this point further below.

Proceeding with the current approach appears to prioritize accountability (state and perpetrator); however, there are no clear gains in victim-survivor safety. In fact, there is good evidence that an incarceration-focused response, including bail refusal, prolonged periods on remand and imprisonment, does not keep women safe in the longer term or rehabilitate and reintegrate offenders (Goodmark, 2018). In fact, the focus on imprisonment as a response to NFS is likely to contribute to many women's efforts to withdraw from the criminal process (Gruber, 2020, p. 194) and may exacerbate her danger. Her danger may be exacerbated, for example, where the risk and danger associated with strangulation is made invisible on the offender's record through plea negotiation to less-serious offenses, such as assault, that do not reflect her future risk. In those contexts where women attempt to withdraw from the prosecution, especially where they provide more than one version of events to police and prosecutors, their credibility as witnesses in future charges or in other justice procedures, such as child protection or family law, may be tainted (Douglas & Fitzgerald, 2021, p. 363). Depending on how she is treated by police and prosecutors after withdrawing her complaint, she may feel that reporting to the police and other services in the future is no longer an option, thereby closing potential avenues of support.

Furthermore, the nearly inevitable response of imprisonment for an NFS conviction fails to account for the diversity of offenders' and victims' circumstances and the complexity in circumstances surrounding DV and, in short, fails to balance all relevant sentencing factors. Many offenders may not require a penalty of imprisonment to ensure the safety of the victim-survivor. Evidence suggests that short-term prison sentences are no more effective than suspended sentences in deterring future DV offending (Trevena & Poynton, 2016).

Another area of concern is the possible contribution of offenses like NFS to what Leigh has referred to as the "second convict age" in Australia (Leigh, 2020), in which there is significant overrepresentation of First Nations people among those denied bail, charged, and imprisoned. These persistent findings underscore racial bias in the system (Porter & Cunneen, 2020) and have been described as a "national disgrace" (Australian Law

Reform Commission, 2018, p. 22). The bail refusal and imprisonment of First Nations people pursuant to the NFS offense contribute to these figures. If business as usual involves such high levels of detention with little evidence of its effectiveness, something needs to change.

Decriminalization

A possible response to address the severely punitive and unequal outcomes, along with the associated social costs of criminalization, is to argue that NFS should be decriminalized. Some years ago, Christie outlined an argument for the treatment of offending behavior as a social rather than a system responsibility when he stated:

> It seems an important ideal to help to create social systems where people are so close to each other that concepts such as crime and criminals are seen by everybody as being of very limited usefulness. Blame and guilt are essential in social life. But I doubt if offenders and victims are (1986, p. 29; similarly, also Braithwaite, 1989)

His view is a precursor to what has become known as the abolition movement that expressly rejects formal criminal justice interventions of arrest and incarceration, seeking to dismantle rather than reform the system (e.g., Davis et al., 2022).

As Goodmark (2018, p. 26) pointed out, criminalization has its own set of costs, including social stigma, and attracts various restrictions that hamper reintegration following punishment. The decriminalization approach opens the way for restorative and transformative justice approaches (O'Brien et al., 2020) (although some aspects of these may be embarked on in the hybrid approach we outline below).

Notably, while Queensland research suggested that many victim-survivors seek to withdraw from prosecution, some victim-survivors do seek a criminalization response. NFS is a highly gendered crime and its recognition through criminal law may provide a form of justice for many survivors (Fricker, 2007; McGlynn, 2022). A strong evidence-base demonstrates the risks and dangers associated with NFS. While it is true that criminal law has captured an ever-increasing number of DV harms, it might be the case that for some offenses, like NFS, criminalization is warranted, at least for now (Scales, 1992, p. 29). However, despite supporting criminalization as a form of strong public denunciation, many of those same women don't necessarily want their abuser to be incarcerated, particularly under circumstances where the abuser is not given access to a program or support services.

Hybrid Approach for Now—Toward Noncarceral Responses

A third possible way of thinking about how to remedy the most troubling aspects of criminalization, following McGlynn (2022), is to continue to use the strategy of criminalization, at least in certain contexts of NFS, to not only identify responsibility and hold the perpetrator and the state to account, but also decouple criminalization from punitive approaches, the most obvious of which is incarceration. Increasingly, in Australia, the assumption is that if we are serious about a crime, the response must be increased police powers, prosecution, and incarceration (through bail refusal and sentence) with ever higher sentences of imprisonment (Queensland Legislative Assembly, 2020, p. 985). We argue decoupling criminalization from incarceration is in part about taking the multiple aims of sentencing, which include rehabilitation and community safety (both of which may also be viewed as aligned with reintegration of the accused back into the community), seriously and understanding those aims broadly. These arguments have been made elsewhere. For example, Pettit and Braithwaite (1994, p. 318) argued for a "republican approach" to sentencing requiring recognition of the victim, recompense for the harm and reassurance to both the community and the victim that the offender will make up for the damage done so that the community and victim's sense of "dominion" over their lives is restored. Similarly, while Kleinfeld would accept a role for criminalization, this, he argued, should be coupled with a "prosocial" punishment principle that would both "expressively and functionally . . . protect, repair, and reconstruct the normative order" (Kleinfeld, 2017, p. 1479).

There are ways to decouple criminalization from punitiveness vis-à-vis incarceration. In the short term, there are some viable options. A promising approach in Australia are First Nations Courts (in Queensland called Murri Courts), which draw on a range of rehabilitative alternatives to incarceration and are designed primarily to rehabilitate and reintegrate the offender and to respond to intergenerational trauma (Marchetti & Daly, 2007). Guided by elders and respected persons from the community, sentences often include orders that combine programs designed to help offenders identify and connect with their kin and family history, address drug and alcohol use, respond to mental health issues, provide training opportunities toward employment, assist with parenting support, and tackle housing struggles (Radke & Douglas, 2020). These courts already sentence NFS matters in some states (although they currently only operate in the magistrate's court in Queensland) and could be developed for the broader population so that more energy is placed into identifying alternative options that are community based and focused on rehabilitation and community safety through responding to the needs and circumstances of individual offenders and their communities.

What is also clearly required is real investment in broad-range interventions, including housing and social assistance for both perpetrators and victim-survivors. Better interventions are also required for those who are found to be too dangerous to release immediately. This might encompass better prison-based employment, education and training support, treatment, recognition of disability, and reentry services and supports (Martin et al., 2021).

CONCLUSION

Criminalization should not be pursued regardless of other social costs. In circumstances where children's evidence is required to support a charge, there should be real consideration about whether prosecution is in the best interests of the child and the victim-survivor given the secondary trauma associated with court proceedings. Similarly, the victim-survivor's views on prosecution should be central to considerations of moving forward with prosecution. In many cases, survivors are best placed to know what will contribute best to their safety (Boxall et al., 2022), and placing pressure on complainants to take part in prosecutions may result in them providing alternative narratives to try to end the prosecution, making their credibility an issue for future matters.

Long ago, Smart (1989, p. 5) identified the need for feminists to decenter law, to think of "nonlegal strategies" because the law is unlikely to "hold the keys to unlock women's oppression." While recent government reviews of responses to DV (e.g., Women's Safety and Justice Taskforce, 2021) have identified criminal law as one aspect of the range of improvements and reforms needed, public responses invariably leap to recommendations around increased policing, criminalization, and incapacitation. In the context of this chapter, we agree that we need to decenter law, and specifically criminal law, as a response to DV, and more specifically still, we need to decenter imprisonment as an answer to promoting women's safety, except in the rarest of circumstances. Where incarceration is used, it needs to have a therapeutic ambition.

ACKNOWLEDGMENT

Research for this chapter was supported by the Australian Research Council (DP 200101020).

REFERENCES

Armstrong, S., & Weaver, B. (2013). Persistent punishment: User views of short prison sentences. *Howard Journal of Criminal Justice, 52*(3), 285–305. https://onlinelibrary.wiley.com/doi/full/10.1111/hojo.12015

Australian Law Reform Commission, (2018). Pathways to Justice- Inquiry into the Incarceration Rate of Aboriginal and Torres Strait Islander People (ALRC Report 133). Australian Law Reform Commission. https://www.alrc.gov.au/publication/pathways-to-justice-inquiry-into-the-incarceration-rate-of-aboriginal-and-torres-strait-islander-peoples-alrc-report-133/

Bail Act 1980 (Qld). http://www.austlii.edu.au/cgi-bin/viewdb//au/legis/qld/consol_act/ba198041/

Boxall, H., Doherty, L. S., Franks, C., & Bricknell, S. (2022). The "Pathways to intimate partner homicide" Project: Key stages and events in male-perpetrated intimate partner homicide in Australia. ANROWS. https://www.anrows.org.au/publication/the-pathways-to-intimate-partner-homicide-project-key-stages-and-events-in-male-perpetrated-intimate-partner-homicide-in-australia/read/

Braithwaite, J. (1989). *Crime. Shame and reintegration.* Cambridge University Press.

Cale, J., Day, A., Casey, S., Bright, D., Wodak, J., Giles, M., & Baldry, E. (2019). Australian prison vocational education and training and returns to custody among male and female ex-prisoners: A cross-jurisdictional study. *Australian & New Zealand Journal of Criminology, 52*(1), 129–147. https://doi.org/10.1177/0004865818779418

Christie, N. (1986). The ideal victim. In E. Fattah (Ed.), *From crime policy to victim policy: Reorienting the justice system* (pp. 17–30). Macmillan.

Davis, A., Dent, G., Meiners, E., & Richie, B. (2022). *Abolition. Feminism. Now.* Hamish Hamilton.

Douglas, H., & Fitzgerald, R. (2021). Proving non-fatal strangulation in family violence cases: A case study on the criminalisation of family violence. *International Journal of Evidence & Proof, 25*(4), 350–370. https://doi.org/10.1177/13657127211036175

Edwards, S., & Douglas, H. (2021). The criminalisation of a dangerous form of coercive control: Non-fatal strangulation in England and Wales and Australia. *Journal of International and Comparative Law, 8*(1), 87–119. https://www.proquest.com/openview/1902c5b5750cacd6c92dbb5f8a4a16d8/1?pq-origsite=gscholar&cbl=4364864

Epstein, D., & Goodman, L. (2018). Discounting women: Doubting domestic violence survivors' credibility and dismissing their experiences. *University of Pennsylvania Law Review, 167*, 399–461. https://scholarship.law.georgetown.edu/facpub/2037/

Fitzgerald, R., Douglas, H., & Heybroek, L. (2021). Sentencing, domestic violence, and the overrepresentation of Indigenous Australians: Does court location matter? *Journal of Interpersonal Violence, 36*(21), 10588–10613. https://doi.org/10.1177/0886260519885916

Fitzgerald, R., Douglas, H., Pearce, E., & Lloyd, M. (2022). *The prosecution of non-fatal strangulation cases: An examination of finalised prosecution cases in Queensland, 2017–2020.* University of Melbourne and University of Queensland.

Fricker, M. (2007). *Epistemic injustice: Power and the ethics of knowing.* Oxford University Press.

Gombru, A., Brignell, G., & Donnelly, H. (2016). *Sentencing for domestic violence* (Sentencing Trends and Issues 45). Judicial Commission of NSW. https://www.judcom.nsw.gov.au/wp-content/uploads/2016/07/sentencing_trends_45.pdf

Goodmark, L. (2018). *Decriminalizing domestic violence: A balanced policy approach to intimate partner violence.* University of California Press.

Gruber, A. (2020). *The feminist war on crime: The unexpected role of women's liberation in mass incarceration*. University of California Press.

Kim, M. (2018). From carceral feminism to transformative justice: Women-of-color feminism and alternatives to incarceration. *Journal of Ethnic & Cultural Diversity in Social Work*, 27(1), 219–233. https://doi.org/10.1080/15313204.2018.1474827

Kleinfeld, J. (2017). Three principles of democratic criminal justice. *Northwestern University Law Review*, 111(6), 1455–1490.

Leigh, A. (2020). *The second convict age: Explaining the return of mass imprisonment in Australia* (Paper number 13025, IZA Institute of Labor Economics). https://www.iza.org/publications/dp

Marchetti, E., & Daly, K. (2007). Indigenous sentencing courts: Towards a theoretical and jurisprudential model. *Sydney Law Review*, 29, 415–443. https://www.griffith.edu.au/__data/assets/pdf_file/0027/227718/2007-Marchetti-and-Daly-Indigenous-sentencing-courts-PUBversion.pdf

Martin, C., Reeve, R., McCausland, R., Baldry, E., Burton, P., White, R., & Thomas, S. (2021). *Exiting prison with complex support needs: The role of housing assistance* (AHURI Final Report). Australian Housing and Urban Research Institute Limited. https://www.ahuri.edu.au/research/final-reports/361

McGlynn, C. (2022). Challenging anti-carceral feminism: Criminalisation, justice and continuum thinking. *Women's Studies International Forum*, 93, 102614. https://doi.org/10.1016/j.wsif.2022.102614

McNamara, L., Quilter, J., Hogg, R., Loughnan, A., Douglas, H., Brown, D., & Farmer, L. (2021). Understanding *processes* of criminalisation: Insights from an Australian study of criminal law-making. *Criminology and Criminal Justice*, 21(3), 387–407. https://doi.org/10.1177/1748895819868519

New South Wales Bureau of Crime Statistics and Research. (2021). Criminal court statistics. https://www.bocsar.nsw.gov.au/Pages/bocsar_datasets/Courts.aspx

O'Brien, P., Kim, M., Beck, E., & Bhuyan, R. (2020). Introduction to special topic on anticarceral feminisms: Imagining a world without prisons. *Affilia*, 35(1), 5–11. https://doi.org/10.1177/0886109919897981

Payne, J. (2007). *Criminal trial delays in Australia: Trial listing outcomes*. Australian Institute of Criminology.

Pettit, P., & Braithwaite, J. (1994). The three Rs of republican sentencing. *Current Issues in Criminal Justice*, 5(3), 318–325. http://classic.austlii.edu.au/au/journals/CICrimJust/1994/14.pdf

Porter, A., & Cunneen, C. (2020). Policing settler colonial societies. In P. Birch, M. Kennedy, & E. Kruger (Eds.), *Australian policing: Critical issues in 21st century police practice* (pp. 397–412). Routledge.

Pritchard, A., Reckdenwald, A., & Nordham, C. (2017). Non-fatal strangulation as part of domestic violence: A review of research. *Trauma, Violence and Abuse*, 18(4), 407–424. https://doi.org/10.1177/1524838015622439

Productivity Commission. (2021). *Australia's prison dilemma: Research paper*. Australian Government. https://www.pc.gov.au/research/completed/prison-dilemma/prison-dilemma.pdf

Queensland Government. (2021). *Queensland's Aboriginal and Torres Strait Islander population, Census 2021 snapshot*. Queensland Government. https://www.qgso.qld.gov.au/issues/11586/qlds-aboriginal-torres-strait-islander-population-census-2021-snapshot.pdf

Queensland Criminal Code 1899 (Qld). http://www.austlii.edu.au/cgi-bin/viewdb/au/legis/qld/consol_act/cc189994/

Queensland Legislative Assembly. (2020). *Parliamentary debates*. 20 May. https://documents.parliament.qld.gov.au/events/han/2020/2020_05_20_WEEKLY.PDF

Radke, A., & Douglas, H. (2020). Indigenous Australians, specialist courts, and the intergenerational impacts of child removal in the criminal justice system. *International Journal of Children's Rights, 28*(2), 378–400. https://doi.org/10.1163/15718182-02802005

R v. HBZ [2020] QCA 73. http://www.austlii.edu.au/cgi-bin/viewdoc/au/cases/qld/QCA/2020/73.html

R v. Ragg [2020] NSWDC 210. http://www.austlii.edu.au/cgi-bin/viewdoc/au/cases/nsw/NSWDC/2020/210.html?context=1;query=Ragg;mask_path=au/cases/nsw/NSWDC

Scales, A. (1992). Feminist legal method: Not so scary. *UCLA Women's Law Journal, 2*(1), 1–34. https://doi.org/10.5070/L321017558

Sharman, L., Fitzgerald, R., & Douglas, H. (2022). *Non-fatal strangulation offence convictions and outcomes: Insights from Queensland Wide Inter-linked Courts data, 2016/2017–2019/2020*. University of Melbourne and University of Queensland.

Smart, C. (1989). *Feminism and the power of law*. Routledge. http://refhub.elsevier.com/S0277-5395(22)00055-3/rf202205280900005774

Sofronoff, W. (2016). *Queensland parole system review: Final report*. https://parolereview.premiers.qld.gov.au/assets/queensland-parole-system-review-final-report.pdf

Sorenson, S., Joshi, M., & Sivitz, E. (2014). A systematic review of the edidemiology of nonfatal strangulation, a human rights issue and health concern. *American Journal of Public Health, 104*(11), e54–61. https://ajph.aphapublications.org/doi/full/10.2105/AJPH.2014.302191

Special Taskforce on Domestic and Family Violence. (2015). *Not now, not ever. Special Taskforce on Domestic and Family Violence*. Queensland Government. https://www.publications.qld.gov.au/dataset/not-now-not-ever/resource/533db62b-b2c9-43cc-a5ff-f9e1bc95c7c7

Stansfield, R., & Williams, K. R. (2021). Coercive control between intimate partners: An application to nonfatal strangulation. *Journal of Interpersonal Violence, 36*(9–10), NP5105–NP5124. https://doi.org/10.1177/0886260518795175

Strack, G., & Gwinn, C. (2011). On the edge of homicide: Strangulation as a prelude. *Criminal Justice, 26*(3), 1–5. https://dfcs.alaska.gov/ocs/Documents/childrensjustice/strangulation/1.%20On%20the%20Edge%20of%20Homicide-%20Strangulation%20as%20a%20Prelude-%20Strack%20and%20Gwinn%202011.pdf

Strack, G., McClane, G., & Hawley, D. (2001). A review of 300 attempted strangulation cases, part II: Clinical evaluation of the surviving victim. *Journal of Emergency Medicine, 21*(3), 311–315. https://doi.org/10.1016/s0736-4679(01)00400-0

Thorburn, H., & Weatherburn, D. (2018). Effect of Indigenous status on sentence outcomes for serious assault offences. *Australian and New Zealand Journal of Criminology, 51*(1), 434–453. https://doi.org/10.1177/0004865817748179

Trevena, J., & Poynton, S. (2016). Does a prison sentence affect future domestic violence reoffending? NSW Bureau of Crime Statistics and Research, Crime and Justice Bulletin 190. https://www.bocsar.nsw.gov.au/Publications/CJB/Report-2016-Does-a-prison-sentence-affect-future-domestic-violence-reoffending-cjb190.pdf

Wakefield, S., & Andersen, L. H. (2020). Pretrial detention and the costs of system overreach for employment and family life. *Sociological Science, 7*, 342–366. https://doi.org/10.15195/v7.a14

Wechsler, R. (2022) Victims as instruments. *Washington Law Review, 97*, 101–174. https://papers.ssrn.com/sol3/papers.cfm?abstract_id=3923051

Women's Safety and Justice Taskforce. (2021). *Hear her voice: Report one—Addressing coercive control and domestic and family violence in Queensland.* https://www.womenstaskforce.qld.gov.au/publications

PART 3

Making Sense of Criminalization

Concepts, Context, Activism

12

Human Rights Penality, the Inter-American Approach to Violence Against Women, and the Local Effects of Centering Criminal Justice

SILVANA TAPIA TAPIA ■

INTRODUCTION

This chapter offers a critical overview of the standards developed by the Inter-American Human Rights System (IAHRS) in the domain of violence against women (VAW) and interrogates the central role of criminal justice in the relevant case law. Then, using the case of Ecuador, the chapter exemplifies how this "human rights penality" can appear in local legal systems. The result is a model that can displace survivors' needs and mask the reduction of services required to materially protect women and enable them to overcome gender-based violence. Victim-survivors are put in a position whereby litigation is all but the only mechanism available to obtain protection, which presupposes various forms of privilege.

Silvana Tapia Tapia, *Human Rights Penality, the Inter-American Approach to Violence Against Women, and the Local Effects of Centering Criminal Justice* In: *The Criminalization of Violence Against Women*. Edited by: Heather Douglas, Kate Fitz-Gibbon, Leigh Goodmark, and Sandra Walklate, Oxford University Press. © Oxford University Press 2024. DOI: 10.1093/oso/9780197651841.003.0013

Despite being challenged by multiple critical traditions—including feminist, Marxist, decolonial, and queer studies—liberal legalism has largely shaped contemporary human rights advocacy, including in the realm of VAW. In Latin America and globally, largely due to the push of international organizations and nongovernmental organizations (NGOs), a "gender perspective" (*enfoque de género*) has been widely adopted as *the* framework to promote women's rights, with an ostensible impact on law and policy. As de Ávila shows in Chapter 2 of this book, the recognition of domestic violence as a violation of women's human rights has translated successfully into local specialized legislation like the "Maria da Penha Law" in Brazil. However, this law-centric approach is a matter of contestation by counterhegemonic critics as it has often disregarded the systemic, racialized, and economic oppression of women in favor of a liberal framing that foregrounds individual rights, formal equality, and the rule of law.

In this context, although human rights have historically stood as moderators of state coercion, the idea that activating the penal apparatus is indispensable to deliver justice is nearly self-evident today. Genealogical accounts suggest that there was a punitive turn in human rights in the late twentieth century (Engle, 2015, 2016), which operated distinctively in the field of VAW. In fact, domestic laws criminalizing VAW were enacted all across Latin America through the 1990s (Tapia Tapia, 2022, Chapter 3). Before that, as an early concern of disciplines like gender and development, VAW had more often been linked to poverty and women's insufficient access to public services. Seminal works did not point at policing and prosecuting as efficient courses of action, especially for low-income sectors (Bedford & Tapia Tapia, 2021; McIlwaine & Moser, 2001).

More recently, however, encouraging states to address human rights violations through criminalization has been a priority of international agencies such as the United Nations, the European Court of Human Rights, and the Inter-American Human Rights System (IAHRS). This human rights penality has also been deployed in mainstream campaigns on VAW, which have revolved around demanding the creation of offenses like femicide/feminicide, with proactive responses from Latin American legislatures (CLADEM, 2007). As I argue here, this is likely in detriment of social justice agendas, which include committing states to enhance public services for women and carry out economic redistribution to materially improve their living conditions.

Importantly, the dominance of criminal justice has been interrogated, not only because criminalization and incarceration differentially affect groups that are already stigmatized and marginalized (Darke & Garces, 2017; Snowball & Weatherburn, 2006; Sudbury, 2005; Wacquant, 2009), but also because the penal apparatus does not necessarily serve the interests of violence survivors in their search for protection (De Aquino, 2013; Goodmark, 2018; Tapia Tapia, 2021). Moreover, there are critiques of criminal justice and human rights that point at their colonial and imperialist foundations (Barreto, 2018; Douzinas, 2007; Kapur, 2006; Kennedy, 2004; López Hidalgo & Tapia Tapia, 2022), as well as the ontic and epistemic violence these systems continue to exert over alternative understandings of justice (Burman, 2017; Mendoza, 2016; Tapia Tapia, 2016, 2019). Such critiques have been reignited at a time when awareness of racialized police violence is being reawakened (French, 2013; Oriola & Knight, 2020).

In her classic feminist critique of law, Carol Smart (1989) gave a visionary warning about the perils, for feminists, of excessively focusing on legal strategies. Along those lines, this chapter shows that criminal law-centric approaches to violence entail the advantage, for governments, of giving the impression that they are "dealing" with gender-based violence, even when they are not funding mechanisms to address the deep roots of VAW and alleviate its effects. Just like the recognition of new rights entails the risk of looking at systemic exclusion as if it were resolved, the risk in criminal justice is that structural, social, and political violence may be deemed overcome merely because the possibility of initiating a criminal trial exists.

As shown here, the Inter-American system reproduces a legalistic model of justice that hardly tackles the socioeconomic aspects of VAW and does not urge states to listen and respond to the expectations of victim-survivors. State obligations are reductively understood within a narrow framing in which complex social problems are "tackled" via law reform and the threat of carceral punishment. The Inter-American standards, moreover, afford multiple functions and "virtues" to criminal law, taking for granted its effectiveness to prevent violence and reduce harms, despite a general lack of evidence in that regard. Criminal justice has been rationalized and normalized to the point of being presented as a common sense pathway to integrally protect women. At the same time, the case law does not consider the brutal forms of violence that penal systems foster in reality, including for violence survivors themselves, who may not only be revictimized, but even criminalized (Coker, 2001; Goodmark, 2021). As Balawyn Jones suggests in Chapter 15 of this volume, violence committed by the state in the form of bureaucratic negligence puts victim-survivors at an exacerbated or perpetuated risk.

Given that both international and domestic laws on VAW tend to equate criminal investigation and prosecution to integral justice, often disregarding socioeconomic aspects as well as penal violence, a nuanced critique of human rights penality is essential. To contribute to this, in the next section I identify and question the standards promoted by the IAHRS.

THE INTER-AMERICAN HUMAN RIGHTS STANDARDS: IMPUNITY, DUE DILIGENCE, AND CRIMINAL JUSTICE

The IAHRS was born with the American Declaration of the Rights and Duties of Man (Bogota, 1948). Its main institutions are the Inter-American Commission on Human Rights (IACHR), created by the Organization of American States in 1959, and the Inter-American Court of Human Rights (IACtHR), installed in 1979. Both produce the Inter-American case law and make up the IAHRS. In the domain of VAW, the key instruments are the American Convention on Human Rights (Pact of San José, 1978) and the Inter-American Convention on the Prevention, Punishment and Eradication of Violence Against Women (Belém do Pará Convention, 1994), which establishes the right to a life free of violence, defining physical, sexual, and psychological VAW in the public and private sphere.

While it incorporated the views of feminist advocates and gender experts of the time, Belem do Pará largely centers formal equality and individual liberties (Tapia Tapia, 2022, Chapter 3). Most of the states' positive obligations (Article 7) entail law reform and enforcement, with a strong focus on enabling criminal prosecution for aggressors. State obligations include applying due diligence to prevent, investigate, and impose penalties for VAW; creating or reforming laws to prevent, punish, and eradicate VAW; and establishing legal procedures for women who have been subjected to violence. It is thus generally assumed that activating the penal apparatus is indispensable to protect women. Albeit the convention recognizes social and economic rights, there is no such thing as a "right to a simple and prompt recourse to shelter and health services for victims," for example.

Accordingly, the Inter-American case law emphasizes law reform and criminal investigation. The model is largely based on the idea that judicial failure to punish creates an environment that facilitates the recurrence of VAW. In the emblematic case of Gonzáles et al. (*["Cotton Field"] v. Mexico*, 2009), the IACtHR affirmed that impunity "encourages the repetition of human rights violations" and that "289.... The State's obligation to investigate must be diligently fulfilled in order to avoid impunity and the recurrence of [VAW]." Impunity is defined, in another judgment, as a breach of the states' obligations to ensure the prosecution and punishment of the perpetrators of violence (*Ana, Beatriz y Celia González Pérez v. México*, 2001).

The focus on impunity is associated with the penal doctrine of general prevention, by which punishing an infraction is believed a priori to produce a social perception of the willingness and effectiveness of the state to sanction crimes, thus discouraging citizens from (re)offending. This is also linked to the idea that criminalization expresses the social rejection of a conduct: Through criminalization, the state acknowledges that hurting women is not acceptable. For example, the IACtHR has affirmed: "177.... When faced with an act of violence against a woman, it is particularly important that the authorities in charge of the investigation carry it out with determination and effectiveness, bearing in mind *society's duty to reject violence against women*" (*Rosendo Cantú y otra v. México*, 2010, emphasis added). Here, criminal law is construed as a signifier of social morality. On these foundations, criminal justice emerges as a mechanism that can perform multiple functions, not only the traditional one of attributing criminal responsibility, but also integrally addressing violence. In other words, prosecution and punishment are not only regarded as ex post responses, but also presented as having the capacity to prevent violence, protect survivors, and remedy harms.

In addition, the obligations that states acquire are "of means, not of results" (González et al., *["Cotton Field"] v. Mexico*, 2009), and the means are, of course, criminal trials. In *Raquel Martín de Mejía v. Peru* (1996), the IACHR established that the right to judicial protection enshrined in Article 25 of the Pact of San José should be understood as "the right of every individual to recourse to a tribunal to obtain judicial protection when he believes he has been a victim of violation of any of his human rights" and to "obtain a judicial investigation by a court." The report also stated that the obligation to investigate means that the state will act with due diligence, which is described as using the means at its disposal to arrive at a penal verdict. Furthermore, Belem do Pará instituted "the right to simple and prompt recourse to a competent court for protection against acts that violate [women's] rights" (Article 4, g), again indicating that activating the penal apparatus constitutes "due diligence."

In the landmark case of *Maria da Penha Maia Fernandes v. Brazil* (2001), where Belém do Pará was enforced for the first time,[1] the IACHR concluded that the state had violated the right to judicial guarantees and to judicial protection, and it had not acted with due diligence because it failed to convict and punish the aggressor (Comisión Interamericana de Derechos Humanos, 2015). The commission also stated that the case of Maria da Penha was part of a general pattern of tolerance of domestic violence, manifested in judicial inefficiency. Such conclusion was not the result of an assessment of the incidence of VAW or an appreciation of the state's failure to reduce it; rather, tolerance of VAW was defined as the absence of legal and judicial proceedings undertaken by the state. The resulting standard dictated that human rights are violated when states do not investigate, prosecute, and punish, rather than when they do not take measures, for instance, to physically protect women from ongoing violence. The same is evident in *Ana, Beatriz y Celia González Peréz v. México* (2001): What the System asks of the state is to establish individual criminal responsibility, not to counteract structural VAW by ameliorating women's living conditions.

When it comes to the interactions between victim-survivors and the penal system, the Inter-American case law mostly focuses on procedural rules, such as recovering and preserving evidentiary material and identifying witnesses to obtain their statements (*Rosendo Cantú y otra v. México*, 2010). Even though the IACtHR has issued good practice recommendations regarding the treatment of victim-survivors (e.g., providing a safe environment for witnesses and limiting the need for repetition), there are cases in which, despite acknowledging the risks to which women are exposed when entering the penal system, activating criminal justice is still strongly encouraged. For example, in *Raquel Martín de Mejía v. Peru* (1996), the ICHR stated:

> Raquel Mejía informed the Commission that when, on June 20, 1989, she filed her declaration with the Oxapampa police concerning the abduction and subsequent homicide of her husband, she did not report the sexual abuse to which she had been subjected because: *[I was] fearful that the violations committed against my person would have caused me to be ostracized and exposed me to greater danger* or physical harm (emphasis added).

In the same report, the ICHR added:

> Women who have been raped by members of the security forces do not report these assaults for two reasons: public humiliation and the perception that those responsible will never be punished. In addition, they are usually threatened with reprisals against themselves or their families if they do report them.

As we see, despite recognizing that reporting VAW to a criminal court entails perils for the complainant, the commission did not delve into the systemic reasons why women are reluctant to report violence or highlight other possible protective mechanisms to minimize the danger. Rather than treating women's experiences as manifestations of a structural problem related to the patriarchal and adversarial nature of the system, the commission insisted on demanding a penal response from the state. Such a dynamic is reflected in various aspects of local Latin American legislations, such as that of Ecuador, which I address next.

LEARNINGS FROM ECUADOR: CRIMINAL LAW, THE DISPLACEMENT OF SURVIVORS, AND THE REDUCTION OF SERVICES FOR WOMEN

As shown above, the Inter-American system emphasizes legislative commitments and criminal prosecution, while construing due diligence as the state obligation to trigger the penal apparatus, notwithstanding women's negative experiences of approaching criminal justice, as well as the systemic nature of VAW. Here, I take the example of Ecuador—a country that has adopted multiple laws on VAW in recent years—to show that centering penality can have detrimental "side effects" for survivors.

Belém do Pará was signed by Ecuador in 1995. That year, the National Congress also approved the first specialized law on domestic and family violence, which was promoted by feminist lawyers and activists but was reframed once at the legislature. Although the law had not originally been conceived as a criminal law, the Congress reframed it to treat most VAW infractions as criminal misdemeanors. This law was implemented by the specialized commissariats for women and the family that had been established in 1994 with relative success in terms of complaints presented, although it performed poorly in terms of solved cases (Jácome Villalba, 2003).

Today, according to the Constitution (2008), judges shall administer justice in accordance with international human rights instruments (Article

172), and human rights treaties shall be applied directly by all justice operators and public servants. Furthermore, when human rights treaties establish rights in a way that is more favorable than the Constitution, they prevail over all other laws (Article 424). That is, human rights instruments are part of the local legal order and are given a privileged place within it. Indeed, the Belém do Pará Convention and the Inter-American case law are widely cited by judges and scholars in their texts and decisions.

In relation to VAW, the Constitution enshrines the principle of nondiscrimination, consecrates gender equality, and mandates that the state implement a "gender approach" in public policy (Article 70). Importantly, the Constitution establishes the fundamental right to physical integrity, which encompasses the right to "a life free of violence in the public and private spheres . . . especially against women, children and adolescents, the elderly, persons with disabilities and all persons in situations of disadvantage or vulnerability" (Article 66. B). This framework has translated largely into criminal justice provisions. In 2013, the "Judicial Units for Violence Against Women and the Family" were established.[2] The 2014 Penal Code incorporated over 70 new criminal offenses, including various forms of "violence against women and members of the family unit" and "femicide."

In the process, there were disagreements between women's organizations and feminist legislators, as well as between social movements and government officials (Tapia Tapia, 2022, Chapter 5). Some activists and NGO-based practitioners believed that VAW should remain in the existing specialized law and warned legislators that using ordinary criminal law would complicate reporting VAW and make access to protective measures more intricate. Yet, various forms of VAW ended up categorized as criminal offenses, where they had been treated as misdemeanors. This obeyed criteria such as communicating the severity of VAW, enabling a better collection of statistics, and permitting the unification of penal legislation. Many arguments also pointed at bringing the mandates of international human rights instruments into the local arena (Tapia Tapia, 2018).

In 2018, the Comprehensive Organic Law for the Prevention and Eradication of Violence Against Women passed. From its exposition of motives, the law invokes the Pact of San José and Belém do Pará. It also states that the 2014 Penal Code was "a new step forward" in the fight against VAW because it criminalized VAW, including femicide. However, although this law was conceived due to the women's movement's perception that the Penal Code was not serving complainants' interests, it continued to center penality. For instance, it established that it is the state's obligation to protect women's human rights by avoiding impunity (Article 5) and uses a rights-based language that is very similar to that found in the IAHRS. Even though the Ecuadorian model has particularities and does include some input from women's movements, its implementation has hardly incorporated feminist perspectives, making standard criminal prosecution the main protagonist again, as shown next.

Criminal Law–Centric Models on the Ground: Reduced Protection and Services

As it happens in so many Latin American countries, VAW is widespread in Ecuador. A comparison between the two most recent national surveys on family violence suggested an increased incidence of VAW.[3] As previously explained, litigation in a criminal court is the primary course of action adopted to counteract VAW. However, the possibility of taking part in a criminal trial is, on the ground, minimally meaningful for victim-survivors and frequently discarded due to the onerous nature of a judicial process. Moreover, the creation of specialized laws and courts has not been matched with an enhancement of services for survivors; rather, it seems to be correlated with their reduction.

To understand the lived experiences of women in their journey through the specialized justice system, my team and I conducted fieldwork in 2019, which revealed a very complex situation (Bedford & Tapia Tapia, 2021; Tapia Tapia, 2021; Tapia Tapia et al., 2020). Coinciding with Elisabeth McDonald's data in Chapter 8 of this book, we found that attrition is extremely high in the domain of intimate partner violence, a fact that was recognized by the majority of legal professionals we interviewed, including judges, caseworkers, private and pro bono attorneys, and judicial clerks. Data provided by the Judicial Council indicated that out of 14,826 trials initiated between 2014 and 2018 at the specialized courts, 6,530 were redirected to the public prosecutor (the courts were not considered competent) and, of the remaining 8,296, only 3,652 were resolved with a judgment. Of those, only 927, that is, a mere 11.1%, resulted in a conviction. In total, 56% of the cases heard by the specialized courts did not receive any type of decision and were often labeled as "abandoned" by the complainant.[4]

The high attrition rate can be in part explained by the fact that most survivors' first priority is, in their own words, protection from ongoing violence and not prosecution. One of the main reasons why they file a complaint is to get hold of a protection/restraining order that, they expect, will discourage the aggressor from approaching them and is not available through a civil or other nonpenal pathway. Likely, women would not pursue a judicial process were it not for the protection/restraining order. However, these orders are conditional, first, on the defendant being notified—which can often be difficult due to unknown whereabouts or because the complainant is expected to deliver the notification herself— and then on the progress of the criminal trial. The central phase of the trial is the hearing, which most complainants do not attend, and then, if the trial is dismissed due to lack of evidence, the protection/restraining orders become ineffective. Furthermore, survivors almost always file a report as a last resort when violence has significantly escalated; therefore, they are at a high risk when they approach a court, which makes these findings extremely worrying.

From the interviews, a pattern was found by which complainants withdrew from the trial due to deficient police intervention, insufficient financial resources, fear of retaliation by the aggressor, fear of losing custody of their children, fear of being ostracized by family and friends, and due to impediments to present valid evidence. As de Ávila argues in Chapter 2 of this book, establishing a causal link between fragmented acts of coercive control and the harm caused can be extremely hard. Additionally, most aspects of the criminal trial are at odds with women's material circumstances: A legal process requires complainants to incur expenses to obtain child care, transportation, and legal advice, as well as time to attend hearings and other proceedings. Sometimes, they are even forced to confront the aggressor despite their fear; therefore, their situation potentially worsens.

On their side, legal professionals tend to attribute women's withdrawal from trials to lack of individual "empowerment" or their reconciliation with the defendant, although the interviews I conducted did not point in that direction. Expectedly, lawyers considered that the "right" way to access justice is through a trial, and again, litigation in a criminal court was made synonymous with integral justice, in line with the Inter-American standards. Such an equation, however, proved hollow for most complainants, whose testimonies conveyed the urgency of protection, economic interventions to allow them to exit abusive relationships, and services to help them start anew. Hence, most women were unhappy with the trial, none continued with the process until the end, and those who had overcome violence did it through services and programs that were mostly provided by NGOs. All the while, the signifiers of the state's obligation to protect women are still legalistic, and social interventions are increasingly losing their relevance as pressing courses of action.

In fact, shelter homes for VAW survivors in Ecuador are not part of the state's social welfare system; rather, where they exist, they are linked to NGOs and/or women's collectives. These shelters aim to offer lodging, food, psychological support, legal aid, and social work services to survivors and their children. Since 2008, the Ecuadorian state has subscribed payment agreements with around 5 shelters and 16 care centers to fund part of their operations; however, from 2018 onward, the state's contributions have been progressively reduced (Robalino, 2020). In 2022, the secretary of human rights, in charge of managing these funds, announced that, rather than directly adjudicating the money to the shelters, it would now hold an open competition for funding (Ponce, 2022). The director of Casa Paula, a home shelter in the Amazon region with over 22 years of experience, explained that the secretary had elaborated the new regulations without the input of shelters' staff regarding budgets and attention models for survivors. Hence, Casa Paula decided not to participate in the competition (Peralta Suárez, 2022). After the adjudications, a spokesperson for the National Network of Shelters said that at least twice as much money would be needed to provide adequate services. She also indicated that out of the five shelters that had previously received state contributions, only three received funding under the new scheme (Peralta Suárez, 2022).

The fact that a comprehensive legal framework exists in Ecuador and its enhancement has coincided with the reduction of services for women leaves us with a lot to reflect on. From a legal perspective, Ecuador is fulfilling its international duties to protect women's human rights as it has enabled the penal prosecution of VAW. However, this has not brought about a reduction of violence or an improvement of women's living conditions.

CONCLUSION: A MEAGER JUSTICE FOR WOMEN

International human rights discourses on VAW, including the Inter-American system, invoke criminal justice as an apparatus that fulfills multiple functions in the fight against violence. The stumbling blocks that appear along the way, including the negative experiences of survivors in interacting with local penal systems, are not addressed as issues that are inherent in the adversarial and invasive nature of criminal justice, but as shortcomings that the system itself can correct. As a result, to fulfill their positive obligations, states are increasingly encouraged to trigger penality.

A closer look at human rights case law shows that the Inter-American standards currently privilege abstraction, doctrinal knowledge, retributive justice, and an individualistic approach to social problems. This is evident in their portrayal of criminal law as capable of solving complex issues, while little attention is paid to real-life protective services and social security for women. The standards instead emphasize judicial adversarial actions and punishment, without establishing a dialogue with existing human rights principles, which contain and restrict the state's coercive power.

Some arguments justifying the resort to penality are of a moral nature and present criminal law as a means to express the social rejection of a conduct, which generally results in a retributive approach to justice. Other arguments are legalistic and self-referential, such as the notion of general prevention. Most arguments assume a priori that criminal justice can prevent violence and eradicate it despite the lack of empirical data to confirm this. As other chapters in this collection demonstrate, the separation between the realm of the social and that of the juridical is impactful. Furthermore, seldom does one come across case law that is based on the knowledge produced by empirical social sciences. Justice operators continue to work with narrow definitions of justice, produced juridically, but unproductive for victims/survivors, which is also reflected in the underreporting that many authors in this volume describe. That is, access to justice is restrictively conceived as access to litigation, and the experience of Ecuador suggests that this model is not survivor oriented on the ground. In enhancing penality, the Inter-American standards facilitate the undermining of survivors' experiences, overlooking alternative, nonpenal, approaches to justice, which could better address women's living conditions and the structural factors that produce VAW.

From an empirical perspective, today's legalism is reproducing women's subordination. Criminal proceedings are precarious mechanisms that provide a passage to a place in which many survivors do not want to be, where they would not go were it not for the hope of a protection that is rarely delivered. In reality, the possibility of reporting violence exists, but not much else is offered, and what is provided—a cumbersome criminal trial—can aggravate women's situations. Then, when complainants decide not to continue with the trial, the state and its agents allege that access to justice does exist, but is not taken advantage of by survivors. From a legal standpoint, it is women who desert justice, not the other way around.

As we see, human rights penality can contribute to creating barriers for women who seek protection from violence and at the same time allow states to fulfill human rights duties in a relatively easy and cheap fashion. The law-centric state is delivering fewer and fewer services and offering more and more laws. As a result, women are not only materially forsaken but also legally "protected," with the paradox that giving access to litigation counts as state progress toward human rights realization.

By way of reflection, it is necessary to consider that promoting a rights-based agenda implies, at least to some extent, bolstering the state and its punitive power. When advocates, activists, and scholars posit VAW as a violation of human rights, we may implicitly be reinforcing a reductive penal model. We may also be—if not deliberately—condoning the suffering produced by the penal system for many underprivileged people, not only inmates, but also victim-survivors who may end up criminalized due to poverty, ethnicity, migratory status, and more. A priority challenge, therefore, is to denaturalize criminal justice, discuss its inherent violence, and reveal its contingency and limitations.

As feminist scholars and practitioners who are sensitive to structural inequalities, we should aim to develop alternative proposals that are survivor oriented. A focus on social and economic rights, which recognizes that VAW is linked to precarity, lack of access to healthcare, housing, employment, and other social and economic rights, could facilitate a less simplistic approach, rendering states accountable for materially ensuring women's dignity.

NOTES

1. This influential case has, in my experience, often been cited by Ecuador's specialized courts in their sentences for violence against women and the family.
2. Article 232 of the Organic Code of the Judiciary determines the competence of judges of violence against women and the family to "hear facts and acts of violence and police offenses when dealing with cases provided for in the law against violence against women and the family."
3. According to the National Survey of 2019, gender-based violence affects approximately 65 out of every 100 Ecuadorian women. The previous National Survey of 2012 suggested a lower incidence: 60% of women said they experienced some type of gender-based violence by any person.
4. For details of the methodology, including the participants' characteristics and numbers, as well as more detailed quantitative data, see Tapia Tapia (2021).

REFERENCES

Ana, Beatriz y Celia González Pérez vs. México, Informe N° 53/01 Caso 11.565 (Comisión Interamericana de Derechos Humanos 2001). https://cidh.oas.org/annual rep/2000sp/capituloiii/fondo/Mexico11.565.htm

Barreto, J. M. (2018). Decolonial thinking and the quest for decolonising human rights. Southeast Asian Journal of Social Science, 46(4–5), 484–502. https://doi.org/10.1163/15685314-04604006

Bedford, K., & Tapia, S. (2021). Specialised (in)security: Violence against women, criminal courts, and the gendered presence of the state in Ecuador. Latin American Law Review, 1(7), 21–42. https://doi.org/10.29263/lar07.2021.02

Burman, A. (2017). The political ontology of climate change: Moral meteorology, climate justice, and the coloniality of reality in the Bolivian Andes. Journal of Political Ecology, 24(1), 921. https://doi.org/10.2458/v24i1.20974

CLADEM. (2007). Feminicidio. Monitoreo sobre feminicidio/femicidio en El Salvador, Guatemala, Honduras, México, Nicaragua y Panamá.

Código Orgánico Integral Penal, Suplemento Registro Oficial N° 180 (2014).

Coker, D. (2001). Crime control and feminist law reform in domestic violence law: A critical review. Buffalo Criminal Law Review, 4(2), 801–860. https://doi.org/10.1525/NCLR.2001.4.2.801

Comisión Interamericana de Derechos Humanos. (2015). Estándares jurídicos vinculados a la igualdad de género y a los derechos de las mujeres en el sistema interamericano de derechos humanos: desarrollo y aplicación. Organización de los Estados Americanos.

Constitución de la República del Ecuador, Pub. L. No. Registro Oficial N° 449 (2008). http://bivicce.corteconstitucional.gob.ec/site/php/level.php?lang=es&component=68

Convención Americana sobre Derechos Humanos. "Pacto de San José", núm. OEA N° 36 – Reg. ONU 27/08/1979 N° 17955, Organización de los Estados Americanos (1969). https://www.oas.org/dil/esp/tratados_B-32_Convencion_Americana_sobre_Derechos_Humanos.htm

Convención interamericana para prevenir, sancionar y erradicar la violencia contra la mujer. "Convención de Belém do Pará", núm. A-61, Organización de los Estados Americanos (1994). https://www.oas.org/juridico/spanish/tratados/a-61.html

Darke, S., & Garces, C. (2017). Surviving in the new mass carceral zone. Prison Service Journal, 229, 2–9.

De Aquino, S. (2013). Organizing to monitor implementation of the Maria da Penha law in Brazil. In M. Al-Sharmani (Ed.), Feminist activism, women's rights, and legal reform (Feminisms and development) (pp. 177–202). Zed Books.

Douzinas, C. (2007). Human rights and empire: The political philosophy of cosmopolitanism. Routledge-Cavendish.

Engle, K. (2015). Anti-impunity and the turn to criminal law in human rights. Cornell Law Review, 100(5), 1069.

Engle, K. (2016). A genealogy of the criminal turn in human rights. In K. Engle, Z. Miller, & D. M. Davis (Eds.), Anti-impunity and the human rights agenda (pp. 15–67). Cambridge University Press.

French, J. H. (2013). Rethinking police violence in Brazil: Unmasking the public secret of race. Latin American Politics and Society, 55(4), 161–181. https://doi.org/10.1111/j.1548-2456.2013.00212.x

González et al. ("Cotton Field") v. Mexico, Series C No. 205 (Inter-American Court of Human Rights el 16 de noviembre de 2009). https://www.corteidh.or.cr/docs/casos/articulos/seriec_205_ing.pdf

Goodmark, L. (2018). Decriminalizing domestic violence: A balanced policy approach to intimate partner violence. University of California Press.

Goodmark, L. (2021). Gender-based violence, law reform, and the criminalization of survivors of violence. International Journal for Crime Justice and Social Democracy, 10(4), 13–25. https://doi.org/10.5204/ijcjsd.1994

Jácome Villalba, N. (2003). Estudio cultural de la práctica jurídica en las comisarías de la mujer y la familia [MSc]. Facultad Latinoamericana de Ciencias Sociales.

Kapur, R. (2006). Human rights in the 21st century: Taking a walk on the dark side. Sydney Law Review, 28(4), 665–687.

Kennedy, D. (2004). The dark sides of virtue. Reassessing international humanitarianism. Princeton University Press.

Ley Orgánica Integral para Prevenir y Erradicar la Violencia Contra las Mujeres, Suplemento al Registro Oficial No. 175 (2018). https://www.registroficial.gob.ec/index.php/registro-oficial-web/publicaciones/suplementos/item/10072-suplemento-al-registro-oficial-no-175

López Hidalgo, S., & Tapia Tapia, S. (2022). Colonialidades legales: La constitucionalización de la justicia indígena y la continuidad del discurso judicial hegemónico en Ecuador. Revista Derecho del Estado, 52, 299–331. https://doi.org/10.18601/01229893.n52.10

Maria da Penha Maia Fernandes v. Brazil, Case 12.051 Report N° 54/01 ___ (Inter-American Commission on Human Rights 2001). http://cidh.org/annualrep/2000eng/ChapterIII/Merits/Brazil12.051.htm

McIlwaine, C., & Moser, C. (2001). Violence and social capital in urban poor communities: perspectives from Colombia and Guatemala. Journal of International Development, 13(7), 965. https://doi.org/10.1002/jid.815

Mendoza, B. (2016). Coloniality of gender and power: From postcoloniality to decoloniality. In L. Disch & M. Hawkesworth, (Eds.), The Oxford handbook of feminist theory (p. 100). Oxford University Press.

Oriola, T. B., & Knight, W. A. (2020). COVID-19, George Floyd and Human Security. African Security, 13(2), 111–115. https://doi.org/10.1080/19392206.2020.1783760

Peralta Suárez, G. (2022). Menos fondos, menos recursos: La pomposa entrega de presupuesto para las casas de acogida, Wambra Medio Comunitario. Wambra Medio Comunitario. https://wambra.ec/menos-fondos-menos-recursos-la-pomposa-entrega-de-presupuesto-para-las-casas-de-acogida/

Ponce, I. (2022). La respuesta de Bernarda Ordóñez que no alcanza, GK. https://gk.city/2022/01/05/respuestas-bernarda-ordonez-sobre-casas-acogida/

Raquel Martín de Mejía v. Perú, Case 10.970 Report No. 5/96 ___ (Inter-American Commission on Human Rights 1996). https://www.refworld.org/cases,IACHR,3ae6b71c6.html

Robalino, J. (2020). Víctimas de violencia de género se quedan sin presupuesto y sin atención. Pichincha Comunicaciones. http://www.pichinchacomunicaciones.com.ec/victimas-de-violencia-de-genero-se-quedan-sin-presupuesto-y-sin-atencion/

Rosendo Cantú y otra Vs. México, Serie C No. 216 ___ (Corte Interamericana de Derechos Humanos 2010). https://www.corteidh.or.cr/CF/jurisprudencia2/ficha_tecnica.cfm?nId_Ficha=339

Smart, C. (1989). Feminism and the power of law. Routledge.

Snowball, L., & Weatherburn, D. (2006). Indigenous over-representation in prison: The role of offender characteristics. Crime and Justice Bulletin, (99), 1–20.

Sudbury, J. (Ed.). (2005). Global lockdown: Race, gender, and the prison-industrial complex. Routledge.

Tapia Tapia, S. (2016). Sumak Kawsay, coloniality and the criminalisation of violence against women in Ecuador. Feminist Theory, 17(2), 141–156. https://doi.org/10.1177/1464700116645324

Tapia Tapia, S. (2018). Feminism and penal expansion: The role of rights-based criminal law in post-neoliberal Ecuador. Feminist Legal Studies, 26(3), 285–306. https://doi.org/10.1007/s10691-018-9380-5

Tapia Tapia, S. (2019). Continuidades coloniales: del discurso de la protección a la familia a la regulación de la violencia contra las mujeres en el derecho ecuatoriano del siglo XX. Universidad Verdad, 1(75), 45–59. https://doi.org/10.33324/uv.v1i75.210

Tapia Tapia, S. (2021). Beyond carceral expansion: Survivors' experiences of using specialised courts for violence against women in Ecuador. Social & Legal Studies, 30(6), 848–868. https://doi.org/10.1177/0964663920973747

Tapia Tapia, S. (2022). Feminism, violence against women and law reform: Decolonial lessons from Ecuador. Routledge (Social Justice).

Tapia Tapia, S., Padrón Palacios, T., Sánchez Palacios, M., López Hidalgo, S. (2020). Women's experiences of using specialised courts for violence against women: Lessons and recommendations from Ecuador. University of Birmingham. https://www.birmingham.ac.uk/schools/law/news/2020/06/bedford-igi-ecuador.aspx

Wacquant, L. (2009). Punishing the poor: The neoliberal government of social insecurity. Duke University Press.

13

Intersectionality, Vulnerability, and Punitiveness

Claims of Equality Merging Into Categories of Penal Exclusion and Secondary Victimization

GEMA VARONA ■

INTRODUCTION

For Hill Collins and Bilge (2020), intersectionality is a concept that helps us to understand the architecture of social and economic injustice and how social inequalities of race, class, gender, sexuality, age, ability, and ethnicity shape one another (Atrey & Dunne, 2020). According to the European Institute for Gender Equality (n.d.), intersectionality represents an analytical tool for studying the ways in which layered identities derived from social relations, history, and the operation of structures of power intersect to contribute to unique experiences of discrimination.

The reality of simultaneous multiple discrimination experiences was highlighted in the 1970s by critical legal studies (La Barbera, 2017), but the term *intersectionality* was coined by Crenshaw (1989) within law and critical race theory. In the context of a structure/agency approach, Crenshaw initially referred to intersectionality as a category to study how

Gema Varona, *Intersectionality, Vulnerability, and Punitiveness* In: *The Criminalization of Violence Against Women*. Edited by: Heather Douglas, Kate Fitz-Gibbon, Leigh Goodmark, and Sandra Walklate, Oxford University Press.
© Oxford University Press 2024. DOI: 10.1093/oso/9780197651841.003.0014

overlapping systems of oppression create distinct experiences for women with diverse identity categories. She illustrated this with the 1976 *De Graffenreid v. General Motors* case regarding Black women whose claim for both racial and sexual discrimination at work was dismissed. Since then, intersectionality has been conceived as a legal concept, an activist practice, a methodology for public policy (Guzmán & Jiménez Rodrigo, 2015; Nash, 2008; Morris & Bunjun, 2007), a criterion for judicial interpretation, and a central element of the fourth wave of feminism (Zimmerman, 2017). Some authors have found profound links between the concept of intersectionality and peripheral, southern, postcolonial, decolonial, and cultural studies (Guzmán & Jiménez Rodrigo, 2015, p. 600), as well as with abolitionist feminism (Lamusse, 2022). There has also been a call for a more or less comprehensive intersectional criminology (Potter, 2015) and justice.

Linked to its origin, intersectionality is being used as a third and more complete analytical feminist framework concerning violence against women (Crenshaw, 1991), understood as a specific form of gender inequality (Bilge, 2013; Jibrin & Salem, 2015; Yuval-Davis, 2006). In this regard, Guzmán and Jiménez Rodrigo (2015, p. 602–603) contended:

a) From a feminism of difference perspective, the main element of analysis is gender, with a focus on the element of being a woman and interpersonal violence, but this brings the risk of reductionism and victimism.
b) From a feminism of equality perspective, social injustice is the key element to addressing cultural and structural violence, but this risks losing sight of personal and contextual differences and agency.
c) From an intersectional feminism perspective, it might be possible to cross social circles (Simmel, 1909/1994) to grasp the reality of complex identities of the exchangeable and diffuse roles of victims (and victimizers, although not mentioned by the authors cited). In those identities a myriad of elements interact differently in time and space to constitute, favor, reinforce,

or oppose diverse positions of subordination, resistance, and domination.

Thus, although coined in relation to law, the notion of intersectionality has extended beyond this realm, and it is presented as progress toward equality. Introduced to the *Oxford English Dictionary* in 2015, activist and political debates soon incorporated it, sometimes in ways that did not refer to the creation of another dimension of disempowerment based on preexistent discriminations. Moreover, for Crenshaw: "The prospect of the creation of new classes of protected minorities, governed only by the mathematical principles of permutation and combination, clearly raises the prospect of opening the hackneyed Pandora's box" (Coaston, 2019, para. 23).

Drawing from these debates on terminology, this chapter describes the relationships between the concepts of vulnerability and intersectionality in connection to the notion of gendered violence victimization in different legal systems. Then it analyzes how introducing the concept of intersectionality in an inherently discriminatory criminal justice system (Balfour, 2013; Dancig-Rosenberg & Yosef, 2019; Fassin, 2018; Wacquant, 2009; Whitby Okafor, 2021) might be problematic, in particular in the context of addressing sexual violence in Spain. In these pages, punitiveness is understood as excessive use of punishment, acknowledging its mythical understanding and the complexity of characterizing something as "excessive" in a system that overall might be more humane in certain jurisdictions and might claim more punishment only in a symbolic way, notwithstanding the historical and cultural embeddedness of punishment as a way of social control (Matthews, 2005).

LEGAL NOTIONS ON VULNERABLE VICTIMS AND INTERSECTIONALITY

The notion of intersectionality relates to inequality in its many forms, but in some jurisdictions, like Spain, it is connected to so-called vulnerable victims. However, intersectionality does not always generate vulnerability and vice versa. Vulnerability can be individual or group based, but intersectionality is experienced individually, although based on the joint action of power structures. Within Fineman's vulnerability theory (2008), what is intersecting are the power systems and privilege structures producing networks of unequal distribution of resources or, in other words, politics of precarity within neoliberalism (Davis & Aldieri, 2021). For this very reason, a responsive state has to act with due diligence and positive obligations, taking adequate measures (not just at the criminal justice level) to avoid violence and abuses of power, including primary and secondary victimizations (Bond, 2003; Brown, 2012). Timmer (2013) stressed that the notion of vulnerability should be used in order to politicize, rather than pathologize, prevailing structures of social dependence. In any case, most authors distinguish compounded vulnerability from intersectionality. This is not always the case when these concepts are introduced in the legal arena.

International Human Rights Standards

The United Nations Committee on the Elimination of Discrimination Against Women monitors the implementation of the Convention on the Elimination of All Forms of Discrimination Against Women and has stressed the need to prohibit intersecting forms of discrimination and their compounded negative impact (Center for Intersectional Justice, 2020). This committee explicitly mentions intersectionality, but it understands it as multiple or double discrimination that, at a practical level, requires having disaggregated data by gender in order to assess it properly.

At the level of the Council of Europe, intersectionality is not mentioned in the Human Rights Convention, probably because, when signed in 1950, the term was nonexistent. Now, the case law of the European Court of Human Rights referring to vulnerability and intersectionality can be read as a critical engagement with alterity and power, but it can also produce a naturalization of certain exclusions of those not deemed vulnerable enough and neglects the need of access to sources of empowerment (Heri, 2021). In any case, the court has discussed the notion of intersectional vulnerabilities. However, until now, it has refused to apply the concept of intersectionality in nondiscrimination cases where it was invoked by third-party interveners.

The court has acknowledged the intersection of grounds for vulnerability depending on the contexts, but it is being more restrictive in the realm of expulsions and asylum. For example, in the case *B.S. v. Spain*[1] (Guzmán & Jiménez Rodrigo, 2015; La Barbera & Cruells, 2019), the court recognized that the applicant was vulnerable "by virtue of not just one but a series of traits, namely her African origin, her gender, and the fact that she was a sex worker" (Heri, 2021, p. 34). This acknowledgment might help empathy and the rediscovering of humanity and individuality, allowing the court to respond to context and respect agency beyond victim essentialism and paternalism. However, after analyzing the emerging jurisprudence at the level of the European Court of Human Rights, Heri (2021) concluded: "Instead of breaking vulnerability down into endless, increasingly specific sub-categories, what is needed is a dynamic approach that balances sources of vulnerability with sources of resilience" (p. 218).

In the specific sphere of legislation about violence against women in the Council of Europe, the 2011 Istanbul Convention on preventing and combating violence against women and domestic violence does not mention intersectionality. Nevertheless, today some authors have defended the intersectional interpretation of this convention with an emphasis on structural intersectionality, taking into account Article 4 on nondiscrimination (Sosa & Mestre, 2022)[2]:

> The focus lies not on "groups" ("migrant women", "Roma women", "women with disabilities", "older women", "lesbian women", "transgender women") but on the categories or "grounds" of discrimination and inequality (e.g. "migrant status", "national minority status", "sexual orientation", "disability", "age") and how these sustain systems of inequality (e.g. "racism", "ageism", "ableism", "lesbophobia", "transphobia"). . . . It confirms the connection of gender-based

violence against women with structural (institutional and social) inequalities and highlights that violence can take place in multiple settings (households, workplace, educational institutions, etc.). (pp. 38-39)

This implies state obligations toward not only prevention, protection, co-ordination, participation of stakeholders, and data gathering, but also state obligations for prosecution and sanctioning, recognizing the need to examine the different structural elements that cause vulnerability, stressing that this is differently experienced, which entails different women victims' needs. In relation to punitiveness, according to Sosa and Mestre (2022, pp. 78-79), intersectionality should have an impact on sanctioning. Based on opportunity theories and Article 46(c) of the Istanbul Convention,[3] these authors proposed adding as aggravating circumstances the commitment of acts of gender-based violence against persons who are placed in different positions of vulnerability. They referred to contexts where perpetrators look for victims less likely to seek prosecution or other forms of reparation because of the multiple forms of discrimination they suffer. Cultural oppression or other forms of discrimination suffered by the victimizer should not justify any kind of violence against women.

European Union Law

In the case of the European Union legislation and case law on gender equality, different binding norms[4] recognized that women are more exposed to the risk of suffering multiple discriminations. Moreover, following La Barbera (2017), the 2013 resolution on women with disabilities (2013/2065/INI) affirmed that they are exposed to multiple discriminations resulting from gender, age, religion, cultural, and social inequality. Finally, the 2014 resolution on violence against women (2013/2004/INL) states that women, due to race, ethnicity, religion or belief, health, marital status, housing, immigration status, age, disability, sexual orientation, and gender identity, may have special needs and be more vulnerable to multiple discriminations. In any case, despite some European Parliament nonbinding resolutions on equality between women and men having explicitly mentioned intersectionality, particularly in relation to Roma women, the list of protected grounds of discrimination might be considered exhaustive (La Barbera, 2017, p. 143) and therefore not open to accommodating claims across identity categories.

Recently, an emerging legal trend to incorporate the notion of intersectionality in European Union norms and distinguish it from multiple discriminations can be observed (European Agency for Fundamental Rights and Council of Europe, 2018, p. 59), with uncertain practical results. The 2020 Gender Equality Strategy 2020–2025 (European Union, 2020) mentions the word *intersectionality* 13 times, understood as a cross-cutting principle, including the need for data gathering and more resources for research on this topic. "To get a complete picture of gender-based violence, data should be disaggregated by relevant intersectional aspects and indicators such as age, disability status, migrant status and rural-urban residence" (p. 5). At the level of public awareness, a campaign will "tackle all spheres of life with an intersectional approach" (p. 6), and the intersectionality of gender with other grounds of discrimination will be addressed across EU policies (p. 16). This includes the labor market, where it is recognized that: "Some women are structurally underrepresented in the labor market, often resulting from the intersection of gender with additional conditions of vulnerability or marginalization such as belonging to an ethnic or religious minority or having a migrant background" (p. 7).

However, other more specific binding norms, like the Directive 2012/29/EU establishing minimum standards on the rights of victims of crime, do not mention intersectionality.[5] This Directive does mention the obligation of an individualized response to victims. Furthermore, vulnerability is a key concept, defined as the exposure to a high risk of harm in the form of revictimization, intimidation, reprisals, or secondary victimization (Preamble, para. 38, and art. 22.7). According to this directive, vulnerability entails special protection needs for some categories of victims, considering certain kinds of crime, contexts, relation to the offender, or sociodemographic profiles. In practice, this open, dynamic, and diffuse concept of vulnerability seems to be creating hierarchies of victims and punitiveness (Moya, 2020). By referring to the concept of secondary victimization, there is an implicit recognition in the directive that the legal system itself creates or reinforces vulnerability of excluded minorities with an intersectional character.

Finally, the 2022 European Commission proposal for a directive of the European Parliament and of the council on combating violence against women and domestic violence calls for harmonization in criminal law to protect E.U. values through a basic criminalization of rape, female genital mutilation, and certain forms of cyber violence (Rigotti, 2022). In relation to intersectionality as disempowerment or power imbalances, this directive does not preclude restorative justice (it mentions that restorative justice services should receive adequate training) in contrast to the agreed prohibition proposal by the 2022 Spanish Equality Commission report, which is mentioned further in the chapter. The E.U. proposal mentions intersectionality in its preamble: "Member States should therefore pay due regard to victims affected by such intersectional discrimination, through providing specific measures where intersecting forms of discrimination are present" (para. 11). In particular, lesbian, bisexual, trans, nonbinary, intersex, and queer (LBTIQ) women, women with disabilities, and women with a minority racial or ethnic background are said to be at a heightened risk of experiencing gender-based violence. Moreover, it underlines that public opinion considers sanctions as insufficient, and vulnerability is again related to the need for aggravating circumstances.

THE CONCEPT OF INTERSECTIONALITY IN SPANISH CRIMINAL POLICY ON GENDERED VIOLENCE: SPECIAL FOCUS ON SEXUAL VIOLENCE

The Spanish Comprehensive Law 15/2022 for equal treatment and nondiscrimination mentions the term *intersectionality* nine times. Article 6 defines intersectionality and differentiates it from multiple discrimination.

According to this law, intersectional discrimination occurs when various causes concur or interact, generating a specific form of discrimination. In any case, the various concurrent discriminatory motivations must be alleged, which can pose difficulties in practice.

The Spanish 1/2004 Organic Law of Measures of Integral Protection Against Gender-Based Violence does not mention the concept of intersectionality, probably because this notion was not present in the general academic and activist debate at the time of its passage. Following E.U. legislation, the 1/2004 law contains the concept of mainstreaming[6] as a gender-sensitive global public policy. By contrast, the 2022 Organic Law on Integral Guarantee of Sexual Liberty (Cortes Generales, 2022) mentions intersectionality 12 times and vulnerability 6 times. Drawing from much contested Spanish judicial cases, within the global discussions on consent and the global *#MeToo* movement, this draft was passed by the Spanish Congress in August 2022. Only the right-wing parties in Congress voted against it.

Mirroring the above-mentioned 2022 European Commission proposal for a directive of the European Parliament and of the council on combating violence against women and domestic violence, the preamble of the Spanish law states the following:

> This Organic Law adopts intersectionality as a basic concept to describe the obligations of the State in the face of discrimination and its impact. Gender discrimination is indivisibly linked to other discrimination factors such as disability, racial or ethnic origin, sexual orientation, sexual identity, social class, administrative status, country of origin, religion, conviction or opinion or marital status. (para. 10)

According to Article 2(e), "Considering Intersectional and Multiple Discrimination," intersectionality is one of the main principles of this law. Thus, in its application, the institutional response must take into special consideration the victims of sexual violence affected by factors of discrimination. In a nonexhaustive way, besides the variables expressed in the preamble, the law refers to the age, health, social class, migration, or other circumstances that imply more disadvantageous positions for certain populations in their effective exercise of their rights.

In the drafting of this law, the equality minister expressed the view that this legislation rests more on the offender's accountability rather than on punitiveness. She highlighted the need for sexual reeducation treatments for offenders, thought to be mandatory for juveniles and included as a condition for probation. She also underlined that mediation could take place only if the victim requests it. The minister also conceptualized the right to reparation in terms of institutional responsibility. However, the Organic Law finally passed, after much political debate, in its 10th final provision and includes an amendment to Article 3.1 of the Spanish Law 4/2015, of April 27, on the Statute of the Victim of Crime, stating that: "In any case, mediation and conciliation shall be prohibited in cases of sexual violence and gender violence." It also stresses the notions of vulnerability, in relation to not only the state's protection and responses to victims but also sanctioning via aggravating circumstances. These aggravating circumstances might provoke an excess of punishment, according to the interpretation of some legal scholars concerned with defendants' rights (Moya, 2020). At the same time, they might be very difficult to apply in practice because of the evidence needed to confirm the intention of taking advantage of the situation of vulnerability or the intersectional vulnerability.

These observations are in line with other reforms in Spanish criminal law. The Spanish Criminal Code mentions the notion of vulnerability on 20 occasions, including the aggravated subcategory of offenses based on the special vulnerability of the victim (because of age, disability, illness, etc.). An analysis by Moya (2020) concluded that the treatment given by the Criminal Code to the aggravating circumstance is incoherent and the jurisprudence contradictory. This is so because, as it might happen with intersectionality, in a contested social field, judges will have too broad discretion regarding a very vague term that does not necessarily lead to more contextualization of individual cases.

Paradoxically, as is the case in other countries (Cabrera, 2009; Ravecca et al., 2022), in Spain strange allies reject the kind of punitiveness favored by some intersectional legal standpoints. On one side, the extreme right believes that what they call the gender ideology (including intersectionality) criminalizes white cisgender men (Álvarez-Benavides & Aguilar, 2021). The extreme right contends that it creates not only hierarchies of victimhood but also women victimism and provokes victimization of men as well. On the other side, many criminal law professors, based on the defense of principles of legality and *ne bis in idem* (under which a person cannot be punished twice for the same facts), criticize the application of the concepts of vulnerability and intersectionality because they aggravate punishment. Those legal professionals, on the right or the left, tend to reject diffuse concepts and political activism because they are seen as endangering universal legal safeguards for the accused. This position does not mean that the state should not address the causes of vulnerability or intersectionality. Moreover, some authors pointed out that the growing legal and political interest in the concept might cause a depoliticization of power imbalances and concentration on individual subjectivities, comparing and commodifying difference without considering the sources of cultural and structural violence (Conaghan, 2009). At the same time, when rereading Crenshaw, we realized that perhaps the application in law tends to understand intersectionality as something additive and not reconstitutive like Crenshaw meant.

FINAL POINTS TO RECAP AND PROPOSE FURTHER ISSUES FOR RESEARCH AROUND AN UNFINISHED DEBATE

Intersectionality is a real experience that cannot be captured in the hegemonic criminal law. The juridification of that complex experience might favor more oppression for some groups. By juridification it is understood the creation of legal norms that affect the criminal justice system. The equality aimed for by the law is a formal one, at least in the Spanish context where, despite feminist political activism, when confronted with violence most affected women show a high degree of legal cynicism

(García-Hombrados & Martínez-Matute, 2021; Sendroiu et al., 2021): Most women victims do not trust the criminal system.

We can conclude that the entrance of the notion of intersectionality into E.U. and Spanish criminal substantive law and jurisprudence, promoted mainly by an activist feminist approach in the case of Spain, has brought ambivalent results. On the one hand, with limited resources it has made the state more responsive to the reality of complex systems of social exclusion, including the criminal one, and might favor creative methodologies to assess discrimination (Rodó Zárate, 2014, 2021). On the other hand, there are signs that this notion might be co-opted by a system driven by punishment where victim protection and reparation tend to be assimilated to the desire for more severe sanctions, particularly for certain populations.

Beyond the divergent Spanish voices against the concept of intersectionality in violence against women, there are at least two pending debatable questions related to the conclusions of this chapter. First, the application of the notion of intersectionality to other forms of discrimination may affect people beyond their gender identity. Second, the reflection on the notions of resistance and resilience, even if the latter concept needs to consider the relevance of political and collective emancipation versus a too narrow neoliberal individual concept of resilience to victimization where this is understood just as an equal risk for all, instead unequally distributed social harm (Barrère, 2016; Davis & Aldieri, 2021).

As for the first pending question, this is related to the current Spanish feminist debate on the so-called identity of difference (Valcárcel, 2023). In the 2022 Draft Law on Real and Effective Equality of Trans People and for the Guarantee of the Rights of Lesbian, Gay, Trans, Bisexual, and Intersex People, we found an article on the special attention to multiple and intersectional discriminations that seems clearer than the definitions contained in the realm of gendered violence (Romero, 2022). The draft on trans people clearly states that, in intersectional discrimination, the multiple causes of discrimination operate and interact with each other in an inseparable way, resulting in a different and specific type of discrimination. However, once again, according to this draft, multiple or intersectional discrimination implies an increase in administrative sanctioning (Esteve & Nonell, 2021). Future research will be needed to assess whether this is just symbolic law and if it really leads to more sanctioning, or more attention to sanctioning, rather than to the actual causes of discrimination addressed in the name of that draft when calling equality as "real and effective."

As for the second pending question, in a parallelism with the notion of sex (Currah, 2022), the word *intersectional* has been included in the law, which can be understood as a state construction of equality. As happens with other concepts (Sosa et al., 2022), the institutionalization (Zugaza, 2020) and legalization of the concept of intersectionality might be being done in a distorted way in which we tend to forget what Jemal (2021) stressed: "Every person is intersectional and to deny that complexity is to dehumanize" (p. 520). That assertion includes the different and exchangeable roles a person can take in the criminal system. Abolitionist feminism and anticarceral feminism stress their overlapping political goals with intersectional feminism by considering the penal system's contribution toward general violence (Lamusse, 2022). In this regard, the law is related to the force of law and the practicalities of governing inequalities, perhaps with an individualistic or patronizing lens. It is uncertain whether the integration of the notion of intersectionality will bring significant punitiveness in practice. In principle, there is a high probability of it in a climate of political antagonism and polarization. In that climate, the formal law encapsulates binarism (women/men; consent/nonconsent even if the law has taken into account feminist claims on sexual freedom) (Angel, 2021; Robcis, 2021), something that seems just the opposite of what a notion of intersectionality aims at in its original emancipatory conception.

An intersectional perspective might be interesting as a general standpoint in public policies aimed at social justice where the axis should be avoiding domination and addressing institutional vulnerability (state incapacity or unwillingness) to protect all human rights, considering particularly those more exposed to interpersonal, state, corporate, or systemic abuses (Pomares & Maqueda, 2022), aiming at a more transformative justice (Emakunde, 2021; Varona, 2015). In this regard, intersectionality seems to be problematic as a legal concept to be used to justify more severe punishment, and it might work better as an analytical eye-opener to transform formal or narrow (essentialist, antagonist, patronizing, or pathological) legal notions about vulnerability.

On the different positions we might occupy simultaneously and provisionally in diverse social circles, reinterpreting Simmel's metaphors (1909/1994) about the bridge and the door, the intersection of categories of exclusion in criminal legal paradigms might act as separation—needed sometimes as a door for not only guaranteeing refuge and visibility, but also risking secondary victimization and further social oppression. Simultaneously, a deep understanding of what intersectionality entails, beyond its legal use, might act as a bridge or connection for complex social justice demands, including the demands of harm doers. The interpretation of intersectionality should avoid focusing on just one or several elements of individual or collective identities (gender, age, or sexual orientation) or domination (patriarchy). Instead, it could try to integrate, in a nonexhaustive way, other identity categories and domination systems (racism, classism, heteronormativity, global capitalism) (Bargu & Bottici, 2017). Thus, we can grasp how violence against women through the interaction of differences and inequalities structures the lives of different persons in diverse contexts (Guzmán & Jiménez Rodrigo, 2015, pp. 601, 608–609).

NOTES

1. Other cases quoted by Heri (2021) are *Mubilanzila Mayeka and Kaniki Mitunga v. Belgium* (an unaccompanied minor with an irregular status); *I.G. and Others v. Slovakia* (pregnant Roma minors); *Valentin Câmpeanu v. Romania* (a Roma minor, deprived of liberty with an intellectual disability, diagnosed with HIV); and *Lacatus v. Switzerland* (an illiterate and destitute young Roma woman).
2. In this text of 60 pages, intersectionality is mentioned 156 times.
3. Following Article 46, among the aggravating circumstances, it should be considered that the offense was committed against a person made vulnerable by particular circumstances and/or that the offense resulted in severe physical or psychological harm for the victim.
4. See the 2000 Racial Equality Directive (2000/43/EC) pursuing the implementation of the principle of equal treatment without distinction of racial origin, and

the Equality Framework Directive (2000/78/EC) establishing a general framework for combating discrimination on the basis of religion or belief, disability, age, and sexual orientation at work (La Barbera, 2017).
5. The communication from the Commission to the European Parliament, the council, the European Economic and Social Committee, and the Committee of the Regions on the EU Strategy on victims' rights (2020-2025) only mentions: "Hate crime also disproportionately affects certain communities such as Jews, Roma, Muslims, people of African descent, migrants and the LGBTI+ community, notably those who are *targeted on multiple grounds*" (p. 65). Italics come from the original text.
6. Gender mainstreaming requires that gender representation and gender-responsive content need to be taken into consideration in all phases of the policymaking process in different areas.

REFERENCES

Álvarez-Benavides, A., & Aguilar, F. J. (2021). La contraprogramación cultural de Vox: secularización, género y antifeminismo. *Política y sociedad*, 58(2), 14. https://dialnet.unirioja.es/servlet/articulo?codigo=8057599

Angel, K. (2021). *Tomorrow sex will be good again: Women and desire in the age of consent*. Verso.

Atrey, S., & Dunne, P. (Eds.). (2020). *Intersectionality and human rights law*. Bloomsbury Publishing.

Balfour, G. (2013). Theorizing the intersectionality of victimization, criminalization, and punishment of women: An introduction to the special issue. *International Review of Victimology*, 19(1), 3-5. https://doi.org/10.1177/0269758012447212

Bargu, B., & Bottici, C. (Eds.). (2017). *Feminism, capitalism and critique. Essays in honor of Nancy Fraser*. Palgrave.

Barrère, M. A. (2016). Martha A. Fineman y la igualdad jurídica: ¿Vulnerabilidad vs. subordiscriminación? *Cuadernos Electrónicos de Filosofía del Derecho*, 34, 17-34. https://dialnet.unirioja.es/servlet/articulo?codigo=5797227

Bilge, S. (2013). Intersectionality undone: Saving intersectionality from feminist intersectionality studies. *Du Bois Review*, 10(2), 405-424. https://doi.org/10.1017/S1742058X13000283

Bond, J. E. (2003). International intersectionality: A theoretical and pragmatic exploration of women's international human rights violations. *Emory Law Journal*, 52(1), 71-186.

Brown, G. (2012). Ain't I a victim? The intersectionality of race, class, and gender in domestic violence and the courtroom. *Cardozo Journal of Law & Gender*, 19, 147-183.

Cabrera, P. M. (2009). *Violencias interseccionales: debates feministas y marcos teóricos en el tema de pobreza y violencia contra las mujeres en Latinoamérica*. Central America Women's Network. https://gabrielamoriana.es/wp-content/uploads/2017/05/Patricia_Munoz-2011-Violencias-Interseccionales.pdf

Center for Intersectional Justice. (2020). *Intersectional discrimination in Europe: Relevance, challenges and ways forward* [Report]. https://www.intersectional justice.org/img/intersectionality-report-FINAL_yizq4j.pdf

Coaston, J. (2019, May 28). The intersectionality wars. *Vox*. https://www.vox.com/the-highlight/2019/5/20/18542843/intersectionality-conservatism-law-race-gender-dis crimination

Conaghan, J. (2009). Intersectionality and the feminist project in law. In E. Grabham, D. Cooper, J. Krishnadas, & D. Herman, (Eds.), *Intersectionality and beyond. Law, power and the politics of location* (pp. 21–48). Routledge.

Cortes Generales. (2022). *Proyecto de Ley Orgánica de garantía integral de la libertad sexual. Boletín Oficial de las Cortes Generales*, XIV Legislatura, 62–66.

Crenshaw, K. (1989). Demarginalizing the intersection of race and sex: A black feminist critique of antidiscrimination doctrine, feminist theory and antiracist politics. *University of Chicago Legal Forum*, 1, 139–167. https://chicagounbound.uchicago.edu/cgi/viewcontent.cgi?article=1052&context=uclf

Crenshaw, K. (1991). Mapping the margins: Intersectionality, identity politics, and violence against women of color. *Stanford Law Review*, 43, 1241–1299. https://doi.org/10.2307/1229039

Currah, P. (2022). *Sex is as sex does: Governing transgender identity*. NYU Press.

Dancig-Rosenberg, H., & Yosef, N. (2019). Crime victimhood and intersectionality. *Fordham Urban Law Journal*, 47, 85–116. https://ir.lawnet.fordham.edu/ulj/vol47/iss1/3/

Davis, B. P., & Aldieri, E. (2021). Precarity and resistance: A critique of Martha Fineman's vulnerability theory. *Hypatia*, 36(2), 321–337. https://doi.org/10.1017/hyp.2021.25

DeGraffenreid v. GENERAL MOTORS ASSEMBLY DIV., ETC., 413 F. Supp. 142 (E.D. Mo. 1976) U.S. District Court for the Eastern District of Missouri - 413 F. Supp. 142 (E.D. Mo. 1976) May 4, 1976. https://law.justia.com/cases/federal/district-courts/FSupp/413/142/1660699/

Emakunde. (2021). *Actuaciones locales para la reparación de las víctimas de violencia machista: Guía didáctica para la aplicación del principio de reparación en los municipios*. Emakunde. https://www.emakunde.euskadi.eus/contenidos/informac ion/documentacion_ipp/es_def/adjuntos/actuaciones_locales_reparacion_vvm.pdf

Esteve, L., & Nonell, A. (2021). Análisis del Anteproyecto de Ley para la igualdad real y efectiva de las personas trans y para la garantía de los derechos de las personas LGTBI. *InDret*, 3, 267–290. https://indret.com/wp-content/uploads/2021/07/1642-2-1.pdf

European Agency for Fundamental Rights & Council of Europe. (2018). *Handbook on European non-discrimination law*. Publications Office of the European Union.

European Institute for Gender Equality. (n.d.). Intersectionality [Glossary]. https://eige.europa.eu/thesaurus/terms/1263

European Union. (2000). *Council Directive 2000/43/EC of 29 June 2000 implementing the principle of equal treatment between persons irrespective of racial or ethnic origin*. https://eur-lex.europa.eu/legal-content/EN/ALL/?uri=CELEX%3A32000L0043

European Union. (2000). *Council Directive 2000/78/EC of 27 November 2000 establishing a general framework for equal treatment in employment and occupation*. https://eur-lex.europa.eu/legal-content/EN/TXT/?uri=celex%3A32000L0078

European Union. (2020, March 5). *Communication from the commission to the European Parliament, the Council, the European Economic and Social Committee and the Committee of the Regions. A union of equality: Gender Equality Strategy 2020–2025* [COM(2020) 152 final].

European Union. (2022, March 8). *Proposal for a directive of the European Parliament and of the council on combating violence against women and domestic violence* [COM(2022) 105 final].

Fassin, D. (2018). *The will to punish.* Oxford University Press.

Fineman, M. (2008). The vulnerable subject: Anchoring equality in the human condition. *Yale Journal of Law and Feminism, 20*(1), 1–24. https://openyls.law.yale.edu/bitstream/handle/20.500.13051/6993/03_20YaleJL_Feminism1_2008_2009_.pdf?sequence=2&isAllowed=y

García-Hombrados, J., & Martínez-Matute, M. (2021). Specialized courts and the reporting of intimate partner violence: Evidence from Spain [I Z A Institute of Labor Economics Discussion Paper, 14936]. I Z A Institute of Labor Economics. https://docs.iza.org/dp14936.pdf

Guzmán Ordaz, R., & Jiménez Rodrigo, M. (2015). La interseccionalidad como instrumento analítico de interpelación en la violencia de género. *Oñati Socio-Legal Series, 5*(2), 596–612. https://opo.iisj.net/index.php/osls/article/view/443/679

Heri, C. (2021). *Responsive human rights: Vulnerability, ill-treatment and the ECTHR.* Hart Publishing.

Hill Collins, P., & Bilge, S. (2020). *Intersectionality.* John Wiley & Sons.

Jemal, A. (2021). Liberation-based social work theory in progress: Time to practice what I teach. *Qualitative Social Work, 20*(1–2), 516–523. https://doi.org/10.1177/1473325020981085

Jibrin, R., & Salem, S. (2015). Revisiting intersectionality: Reflections on theory and praxis. *Trans-Scripts, 5,* 7–24.

La Barbera, M. (2017). La interseccionalidad y sus viajes: De las teorías feministas contrahegemonicas al derecho de la democracia europea multinivel. *Investigaciones Feministas, 8*(1), 131–149. https://doi.org/10.5209/INFE.54858

La Barbera, M., & Cruells Lopez, M. (2019). Toward the implementation of intersectionality in the European multilevel legal praxis: BS v. Spain. *Law & Society Review, 53*(4), 1167–1201. https://doi.org/10.1111/lasr.12435

Lamusse, T. (2022). Feminist prison abolitionism. In A. Gibbs & F. E. Gilmour (Eds.), *Women, crime and justice in context: Contemporary perspectives in feminist criminology from Australia and New Zealand* (pp. 239–252). Routledge.

Matthews, R. (2005). The myth of punitiveness. *Theoretical Criminology, 9*(2), 175–201. https://doi.org/10.1177/1362480605051639

Morris, M., & Bunjun, B. (2007). *Using intersectional feminist frameworks in research: A resource for embracing the complexities of women's lives.* Canadian Research Institute for the Advancement of Women.

Moya, C. (2020). La especial vulnerabilidad como circunstancia agravante. Resultados de una investigación sobre la jurisprudencia penal española. *Revista de Derecho Penal y Criminología, 24,* 13–58. https://doi.org/10.5944/rdpc.24.2020.28085

Nash, J. C. (2008). Re-thinking intersectionality. *Feminist Review*, 89(1), 1–15. https://doi.org/10.1057/fr.2008.4
Pomares, E., & Maqueda, M. L. (2022). Mujeres: Entre la igualdad y un nuevo orden moral. *Mientras Tanto*, 210. https://mientrastanto.org/210/notas/mujeres-entre-la-igualdad-y-un-nuevo-orden-moral/
Potter, H. (2015). *Intersectionality and criminology. Disrupting and revolutionizing studies of crime*. Routledge.
Ravecca, P., Schenck, M., Forteza, D., & Fonseca, B. (2022). Interseccionalidad de derecha e ideología de género en América Latina. *Analecta Política*, 12(22), 1–29. https://doi.org/10.18566/apolit.v12n22.a07
Rigotti, C. (2022). A long way to end rape in the European Union: Assessing the commission's proposal to harmonise rape law, through a feminist lens. *New Journal of European Criminal Law*, 13(2), 153–179. https://doi.org/10.1177/20322844221100046
Robcis, C. (2021). France and the question of consent. *Public Books*. https://www.publicbooks.org/france-and-the-question-of-consent/
Rodó Zárate, M. (2014). Developing geographies of intersectionality with relief maps: Reflections from youth research in Manresa, Catalonia. *Gender, Place & Culture*, 21(8), 925–944. https://doi.org/10.1080/0966369X.2013.817974
Rodó Zárate, M. (2021). *Interseccionalidad: Desigualdades, lugares y emociones*. Bellaterra.
Romero, C. (2022). Interseccionalidad en tiempos de transfobia, o los peligros de leer las luchas feministas como olimpiadas de la opresión. In S. Reverter & A. Moliní (Eds.), *La praxis feminista en clave transformadora* (pp. 81–100). Universitat Jaume I.
Sendroiu, I., Levi, R., & Hagan, H. (2021). Legal cynicism and system avoidance: Roma marginality in Central and Eastern Europe. *Social Forces*, 101(1), 281–308. https://doi.org/10.1093/sf/soab125
Simmel, G. (1994). Bridge and door. *Theory, Culture & Society*, 11(1), 5–10. (Original work published 1909) https://doi.org/10.1177/026327694011001002
Sosa, L., & Mestre, R. M. (2022). *Ensuring the non-discriminatory implementation of measures against violence against women and domestic violence: Article 4, Paragraph 3, of the Istanbul Convention. A collection of papers on the Council of Europe Convention on preventing and combating violence against women and domestic violence*. Council of Europe.
Sosa, L., Thiele, K., & Timmer, A. (2022). Workshop on structural inequality and the complexity of power: Understanding why transformative legal concepts hit a glass ceiling. Oñati International Institute for the Sociology of Law. https://www.iisj.net/sites/default/files/220509_final_programme_v1_0.pdf
Timmer, A. (2013). A quiet revolution: Vulnerability in the European Court of Human Rights. In M. A. Fineman & A. Grear (Eds.), *Vulnerability: reflections on a new ethical foundation for law and politics* (pp. 147–170). Ashagate.
Valcárcel, A. (2023). *La civilización feminista*. La Esfera de los Libros.
Varona, G. (2015). Beyond cartographies of women's fear of crime: Intersectionality, urban vulnerability and resilience through women safety audits in the Basque Country. *Eguzkilore: Cuaderno del Instituto Vasco de Criminología*, 29, 325–344.
Wacquant, L. (2009). *Punishing the poor*. Duke University Press.

Whitby Okafor, P. A. (2021). *Punishment injustices: An analysis exploring intersectionality, racial/ethnic threat, and punitive outcomes* [Doctoral thesis]. Florida State University. https://purl.lib.fsu.edu/diginole/2021_Summer_WhitbyOkafor_fsu_0071E_16659

Yuval-Davis, N. (2006). Intersectionality and feminist politics. *European Journal of Women's Studies, 13*(3), 193–209.

Zimmerman, T. (2017). #Intersectionality: The fourth wave feminist Twitter community. *Atlantis: Critical Studies in Gender, Culture & Social Justice, 38*(1), 54–70.

Zugaza, U. (2020). Apuntes críticos sobre las dinámicas de institucionalización de la interseccionalidad. *Revista Internacional de Sociología* (RIS), *1*(8), 1–7.

14

Dangerous Liaisons

Restorative Justice and the State

APARNA POLAVARAPU ■

INTRODUCTION

Restorative justice is hardly new, but in the United States it is increasingly gaining attention as a noncriminal option to address gender-based violence. As a general matter, interest in restorative justice is exploding. The National Association for Community and Restorative Justice saw 1,707 people register to attend their national conference in 2022, compared to 183 attendees in 2007 (National Association of Community and Restorative Justice, n.d.). As antiviolence advocates are grappling with the harms the criminal legal system commits against their clients, they are also exploring new opportunities for supporting clients in navigating the violent situations in their lives.

Various statewide coalitions against domestic violence and sexual assault have begun requesting increased education about restorative practices as an option for addressing partner and sexual violence. Several have begun to take open stances against carceral policies and are considering community-based responses such as restorative justice (Kim, 2020). While this would suggest an interest in practices separated from the state, the state has also inserted itself in the restorative justice conversation. The

Aparna Polavarapu, *Dangerous Liaisons* In: *The Criminalization of Violence Against Women*. Edited by: Heather Douglas, Kate Fitz-Gibbon, Leigh Goodmark, and Sandra Walklate, Oxford University Press. © Oxford University Press 2024.
DOI: 10.1093/oso/9780197651841.003.0015

United States federal government, for example, accounts for restorative justice responses to sexual and partner violence in Title IX regulations and the 2022 Violence Against Women Act Reauthorization Act.

In addition, some practices seek to work with the state. Some earlier models of restorative justice practices to respond to domestic violence or sexual assault, such as the RESTORE program in Arizona, are firmly connected to the criminal legal system (Koss, 2014). Perhaps this is to be expected for practices developed prior to the current moment, in which advocates for survivors are more seriously contemplating the harms of policing, the criminal system, and incarceration. Yet even now, restorative justice practices continue to be developed in collaboration with the state.

In this chapter, I consider the impact of state involvement in restorative justice responses to interpersonal violence, and I suggest caution. I examine what restorative justice is meant to be and how it is often positioned in opposition to criminal processes. Based on my own experiences as a restorative justice advocate and analysis of existing programs self-labeling as restorative justice, I pinpoint some of the dangers of state encroachment. While restorative justice programs developed alongside courts provide necessary alternatives to the criminal process, they also run the risk of being limited or co-opted by the state and simply reinforcing existing criminal paradigms.

THE WHAT AND WHY OF RESTORATIVE JUSTICE

There is no centrally agreed upon definition of restorative justice. For purposes of this chapter, I borrow from the definition I have set out elsewhere. This definition seeks to both bound the term and permit a full range of possibilities for restorative justice practice. As I use this term in this chapter, I limit restorative justice to those practices that seek to repair harm. While restorative practices—such as community-building circles—can make repair harm practices within the community even more robust and effective, repair harm processes can also occur absent those practices.

When describing restorative justice, I describe a practice that:

(1) Reframes how we consider harm by focusing on the harm that has been committed, what needs must be fulfilled, and who bears the obligations to fulfill those needs; (2) involves a process that brings together the interests of the responsible party, the harmed party, and community stakeholders; (3) allows all parties to engage in a free discussion and exploration of the harm and the circumstances surrounding it; (4) includes collaborative determination of what accountability looks like; and (5) seeks to support the responsible party in arriving at accountability and reintegrating into the community, which requires making reparation, taking responsibility for the harm and its impacts, and sometimes also taking steps to avoid committing future harm. Encapsulated in this definition is the notion that parties will be treated with dignity and respect for their humanity. (Polavarapu, 2023)

Animated by, inter alia, a focus on harm (rather than crime), how we can repair the harm (rather than simply punish), and how to support responsible parties in holding themselves accountable (often largely ignored in state systems) (Zehr, 2015), restorative justice is an attractive option when compared against the documented harmful practices of the criminal legal system. When restorative justice processes are implemented properly, survivors are able to tell their whole story, a particular contrast to jurisdictions with adversarial systems in which testimony is often limited by procedural rules or lawyers' interventions. Both restorative and transformative justice practitioners speak of how survivors' needs can be centered even as a process creates space for the responsible party and community members to openly share their stories and perspectives (Barnard Center for Research on Women, 2020). Survivors are given the space to discuss in full the harm they have experienced as well as its impacts.

Restorative justice is expansive in ways that courts struggle with. The legal system's classification of parties as either "victim" or "offender" allows interpersonal violence to be viewed as binary and unidirectional when in reality it can be much more complex and nuanced. Harm can travel in both directions between the parties or in multiple directions among several parties. Communities can play a significant role in facilitating violence. For example, in-laws can be a significant contributing factor to violence committed by a partner. In some countries, widow eviction, which is the act of in-laws forcibly evicting widows from their marital property, is a significant form of economic domestic violence (Polavarapu, 2019). In families and communities inside or outside the United States, in-laws can be the source or instigator of violence against spouses. Community-wide norms relating to issues like dowry expectations, conceptions of appropriate roles within marital and family relationships, and contempt of divorce all contribute to abusive marital dynamics. Research has shown that men who commit abuse are able to view themselves as victims because the people around them support that view (Coker, 2002). Community relationships or norms can also contribute to incidents of sexual assault. Rape culture is commonly referenced in conversations about sexual assault on college campuses in the United States, yet the role of these community norms in facilitating the violence cannot be adequately addressed in formal legal processes. Restorative justice processes, on the other hand, are not limited by a binary understanding of harm and can accommodate the varying nuances of different interpersonal relationships and community dynamics. Understanding that multiple truths can coexist, the process permits fuller understanding of the harms that have occurred and are ongoing. Still, because the community can be complicit in harm, great care must be taken to ensure the process does not simply reflect harmful community norms perpetuating violence.

A key feature of restorative justice is its definition of harm. Within the criminal legal system, harms experienced by survivors of violence are not always afforded remedies under law. A restorative justice practice delves into the full extent of the harms that have been suffered without being constrained by whether the acts constitute crimes under the law. For example, economic violence as a form of partner violence can be severe, and yet it is rarely adequately addressed by legal responses. Examples of economic violence include withholding resources or eviction from property to which all partners have contributed, whether or not that contribution is financial. This is particularly problematic when the evicted partners do not have the benefit of marital legal protections because in such cases, the law does not always offer a remedy (Polavarapu, 2019).

Still, restorative justice is often met with skepticism. Even as antiviolence advocates acknowledge the harms and shortcomings of the criminal legal response, it can be difficult to embrace restorative justice. In cases of partner violence and sexual assault, a stumbling block for those considering restorative justice is the notion that the needs of the responsible party ought to be met. "Isn't that simply justifying the behavior?" is what I commonly hear. Why should the responsible party be considered at all?

Sometimes certain needs must be met before a person can effectively embrace accountability. This concept is somewhat easier to understand with children, who may need mentorship, access to nutrition, or afterschool resources, but it is also true for adults. Meeting social and other needs of responsible parties allows them to allocate greater focus to accountability. Studies evaluating the Circles of Support and Accountability in Canada, a program that began as a grassroots community movement to support reintegration of those who are considered to have the highest risk of recidivism for sexual offenses, found extraordinary reductions in recidivism among program participants (Wilson et al., 2009). At least some of this is credited by researchers to the intensive psychosocial support that is offered to participants in the program.

Pushback can also stem from the perception that restorative practices are too easy. A former law enforcement officer who recently questioned me on the value of restorative justice derided restorative practices as simply "talking things out" with no punishment. It is true that restorative justice does not emphasize punishment. However, that does not mean there are no consequences. Consequences are tailored to the circumstances of the harm and the people involved and are a key aspect of accountability. Consequences, which can include outcomes such as ending a relationship or losing a job, can feel quite acute to the person experiencing them. In addition, describing practices as simply "talking things out" diminishes how difficult it is for a person to face the people they have harmed and openly admit to what they have done and the harm it has caused. This is something that is so discouraged by the American legal system that civil settlements often include written statements denying the assignment of fault.

There is also the simple fact that many survivors of violence do not feel served by the criminal system or do not seek carceral outcomes. At least some of the restorative justice practices that serve survivors of partner violence are serving those who are purposefully avoiding the state (Kim, 2022; South Carolina Restorative Justice Initiative, 2021a). In a national survey of victims of violent crime, a majority of respondents reported that to the extent they received help after being victimized, that help came from family, friends, or healthcare systems, not the criminal legal system. The survey also reported that a majority of victims prefer rehabilitation over punishment (Alliance for Safety and Justice, 2022). Restorative justice practices, particularly community-based restorative justice practices, offer alternatives that can serve these survivors.

WHAT ROLE FOR THE STATE?

Even as restorative justice can be described in opposition to the state, as I do here, restorative justice practices have engaged with the state. Practical considerations may require a certain degree of interaction with the criminal system as some people seeking restorative justice are already entangled with law enforcement or courts. For example, community practices can agree to take referrals from the criminal system. In other cases, restorative justice practices are designed to work closely with the criminal legal system from the outset. Perhaps this is unsurprising. In addition to being simpler to append practices to preexisting institutions, it can be difficult to imagine a justice practice that is completely severed from the criminal system.

Popular conceptualizations of partner violence prevent some advocates from viewing community-based restorative justice options as suitable (South Carolina Restorative Justice Initiative, 2021b). My own conversations with advocates from various geographic regions in the United States have revealed a resistance to leaving the state behind. Antiviolence advocates question whether we can be sure that the parties are being authentic in the restorative justice process or that power dynamics are not influencing the process. I point out that those are also concerns that the criminal legal system does not adequately address, but that a well-constructed restorative justice process can. Still, no practice is perfect, and I do not contend that no one has ever manipulated a restorative justice process. Questions continue to be raised about whether restorative justice ought to be available as a response to gender-based violence because of safety concerns, whether community participants may justify the violence, and whether facilitators are capable of navigating abusive relationships (Coker, 2002, 2020; Singer, 2019; Daly & Stubbs, 2006). These concerns are legitimate and must be carefully considered as restorative practices are being developed and implemented.

Collaboration with the state is not limited to those who work in gender-based violence cases. There are examples of youth-focused practices that are predicated on referrals from people like school resources officers, police officers, or courts (Baliga et al., 2017). In fact, early restorative justice practices developed alongside and in cooperation with the criminal legal system (Kim, 2021). Noted restorative justice scholar and advocate Howard Zehr has stated that while "restorative justice advocates dream of a day when justice is fully restorative," he imagines a world in which the criminal system would be used as a backup or last resort (Zehr, 2015, p. 76).

Restorative justice practices working with state criminal institutions range in the degree of their connection to the state. Even in the context of partner violence, some practices seek to avoid law enforcement and the criminal system altogether (Kim, 2022; South Carolina Restorative Justice Initiative, 2021a). Others operate in the community but will support cases referred by the state. In South Africa, for example, a victim–offender conferencing (VOC) practice is implemented by community organizations that will receive community walk-ins and also take referrals from courts and other organizations (Dissel & Ngubeni, 2003). Other practices, such as the Men as Peacemakers' Domestic Violence Restorative Circles (DRVC) in the United States, are more closely tied to the criminal system.

The DVRC program in Duluth, Minnesota, was developed to work with men who had been through battering intervention but continued to reoffend. Participants in the program are those who have experienced legal consequences for committing abuse (Men as Peacemakers, n.d.). The program is technically open to anyone, but as of 2020, the then-coordinator of DVRC noted that most of the participants had been cisgender, heterosexual men who had used violence in monogamous relationships with cisgender, heterosexual women and had been referred by actors within the criminal system—attorneys, parole officers, judges, or social workers (South Carolina Restorative Justice Initiative, 2021a). Circles include trained community volunteers who work with the participant and conclude with an agreement that must be approved by the circle members, program staff, probation officer, and judge. Participants are expected to have acknowledged the harm they have committed, take steps to repair that harm, and take steps to change their future behavior (Men as Peacemakers, n.d.).

To address safety concerns and gain support for the program, DVRC does not allow survivors and responsible parties to be in a circle together. Survivors are offered the opportunity to participate in their own support circles. This prohibition against face-to-face dialogue can be limiting. Restorative justice practices should certainly not mandate face-to-face dialogue, and in fact numerous practices have methods to avoid it should the survivor so request. Practices can include finding proxies to serve as stand-ins for the survivor or exchanging letters instead of engaging in face-to-face dialogue. However, some survivors do want face-to-face interaction. For some, it is an important step toward healing. In other cases, especially with relationship violence, the face-to-face dialogue is necessary in relationships that will continue after the conclusion of the restorative process. Participants in South Africa's VOCs, for example, valued the ability to speak about their experiences directly to violent partners in a safe space (Dissel & Ngubeni, 2003).

An early qualitative study of the DVRC pilot program suggested positive outcomes. The study, reviewing three pilot cases, reported a decrease or cessation of violence and increased "level of positive social support . . . through reconnection with family, new relationships with circle members and referrals to recovery groups, mental health services and work or school programmes" (Gaarder, 2015, p. 356). This assessment suggested that a positive aspect of the DVRC program is that the legal system is always operating in the backdrop as a coercive partner. In the pilot cases, what this meant was that while the circles ended with accountability agreements, jail and prison were also used as safety measures (Gaarder, 2015).

This study described a program that stayed somewhat close to the concept of restorative justice while addressing the safety concerns espoused by concerned advocates and scholars. So what is the cause for concern?

Limitations Created by the State

A primary concern is that when practices are predicated on referral, they become limited to those already entangled with the state. Though partner violence is not limited to monogamous, heterosexual relationships between two cisgender people, this is the primary group participating in DVRC. There is no documented reason why this is so—as far as I know—yet it is unsurprising for the informed observer. Commentators have pointed out the ways in which the criminal legal system, the DVRC's source of referrals, is hostile to certain populations (Coker, 2001; Goodmark, 2008, 2013). In terms of partner violence, the system struggles to recognize relationship violence that does not involve the image of a perfect victim, discouraging those who do not fit the typology from engaging with the system. Even those that do fit the mold may avoid the criminal legal system for any number of reasons. In addition, in the United States, domestic violence and sexual assault are underreported to police (Morgan & Smith, 2022; Reaves, 2017). Appending a practice to the state's criminal system thus can immediately narrow the scope of people who have access to that practice. In addition, if accessibility to the practice depends on referrals, any bias present within the system or any system actor can influence which parties are deemed appropriate for restorative justice.

We must also question whether such practices can maintain their integrity as restorative justice when they become an arm of the state. Though legal system involvement is highlighted as a positive by some for its coercive power, the involvement of the system can alter the program entirely. There is danger attendant to opening the door to working with the state, even if some state-related practices operate in line with restorative justice principles. States have increasingly begun using the term *restorative justice* to describe practices that drift further and further away from the core of restorative justice. In Minnesota, for example, a Veterans Restorative Justice Act (VRJA) was signed into law in 2021 (Skluzacek, 2021). Despite its title, the legislation simply creates a sentencing alternative. The act empowers a judge, on a finding or plea of guilt, to determine whether a veteran defendant is eligible for a "probationary period" under the VRJA. Eligibility is only available for those veterans whose military records show that the offense was committed in connection with a service-related condition. During the probationary period, the veteran is required to participate in treatment, education, and/or rehabilitation programs, at the conclusion of which the court determines whether the conditions of probation have been met (Minnesota Veterans Restorative Justice Act, 2022). At no point in this description is there a reference to restorative justice practices. In fact, supporters of an earlier iteration of the bill argued that the goal was to bring services to areas that lacked veterans' treatment courts and guide those counties seeking to start such courts (Walker, 2020).

While this is arguably a positive step for Minnesota's veterans, there is a risk to labeling this practice as restorative justice. First, it simply relabels a somewhat minor alteration to an existing practice with a more amenable term. While the VRJA may have created a change in Minnesota, the creation of sentencing alternatives requiring participation in state-approved programs is not novel and is simply a new stop along criminal and carceral pathways. Second, it empowers state actors to claim that they are already supporting restorative justice practices and to shut down opportunities to engage in more robust alternatives to the criminal legal system. I have come across this problem in my own advocacy. In conversations with various prosecutors or other officials affiliated with state criminal and carceral systems, I have been told there is no need for restorative justice because the state is already doing it, with citations to the use of drug treatment programs or mandatory curricula for at-risk populations about how to make better life choices. Ultimately, state co-optation of the phrase facilitates the continuation of existing criminal practices with little to no change and creates obstacles to the implementation of restorative justice practices.

Absorption by the State

States claiming ownership over restorative justice practices also perpetuate a system in which community interests are set aside in favor of state interests. For example, states have begun embracing state-run victim–offender dialogues (VODs) with people who are incarcerated, locating these programs in their department of corrections rather than in community initiatives. Most states with legislation providing for access to VODs do not explicitly provide for confidentiality within those laws (National Crime Victim Law Institute, 2017). When housed in the Department of Corrections, VODs are also controlled by the Department of Corrections and maintain the trappings of a carceral system. At least some states' policies contemplate a facilitator who is either corrections staff or who is accompanied at all times by corrections staff. In Kansas, not only must one of the facilitators be corrections staff, but also support persons for the incarcerated party must be either corrections employees, contract staff, or a volunteer that has worked with the incarcerated party (Kansas Department of Corrections, 2023). In contrast, the only requirement for victims' support persons is that they sign a "Support Person Agreement." (Kansas Department of Corrections, 2023). The South Carolina Department of Corrections policy is considered "restricted" and not permitted to be shared with the public. The end result is an enclosed process that is under strict state control and fails to create the degree of trust necessary to support an open dialogue facilitating accountability and repair.

The state interest in retaining control rears its head time and again. I have been asked by prosecutors whether I would be in support of a few edits in the legal process to create a "restorative justice court." I was and am not.

A court cannot simply be slightly altered to contain a restorative justice process. Restorative justice is more than process; it is driven by an underlying ethic that is fundamentally different from what motivates the criminal legal system. Ensuring restorative justice is available to anyone, including those already affected by the criminal system, requires some interaction with the state. However, any relationship with the state must be thoughtfully developed and subject to constant reevaluation to maintain the integrity of restorative justice practice.

CONCLUSION

Restorative justice offers great opportunities to repair harm. As a promising idea that continues to develop and adjust, restorative justice creates space for multiple forms of implementation. While some restorative justice practitioners work freely with the state, others envision a future without it. Even for abolitionist practitioners and advocates, working with the state is sometimes a necessity to reach the many people who are already entangled with the state.

But, working with the state creates a danger of state encroachment. It is not uncommon for state practices to claim the label "restorative justice" while continuing to perpetuate the harms of the state or patriarchy. Even restorative practices developed by "community" can perpetuate shortcomings of the state if they are too closely aligned or completely reliant on the criminal system. Yet even as individuals, service providers, and other organizations are now reexamining their relationships with law enforcement and other criminal/carceral institutions, they continue to struggle against the instinct to work with those same institutions.

It is perhaps the proliferation of restorative justice practices that have aligned themselves with the criminal legal system that has led to the belief that restorative justice necessarily involves working with the state, setting restorative justice in opposition to transformative justice. Transformative justice arose as its own concept organically but has also become a destination for those seeking to avoid the state altogether and who see restorative justice as a friend of the state. This dichotomy oversimplifies transformative justice, which is more than just a nonstate alternative to responding to harm. Transformative justice also involves community mobilization and violence prevention and is tied to the politics of liberation (Kim, 2020; Spring Up, 2020). "Transformative justice remains locally driven, anti-state, and anti-institutional" (Kim, 2020, p. 319). However, just as the state has begun to use the word *restorative* to serve its own purposes, so now are state institutions and programs beginning to claim the "transformative justice" label. Williamson County in Texas, with federal funding, recently launched a "Transformative Justice of WC" program that works directly with the criminal system (Bureau of Justice Assistance, n.d.; Transformative Justice of WC, n.d.). Co-optation is always a risk.

To those who find concerns of state absorption overblown, Amy Cohen's genealogy of mediation in the United States is instructive (Cohen, 2022). Though mediation has radical roots—described by Cohen as compatible with today's transformative justice movement—the legal system's involvement reshaped it into a sterile and formal process. Community and transformative mediation continue to exist, but the state-attached process of legal mediation is merely a ghost of mediation's initial promise. Cohen has not given up on mediation, nor have I on restorative justice, although I suspect restorative justice risks a similar fate.

At this moment in time, interacting with the criminal system may be unavoidable when serving certain populations. But restorative justice advocates and practitioners must operate with great care and deliberation if they are to achieve the full potential restorative justice offers.

REFERENCES

Alliance for Safety and Justice. (2022). Crime survivors speak: The first-ever national survey of victims' views on safety and justice. https://allianceforsafetyandjustice.org/wp-content/uploads/documents/Crime%20Survivors%20Speak%20Report.pdf

Baliga, S., Henry, S., & Valentine, G. (2017). *Restorative community conferencing: A study of Community Works West's restorative justice youth diversion program in Alameda County*. Impact Justice & Community Works West.

Barnard Center for Research on Women. (2020, March 11). *Centering the needs of survivors (part 1)* [Video]. YouTube. https://www.youtube.com/watch?v=ZeBuP7VCJyM

Bureau of Justice Assistance. (n.d.). *Wilco transformative justice*. United States Department of Justice, Bureau of Justice Assistance. https://bja.ojp.gov/funding/awards/15pbja-22-gk-04587-mumu

Cohen, A. J. (2022). The rise and fall and rise again of informal justice and the death of ADR. *Connecticut Law Review, 54*(1), 197–242.

Coker, D. (2001). Crime control and feminist law reform in domestic violence law: A critical review. *Buffalo Criminal Law Review, 4*(2), 801–860. https://doi.org/10.1525/nclr.2001.4.2.801

Coker, D. (2002). Transformative justice: Anti-subordination processes in cases of domestic violence. In H. Strang & J. Braithwaite (Eds.), *Restorative justice and family violence* (pp. 128–152). Cambridge University Press.

Coker, D. (2020). Restorative responses to intimate partner violence. In M. Moscati, M. Palmer, & M. Roberts, (Eds.), *Comparative dispute resolution* (pp. 46–63). Edward Elgar Publishing.

Daly, K., & Stubbs, J. (2006). Feminist engagement with restorative justice. *Theoretical Criminology, 10*(1), 9–28. https://doi.org/10.1177/1362480606059980

Dissel, A., & Ngubeni, K. (2003). *Giving women their voice: Domestic violence and restorative justice in South Africa*. Centre for the Study of Violence and Reconciliation.

Gaarder, Emily. (2015). Lessons from a restorative circles initiative for intimate partner violence. *Restorative Justice, 3*(3), 342–367. https://doi.org/10.1080/20504721.2015.1109334

Goodmark, L. (2008). When is a battered woman not a battered woman? When she fights back. *Yale Journal of Law & Feminism, 20*, 75–128.

Goodmark, L. (2013). Transgender people, intimate partner abuse, and the legal system. *Harvard Civil Rights-Civil Liberties Law Review, 48*, 51–104.

Kansas Department of Corrections. (2023). *Victim services: Victim/offender dialogue program*. https://www.doc.ks.gov/kdoc-policies/AdultIMPP/chapter-21/21-103a.pdf

Kim, M. E. (2020). Anti-carceral feminism: The contradictions of progress and the possibilities of counter-hegemonic struggle. *Affilia, 35*(3), 309–326. https://doi.org/10.1177/0886109919878276

Kim, M. E. (2021). Transformative justice and restorative justice: Gender-based violence and alternative visions of justice in the United States. *International Review of Victimology, 27*(2), 16272. https://doi.org/10.1177/0269758020970414

Kim, M. E. (2022). *Non-law enforcement restorative justice addressing domestic and sexual violence: Evaluation results from the CHAT project pilot*. CHAT Project.

Koss, M. P. (2014). The restore program of restorative justice for sex crimes: Vision, process, and outcomes. *Journal of Interpersonal Violence, 29*, 1623–1660. https://doi.org/10.1177/0886260513511537

Men as Peacemakers. (n.d.). *Domestic violence restorative circles*. https://www.menaspeacemakers.org/dvrc

Minnesota Veterans Restorative Justice Act, Minn Stat. § 609.1056. (2022). https://www.revisor.mn.gov/statutes/cite/609.1056

Morgan, R., & Smith, E. (2022). The National Crime Victimization Survey and National Incident-Based Reporting System: A complementary picture of crime in 2021. United States Department of Justice, Bureau of Justice Statistics. https://bjs.ojp.gov/sites/g/files/xyckuh236/files/media/document/ncvsnibrscpc21.pdf

National Association of Community and Restorative Justice. (n.d.). https://www.nacrj.org/

National Crime Victim Law Institute. (2017). Survey of select state laws explicitly addressing the confidentiality of victim offender dialogues. https://nicic.gov/weblink/survey-select-state-laws-explicitly-addressing-confidentiality-victim-offender-dialogues

Nondiscrimination on the Basis of Sex in Education Programs or Activities Receiving Federal Financial Assistance, 34 CFR § 106 (2020).

Polavarapu, A. (2019). Global carceral feminism and domestic violence: What the west can learn from reconciliation in Uganda. *Harvard Journal of Law & Gender, 42*, 123–176.

Polavarapu, A. (2023). Myth-busting restorative justice: Uncovering the past and finding lessons in community. *UC Irvine Law Review, 13*(3), 949–992.

Reaves, B. (2017). Police response to domestic violence, 2006–2015. United States Department of Justice, Bureau of Justice Statistics. https://bjs.ojp.gov/content/pub/pdf/prdv0615.pdf

Singer, V. E. (2019). Restorative approaches and gendered violence: Moving beyond is it possible? [Working paper, May 2019]. Bridges Institute.

Skluzacek, J. (2021, August 10). Walz signs legislation that offers alternative sentences for veterans convicted of crimes. KSTP.com. https://kstp.com/kstp-news/top-news/walz-signs-legislation-that-offers-alternative-sentences-for-veterans-convicted-of-crimes/

South Carolina Restorative Justice Initiative. (2021a, January 8). Restorative justice & intimate partner violence with *Sujatha Baliga* and Chris Godsey—Week 2 [Video]. YouTube. https://www.youtube.com/watch?v=xC5kJQ__Sjk

South Carolina Restorative Justice Initiative. (2021b, April 28). IPV and *restorative justice*: Therapeutic *perspective* with Tod Augusta-Scott—Week 3 [Video]. YouTube. https://www.youtube.com/watch?v=JOYa0_pPz6k&t=1181s

Spring Up. (2020). *Transformative justice workbook zine.*

Transformative Justice of WC. (n.d.). *Transformative justice overview.* https://tj-wc.org/

Violence Against Women Act Reauthorization Act of 2022. S. 3623. 117th Cong (2022). https://www.congress.gov/bill/117th-congress/senate-bill/3623/text

Walker, T. (2020, April 23). *Diversion program would offer veterans help instead of jail time.* Minnesota House of Representatives. https://www.house.leg.state.mn.us/SessionDaily/Story/15251

Wilson, R. J., Cortoni, F., & McWhinnie, A. J. (2009). Circles of support & accountability: A Canadian national replication of outcome findings. *Sexual Abuse, 21*(4), 412–430. https://doi.org/10.1177/1079063209347724

Zehr, H. (2015). *The little book of restorative justice: Revised and updated.* Good Books.

15

Bureaucratic Violence

State Neglect of Domestic and Family Violence Victims in Aceh, Indonesia

BALAWYN JONES ■

INTRODUCTION

In 2004, the Indonesian government passed Law No. 23/2004 regarding the Elimination of Domestic Violence (*Undang-Undang tentang Penghapusan Kekerasan Dalam Rumah Tangga*—"the law"). The law identified domestic and family violence (DFV) as a violation of human rights and human dignity, as well as a form of discrimination (Preamble of the Law; Art. 3 of the law). The law aims to establish state protection for victims of DFV through the legal system. DFV is made a criminal offense by Article 44 of the law, which states that anyone committing DFV shall be punished with imprisonment or a fine; judges are also given the discretion to impose counseling or restraining orders. DFV is defined in Article 1(1) as: "any act against anyone, particularly women, bringing about physical, sexual, psychological misery or suffering, and/or negligence of the household . . . within the scope of the household." The specific focus on women in the drafting of the law acknowledged that DFV is a type of gendered violence and reflects the fact that in the vast majority of DFV cases husbands perpetrate violence against their wives

Balawyn Jones, *Bureaucratic Violence* In: *The Criminalization of Violence Against Women.* Edited by: Heather Douglas, Kate Fitz-Gibbon, Leigh Goodmark, and Sandra Walklate, Oxford University Press. © Oxford University Press 2024. DOI: 10.1093/oso/9780197651841.003.0016

(Jones, 2022, pp. 84, 181). The scope of the household is defined in Article 2(1) to include the husband, wife, children, people who have a family relationship, and individuals working and living in the household.

At the time of writing, DFV had been criminalized under the law for over 18 years. However, there remain substantial barriers to the implementation of the law, a lack of protection for DFV victims and widespread impunity for DFV perpetrators (Jones, 2022). Victims face many barriers to accessing justice via state (as opposed to customary law) justice systems, largely due to stigma, victimblaming, and poor socialization of the law's norms at the community level (Jones, 2020). Victims who overcome these barriers to engage with state systems face further barriers to access to justice within state justice systems, in particular due to gender bias (Jones, 2022). This chapter, however, does not focus on barriers to access to justice in general; rather, it focuses on structural violence committed by the state in the form of bureaucratic negligence, which I term "bureaucratic violence."

Bureaucratic violence is the harm done to victims by a system promising to provide help in law but failing to provide such assistance in practice. As I explain below, the provisions of the law create a number of rights for victims and place correlative responsibilities on the state to fulfill these rights. Where victims have such rights, the failure of the state to fulfill legal promises is not benign because it, in fact, puts victims at an exacerbated and/ or perpetuated risk of violence. I argue that state justice system stakeholders should, in theory (if not yet in practice), be held accountable for the distinct harms caused to DFV victims as a result of defaulting on their promises. In other words, the theory of bureaucratic violence seeks to establish a causal relationship between the failures of the state to operationalize laws relating to DFV and the harms experienced by victims of DFV.

A "GROUNDED" THEORY OF BUREAUCRATIC VIOLENCE

The analysis in this chapter was produced using grounded theory methodology. Broadly speaking, this means that the analysis operates at two levels. The first level of analysis is based on fieldwork data conducted in Banda Aceh (the capital of Aceh, Indonesia) between 2017 and 2019. Approximately 40 interviews were conducted with local women's advocates, academics, government officials, staff from front-line DFV services, police, prosecution, lawyers, community leaders, judges from the religious and criminal jurisdictions, and victims of DFV.[1] The second level of analysis involved drawing theoretical implications from the data. In this chapter, the relevant theoretical implications relate to the role of the state in protecting victim rights. In the next section, I explain what I mean by the terms "bureaucratic" and "violence" before linking this theory to state accountability and the role of the state in protecting victims.

The "Bureaucratic" in Bureaucratic Violence

First, I have used the term "bureaucratic" violence instead of "state" violence because, in the Acehnese context, the phrase "state violence" has connotations of direct, physical attack by the state. Aceh is a postconflict area. The Free Aceh Movement (*Gerakan Aceh Merdeka*) fought a 30-year civil war for independence against the Indonesian government, from 1976 until 2005, when the Helsinki Peace Agreement was finalized (Jones, 2022). The term bureaucratic is therefore used to indicate a more indirect harm caused by the operation of government bureaucracy in implementing the law across and within government departments.

Bureaucracy is used in its ordinary sense to refer to state systems where government administration (including the allocation of government funds) is carried out by government officials, often in accordance with obscure or unnecessarily complicated procedures. Indonesia is well known for its inflated and inefficient bureaucracy (Turner, Prasojo & Sumarwono, 2019), which includes a lack of coordination between levels of government and a resultant "passing of the buck" for responsibility to implement laws between institutional stakeholders. For context, in Indonesia when legislation is implemented, the general practice is for the national government to be responsible for allocating the budget necessary for implementing the law and for the provincial or local government to be responsible for the allocation of land or physical infrastructure.

Second, with respect to bureaucracy as a form of structural violence, structural violence can be defined as violence that is

> invisible, embedded in ubiquitous social structures, normalized by stable institutions and regular experience. Structural violence occurs whenever people are disadvantaged by political, legal, economic, or cultural traditions. Because they are longstanding, structural inequities usually seem ordinary—the way things are and always have been. (Winter & Leighton, 2001, p. 99)

In the context of the Global South, Gupta analyzed "invisible" or "implicit" violence "taken for granted in the routinized practices of state institutions" (Gupta, 2012, p. 5). Specifically, Gupta argued that poverty in the Indian context can be theorized as a form of structural violence stemming from state policies and practices. In doing so, he challenged the idea that the state is not culpable for harm caused to citizens if they are passively "allowed to die" (Gupta, 2012, pp. 16, 19). Like in the context of DFV in Aceh, Gupta acknowledged that while there are government programs in place that attempt to assist citizens to a certain extent, "no matter how noble the intentions of [these] programs, and no matter how sincere the officials in charge of them, the overt goal of helping . . . is subverted by . . . bureaucracy" (Gupta, 2012, p. 23).

Bureaucracy in this sense can be distinguished from the form-filling, box-ticking type of bureaucracy at lower levels of administration. Bureaucratization of government procedures has been identified by many front-line service providers as impeding their ability to meet victim needs in a timely manner (Reinke, 2018). While this type of bureaucratic inefficiency is tangentially relevant in that it may affect access to justice, this is not the kind of bureaucracy I am addressing within the theory of bureaucratic violence. Rather, I am talking about higher level bureaucracy across and within state departments and institutions, particularly a lack of coordination between the national and provincial governments that impedes implementation of the law regarding elimination of domestic violence and has led to the failure of the state to protect DFV victims.

In the context of DFV, Douglas persuasively argued that victims of DFV experience not only direct harms at the hands of their abusive partners but also

> *injuries that come from the bureaucracies within institutions* that do not respond to their needs and instead disrespect and mistreat them and further exacerbate their marginalization. (Douglas, 2021, p. 118, citing Montesanti & Thurston, 2015, p. 11, emphasis added)

It is these injuries that the theory of bureaucratic violence seeks to capture, with a particular focus on the ways in which these harms materialize in the Acehnese context.

The "Violence" in Bureaucratic Violence

In this section, I argue that the failure of the state to fulfill its promises does not result in a type of "neutral negligence" but causes unique forms of harm to victims of DFV. There are, at least, two kinds of harm that DFV victims potentially face if the state fails to provide protection as promised in the law.

The first is an exacerbated risk of violence. It is well known in DFV literature that the risk of violence greatly increases in separation and postseparation contexts. In her recent study, Douglas found that "many women who participated . . . reported that separation, and interacting with the legal system, marked a period of heightened danger and failed to deliver on the promise of safety for them and their children" (2021, p. 216). Therefore, it is not a stretch to say that if a victim engages with the state justice system on the premise of receiving assistance and protection and does not receive it, the state's failure to fulfill its promises is likely to result in an exacerbated risk of violence for the victim. For example, in the absence of operational safe houses (discussed below), the victim may literally have nowhere safe to seek refuge, opening her up to having to return home to her abuser or to another location where she may not be supported or safe or she may face homelessness. As Hill observed: "If women and children don't have somewhere to go, they are left with a set of dangerous options" (2019, p. 238).

With respect to the second form of violence—the risk of perpetuated violence—I argue that each time the state promises to help victims of DFV and fails to do so, it, first, loses the victim's trust and, second, emboldens perpetrators due to the lack of accountability. The state's failure to fulfill promises therefore potentially contributes to the victim's further isolation and abuse (Goldblatt, 2019, p. 366; Hill, 2019, p. 60). To provide an illustration, if you imagine that a victim coming to the state for help is metaphorically coming to the surface of the ocean and taking a breath then if, when she reaches out her hand, the state misses the opportunity to grasp it, the woman may not come to the surface again for a very long time, if at all. The second category of "risk of perpetuated violence" is the sum of this lost opportunity, the dissipation of hope and trust on the part of the victim and the emboldening of abusers by the absence of accountability.

This is not to imply that engaging with the state system by "going to the law" necessarily ensures women's safety long term. In fact, Douglas's recent study in the Australian context found that even years after first engaging with state justice systems, poor legal processes and stakeholder practices can exacerbate the danger of leaving an abusive relationship for women (Douglas, 2021, p. 221). Indeed, iterations of bureaucratic violence can be identified in the failures of state justice system processes over time; however, this chapter's analysis is limited to two examples. The first example—of safe houses—explores DFV victim's initial interactions with the state at one of the points of "entry" to the system. The second example—of rehabilitation as a part of sentencing—focuses on one of the points of "exit" from the system. Of course, in practice, multiple other incidents of bureaucratic violence exist along the spectrum from entry to "exit" as DFV victims engage or disengage with state systems.

Promises Made by the State in the Law—The Example of Safe Houses

In the next two sections, I provide examples of bureaucratic violence in practice. The starting point for this analysis is the identification of victim rights in the law concerning elimination of domestic violence. Chapter 4 of the law, "Victim Rights," states that victims are entitled to "protection," including healthcare and social, religious, and legal support. Chapter 5 of the law, "Obligations of the Government and Public," states that, first, the government is responsible for the efforts to prevent DFV. Second, in order to organize services for victims, the national government and provincial governments should make efforts to "prepare and develop service program cooperation systems and mechanisms that are easily accessible to victims." It is therefore clear in the law that the state is responsible for the provision of care and protection of DFV victims.

Taking the example of safe houses, Chapter 6 of the law makes these obligations even more explicit. For example, Article 16 states that within 24 hours after receiving a DFV report, police are obliged to provide the victim temporary protection. "Temporary protection" is defined as including access to services as well as a protection order from the court. Article 22 provides that one of the services that victims are entitled to is assistance from a social worker. Social workers must, among other things, "take the victim to a safe house or alternative dwelling." Again, the law is explicit and places positive obligations on state stakeholders—stating that the services of a social worker must be conducted "at a safe house belonging to the government, a provincial government, or the public." "Safe house" is further defined as a "temporary dwelling used to provide protection to the victim," and "alternative dwelling" is defined as "a place for the victim to stay if she is forced to be separated or be far from the perpetrator."

The answer to the question of whether victims of DFV are entitled to access a safe house is yes. The answer to the question of who is responsible for such provision and protection is "the state." During my fieldwork in Banda Aceh, I conducted interviews with approximately 20 front-line service providers and DFV experts. Some interviewees stated that there were no safe houses in Banda Aceh. Other interviewees explained that there were, in fact, safe houses in the sense that there was a building that had been allocated for such a purpose (meaning the local or provincial government had allocated land and infrastructure) (e.g., interview with male lawyer, Banda Aceh, December 15, 2017; interview with female commissioner from the Indonesian Women's Commission, Jakarta, January 12, 2018). However, interviewees made it clear that no budget had yet been allocated by the national government for their operation. There was, for instance, no electricity or other amenities and no staff. This means that there were, in effect, no operational safe houses in Banda Aceh available for DFV victims.

A commissioner from the Indonesian Women's Commission (*Komnas Perempuan*) stated:

> If we are talking about implementation, we must also talk about infrastructural support. If the police do not have safe houses, and there are no other safe houses that can be accessed, how do they provide protection [to victims]? (interview with female commissioner from the Indonesian Women's Commission, Jakarta, January 12, 2018)

The head of the Police Women's and Children's Protection Unit (*Bidang Perlindungan Perempuan dan Anak*) explained that it was common practice for women's advocates to "bring [victims] back to our homes, often I have to take [a victim] home to provide protection because there are no safe houses" (interview with the head of the Police Women's and Children's Protection Unit, Banda Aceh, September 24, 2018). This is just one example of the state failing to fulfill their positive obligations under the law.

Establishing an operational safe house relies on coordination between different levels of government. As mentioned, in practice it would require the local or provincial government to allocate land and infrastructure and the national government to allocate a budget and pay staff to run the safe house; in the context of Banda Aceh, it is the latter that has not occurred. Perhaps this is not surprising when considered in the broader context of a political environment where the budget of the Ministry of Women's Empowerment and Child Protection (*Kementerian Pemberbayaan Perempuan dan Perlindungan Anak*) has been repeatedly cut and the Ministry is "considered one of the weakest" in the national cabinet (Perdana & Hillman, 2020, p. 168).

Promises Made by the State in the Law—The Example of Rehabilitation Programs

Building on the example of safe houses above, another example of bureaucratic violence is the failure of the state to establish perpetrator rehabilitation programs as required under Article 50(b) of the law to eliminate domestic violence. Article 50(b) of the law specifies that a judge may impose a sentence in the form of a "ruling that the perpetrator undertake a counselling program under the supervision of a certain institution."

During an interview, a judge from the District Court (*Pengadilan Negeri*) confirmed that perpetrator rehabilitation programs had not been established in Banda Aceh, and, as a consequence, judges have never handed down sentences to this effect (interview with District Court judges, Banda Aceh, September 26, 2018). According to judges interviewed, the responsibility for establishing such services lies with state institutional stakeholders outside the courts; however, no budget has yet been allocated by the national government (interview with District Court judges, Banda Aceh, September 26, 2018). Services for court-mandated counseling are therefore another example of the implementation of the law falling through the cracks of institutional responsibility (i.e., bureaucratic negligence). As with the failure to establish operational safe houses, the failure to establish a court-adjacent system for perpetrator rehabilitation as required under the law results in tangible harms for DFV victims (i.e., bureaucratic violence).

For example, in criminal law cases applying the law, the court stated that sentencing should aim to be "corrective therapy for the defendant so that the defendant can realize the consequences of the deed he did and not repeat [such actions] again in the future" (e.g., Case 1 of 2014, District Court, Banda Aceh). However, the reality is that court-mandated counseling programs targeted toward perpetrators are currently nonexistent. There was also no evidence of any DFV-related rehabilitation programs being run with perpetrator attendance a condition of a suspended sentence or, alternatively, being run in state prisons as part of a carceral sentence.

As one interviewee explained: "If the husband goes to prison, after getting out there will [likely] be more violence because there is no education for the offender ... and he may feel [he was] unfairly imprisoned" (interview with female nongovernmental worker from the women's organization Balai Syura, Banda Aceh, December 19, 2017). As identified by the interviewee, without therapeutic intervention, it is common for perpetrators to conceptualize themselves as the "victim" of criminal prosecution. It should of course be noted that even if these programs were established, the question of their effectiveness in terms of ensuring the safety and protection of DFV victims would still need to be evaluated on an ongoing basis (Bell & Coates, 2022; Mackay et al., 2015).

While the content of the law is promising in its inclusion of counseling for perpetrators, substantive barriers remain to successful implementation of these provisions. It is currently not possible for such orders to be executed by District Court judges. The lack of a system implementing, or making functional, the powers given to the court to impose orders for counseling as part of sentencing under Article 50(b) of the law is particularly concerning considering that contemporary approaches toward DFV generally promote inclusion of rehabilitation pathways for perpetrators instead of solely punitive approaches (Bowen et al., 2003; Day et al., 2010).

It can be concluded that due to bureaucratic negligence, current criminal justice processes do not adequately protect victims of DFV and, in fact, exacerbate risks to victim safety. At present, victims participating in criminal prosecutions do so at great personal risk, with little tangible protection in return (Jones, 2022). While the legal infrastructure for court-ordered rehabilitation programs as a sentence under the law is in place, on-the-ground facilities and programs to carry out the promises of the law have not yet been established by the state. To remedy this, it is crucial to develop perpetrator rehabilitation services to address the root causes of violence and attempt to break the cycle of violence.

Implications for State Accountability

The reason I have drawn bureaucratic negligence and structural violence together in this way is to emphasize state accountability for the harms caused to victims (i.e., bureaucratic violence). I argue that the creation of legal rights and responsibilities by the state should not be assumed to result in positive, or even neutral, outcomes. Rather, in the context of DFV when the state fails to fulfill its legal obligations this results in unique types of harm. This has broader theoretical implications for human rights theory. Bureaucratic violence implicitly draws on concepts of international human rights law, including that the state has a responsibility to protect human rights and that DFV is a violation of women's rights. It is uncontroversial that state parties are responsible for acts or omissions that constitute gender-based violence against women under the Convention on Elimination of All Forms of Discrimination Against Women (CEDAW). Freedman explained: "States' failure to protect women from violence is in itself a human rights violation, and that States must exercise 'due diligence' not only in not perpetrating violence against their citizens, but in actively protecting these citizens from abuse" (2021, p. 69). The theory of bureaucratic violence against DFV victims therefore seeks to identify the harms caused to victims by state negligence in implementing the law to eliminate domestic violence and to emphasize state responsibility for causing such harms.

The theory of bureaucratic violence also implicitly challenges the assumption that the state is a good or neutral actor in international law, even in cases where the state has explicitly enacted laws to implement CEDAW—such as Indonesia did when enacting the law. Freedman explained that in order to combat DFV and seek redress for victims, it is "necessary to push national governments to take more responsibility for protecting the human rights of their citizens" (Freedman, 2021, p. 76). The theory of bureaucratic violence seeks to do this by identifying and naming the harms caused by state failures to implement rights protections—in addition to and distinct from the harms caused by DFV perpetrators. Further, challenging the idea that enactment of a law is a neutral or positive action by the state, Tapia Tapia (Chapter 12, this volume) concluded that the "law-centric state is delivering fewer and fewer services and offering more and more law."

From a more pragmatic perspective, the importance of developing the concept of bureaucratic violence against DFV victims is its ability to iterate a link between the state's responsibility to fulfill legal obligations and the specific kinds of harm that result when the state fails to do so. In establishing this link, the theory of bureaucratic violence may be invoked to promote state accountability and action. In practice, this would mean relying on the theory of bureaucratic violence to call on the state to allocate sufficient funding to fulfill the legal promises made to DFV victims under the law.

CONCLUSION

In this chapter, I argued that the state's failure to implement the law to eliminate domestic violence does not result in a type of "neutral negligence," but rather results in specific harms for DFV victims for which the state should be held accountable. Where the state's failure to protect victims of DFV as promised by the law results in harm, I term these harms bureaucratic violence. I have argued that bureaucratic violence occurs when the state fails to protect victims or otherwise provide services as promised in the law, and, as a result, victims are placed at an exacerbated risk of violence and/or a risk of perpetuated violence. To support this analysis, I provided examples of the Indonesian state's failure to establish operational safe houses and perpetrator rehabilitation programs in Aceh Province. In the Indonesian context and beyond, this theory seeks to emphasize the roles and responsibilities of the state to protect victim rights and promote state accountability.

ACKNOWLEDGMENT

The author wishes to thank Kathleen Birrell for thoughtful feedback on earlier drafts of this chapter.

NOTE

1. Note that these interviews were conducted with ethics clearance granted by the University of Melbourne (Ethics ID: 1749977).

REFERENCES

Bell, C., & Coates, D. (2022). *The effectiveness of interventions for perpetrators of domestic and family violence: An overview of findings from reviews* [ANROWS Report] ANROWS.

Bowen, E., Brown, L., & Gilchrist, E. (2003). Evaluating probation based offender programmes for domestic violence perpetrators: A pro-feminist approach. *Howard Journal of Crime and* Justice, 41(3), 221–236. https://doi.org/10.1111/1468-2311.00238

Day, A., Chung, D., O'Leary, P., Justo, D., Moore, S., Carson, E., & Gerace, A. (2010). *Integrating responses to domestic violence: Legally mandated intervention programs for male perpetrators* [AIC Report]. Australian Institute of Criminology.

Douglas, H. (2021). *Women, intimate partner violence and the law.* Oxford University Press. https://doi.org/10.1093/oso/9780190071783.001.0001

Freedman, J. (2021). Domestic violence through a human rights lens. In J. Devaney, C. Bradbury-Jones, R. J. Macy, C., Øverlien, & S. Holt (Eds.), *The Routledge international handbook of domestic violence and abuse* (pp. 68–78). Routledge.

Goldblatt, B. (2019). Violence against women and social and economic rights: deepening the connections. In Susan Harris Rimmer & Kate Ogg (Eds.), *Research handbook on feminist engagement with international law* (pp. 359–378). Edward Elgar Publishing.

Gupta, A. (2012). *Red tape: Bureaucracy, structural violence, and poverty in India.* Duke University Press. https://doi.org/10.1215/9780822394709

Hill, J. (2019). *See what you made me do: Power, control and domestic abuse.* Black Inc.

Jones, B. (2022). *Reaching out from the ocean: Women's experiences navigating the anti-domestic violence law in Aceh, Indonesia* [Doctoral thesis]. University of Melbourne.

Law No. 23/2004 regarding the Elimination of Domestic Violence (Indonesia), *Undang-Undang tentang Penghapusan Kekerasan Dalam Rumah Tangga*.

Mackay, E., Gibson, A., Lam, H., & Beecham, D. (2015). *Perpetrator interventions in Australia: Part one - literature review* [ANROWS report]. ANROWS.

Montesanti, S., & Thurston, W. (2015). Mapping the role of structural and interpersonal violence in the lives of women: Implications for public health interventions and policy. *BioMed Central Women's Health*, *15*, Article 100. https://doi.org/10.1186/s12905-015-0256-4

Perdana, A., & Hillman, B. (2020). Quotas and ballots: The impact of positive action policies on women's representation in Indonesia. *Asia & the Pacific Policy Studies*, *7*(2), 158–170. https://doi.org/10.1002/app5.299

Reinke, A. (2018). The bureaucratic violence of alternative justice. *Conflict and Society*, *4*, 135–150. https://doi.org/10.3167/arcs.2018.040111

Turner, M., Prasojo, E., & Sumarwono, R. (2019). The challenge of reforming big bureaucracy in Indonesia. (2019). *Policy Studies*, *43*(2), 333–351. https://doi.org/10.1080/01442872.2019.1708301

Winter, D., & Leighton, D. (2001). Structural violence. In D. J. Christie, R. V. Wagner, & D. D. Winter (Eds.), *Peace, conflict, and violence: Peace psychology for the 21st century* (pp. 99–104). Prentice-Hall.

16

Reclaiming Justice

Understanding the Role of the State and the Collective in Domestic Violence in India

NIVEDITHA MENON ■

INTRODUCTION

The concept of justice is hard to define. In general, it can be understood as a fundamental and foundational ethical principle: a concept that captures a normative demand for equality, fairness, and rectitude. Enshrined within public policies or institutionalized through formal and informal agencies, it considers actions, actors, structures, or states with regard to their impact and entitlement on any given action (Stumpf et al., 2016). However, in lived reality, justice is a highly contested concept whose material terms or manifestations are often opaque and fleeting. For example, while justice might mean an investment in the human rights discourse, the focus on individualism, autonomy, bodily integrity, agency, or choice are not so easy to implement or even to discern (Merry, 2006). Although justice as a concept might loosely refer to claims or rights within a community, it has to be seen within a philosophical and ethical framework as well, involving such questions as: Who is the claimant? What is their subject position? What are the power hierarchies in the community? Who are the invisible actors? What is seen or demanded as justice? What are the modalities of doing so?

Thus, a major problem with defining justice, especially when it comes to women's issues, is how to reconcile seemingly diverse interests and identities with a shared imagination of a constituency (Marx Ferree & McClurg Mueller, 2004; Brison, 2006). For the sake of providing the modalities of justice for all, a common set of resolutions, decisions, have been codified into law and policy and eventually into practice (Saxena, 2003). But this also means flattening the diverse oppressive and discursive structures influencing and mitigating the needs and requirements of women. For example, a flattened notion of justice ignores the possibility that a Muslim woman or a Dalit woman addressing domestic violence in the household has to be cognizant of her identity as not only a woman who is subject to patriarchal violence, but also a woman aware of the consequences of sending a Muslim or Dalit man to the custody of the state, which has turned hostile toward these minority groups.

In fact, the resurgence of the (Hindu) Right in India has made it very hard for women to seek any form of justice. The recent controversial move on banning hijabs in schools in Karnataka has brought into question not only the machinations of Islamophobia, but also the targeting of the Muslim woman (Mukherjee, 2022) and her body (Sarkar, 2022). Moreover, in the recent release of rapists who were convicted in the Bilkis Bano case, it is clear that the government has started withdrawing from its critical responsibility of delivering justice for women. Bilkis herself has clearly stated that justice is not an end in itself, but a means to an end:

> Today, I can only say this—how can justice for any woman end like this? I trusted the highest courts in our land. I trusted the system, and I was slowly learning to live with my trauma. The release of these convicts has taken from me my peace and shaken my faith in justice. My sorrow and my wavering faith is not for myself alone but for every woman who is struggling for justice in the courts. (Scroll staff, 2022)

Therefore, even as they are codified often away from the contexts, it is even more critical to create modalities of justice that work for *all* women.

To explore this idea of justice, I would like to examine the interconnecting relationship between the state, the family, and domestic violence by deepening our understanding of the phenomenon of "missing women" who are "returned" to their families from whom they have escaped. In doing this, I am trying to establish that one of the ways that the state engages with justice is to erase the possibility of it. Using the cases of the missing women as an illustration, I want to advocate for creating alternate forms of justice that can cater to, draw from, and be informed by women's definitions of justice.

STATE, FAMILY, AND THE NOTIONS OF JUSTICE

Researchers and activists in India are keenly aware of the fact that the surveys suggesting that between 30% and 40% of women are subject to violent behavior from their husbands provide a gross underestimation of the actual figures (Karp et al., 2015). The fact that only 30% of people in surveys report it is acceptable that a husband beats his wife (for any number of reasons) is also a gross underestimation of the actual belief systems prevalent in India. It is also not surprising to many scholars in India that the National Crimes Records Bureau, a police agency that operates under the Ministry of Home Affairs, has been consistently underreporting crimes against women, especially domestic violence.

There are many reasons for this discrepancy between the experience of violence and the reporting of it, but a primary factor appears to be the role of the police. Most women do not report the violence because they are hesitant, or intimidated, to take the steps to approach the police; feel humiliated at the thought of going to the police; are threatened not to go to the police; feel that it is wrong for others to be involved in their private matters; fear demands for bribes; or anticipate abusive treatment from the police (Karp et al., 2015). These factors also prevent people who might have witnessed violence from reporting it (Karp et al., Marwah &

Manchanda, 2015). Moreover, even if reported, a high percentage of family court cases are dismissed (Iyengar, 2016). Hence, many women find the notion of going to the law to seek any measure of justice futile to begin with (Karp et al., 2015; M. Kumar, 2013; Prison Policy Initiative, 2019).

At the same time, the nature of the state has changed drastically toward gender violence in the past 30 years. Indeed, the state started to take interest in gendering the state—in that it has invested in providing not only resources to women, but also creating ways in which departments could cater to the needs of women (Ramachandran et al., 2012). During this time, many programs, such as the Mahila Samakhya (MS, a national-level program focused on empowering women through collectivization), were developed and provided a good model for bringing women's needs directly into policymaking. Pressure from the women's movement, in prominent cases such as the Banwari Devi rape case or the murder of Nirbhaya in Delhi, also resulted in the state instituting a specific architecture of support services such as the Internal Complaints Committee, women's resource centers, and other services (Rao & Kelleher, 2003). However, in recent years, this interest in incorporating women's voices has significantly waned, and there are indications that the government has moved from the role of being a provider of justice to an enabler of justice mechanisms (Wilson et al., 2018). More and more, it is clear that the state is failing in its essential duties, and this is clearer than in our understanding of the way in which the police respond to citizens' concerns, especially when it comes to violence against women.

The police, as the executive arm of the state, have long been (dis) reputed for their masculinized culture, often associated with brute strength, aggression, and dominance (Carrillo, 2021). These "expected" characteristics of the police translate into an occupational or organizational culture that does not foster sensitivity, understanding, empathy, and cooperation, all of which are foundational in addressing issues related to the most marginalized populations. From another study currently being undertaken, police do not necessarily respond to women's calls of distress when they experience violence (Centre for Budget and Policy Studies, n.d.; interview with women, June 9, 2022). Although the state has set mechanisms by which the police are meant to respond to every distress call, most of the police treat them as "nuisance" calls. They are obligated by law to attend to these calls, so they do come to the house. However, they do not try to resolve the issue to ensure the safety of the woman. They do not even stay long enough to address the women's concerns. Instead, they tell the husband to be quiet, and leave, often escalating the violence thereafter. Unless there is some political or media pressure on particular forms of crime, like stranger rape, dowry cases, or any other high-profile case, the violence that women experience at home at the hands of their husbands is often considered routine and unimportant (Carrillo, 2021).

The reason the police are almost always sensitive only to the politics of visibility is because of the prevailing sociocultural and political norms and agendas. The police run primarily under the aegis of powerful political alliances rather than the law (Bayley, 1971a; Bhowmik, 1986). In fact, many police officers, whether at the junior or the senior level, constantly have to calculate the likely political effect of many enforcement actions and cater only to those who are in a position to influence their actions. (Bayley, 1971a; M. Kumar, 2013; Verma, 2012). Precisely because of this fact, their actions provide a window into the priorities of the state. As the gatekeepers of justice, the police are a lens through which we can understand the way the state wants to deal with violence, what it deems to be suitable action, and when (and if) it should take notice of the violence at hand (Desai, 2009). In fact, there was significant police complicity in destroying evidence in the Bilkis Bano case (referenced previously), as the violence was conducted within an anti-Muslim pogrom. In fact, taking note of this complicity of the police with the rapists, the Supreme Court transferred the case out of the state entirely.

We should note that while this is an indictment of the police and the prevailing culture in which they operate, they themselves have structural challenges to deal with. They are poorly paid and are not sufficiently trained to deal with gender violence. This, in turn, exacerbates a culture of corruption and power brokering within the system (Bayley, 1971b). In addition, as mentioned, police rarely have autonomy over their actions and are often directed by informal power centers (e.g., the Mafia), political parties, or their own chain of command (Verma, 2012). Thus, "organizational ethos, the indifferent styles of administration, and the deliberate alienation from the citizens" (Verma, 2012, p. 5) are some of the many reasons why women do not trust or report violence to the police. Given this predominant relationship between the police and women, it is curious that when Gamana Women's Collective started to examine cases of missing women, the police were *unusually* active in finding them. To understand the context in which the police started to act in ways contrary to general practices, we must understand the context of "missing" women.

CIRCUMVENTING JUSTICE: MISSING WOMEN

The idea that the police were trying to locate "missing women" came about when the Gamana Women's Collective operating in Kolar started noticing a curious notation in police records. The Gamana Women's Collective had been working in the town of Kolar on issues related to violence against women over the past 20 years and has been focusing on community mobilization to ensure the safety and welfare of women in distress. During this process, they noticed that police records appeared to indicate that missing women had been "returned safely" to their families. The initial understanding of this was that these were trafficked women who had safely returned to their homes (Magar, 2012). This was not the case. On investigation,[1] it appeared that many of these so-called missing women had, in fact, left their homes voluntarily as a direct response to the high levels of domestic violence they had faced and were being systematically returned by the police to their violent homes, often under coercive circumstances. They were not minors—they were adult women who had been traced by the police, most of them within a month of their leaving. In fact, those of the women we were able to trace told us that they did not even realize they were considered missing until the police "found" them.

Although some women had not left their homes to escape violence (some had left for varied reasons, including elopement, love, education, etc.), many had left violent familial relationships. This leaving (as coping behavior) also had different motivations and forms. This coping behavior was also diverse. While some had left their homes as a strategic move to ensure that the husbands modified their behavior in response to their leaving, others intended to leave permanently, tired of the abusive behavior from their husbands and their husbands' families. Legally, the police do not have any rights to return the women. The police were very clear that there was, in fact, *no* criminal legislation related to these cases, and that missing women as denoted in the police records (official documents) does not have any legal meaning. Moreover, the police were aware of the multiple reasons why women left their homes. In their explanation, they told the investigators that when families are abusive, when they do not care for the women (emotionally, physically, financially), when they withhold food and are excessively violent toward them, women do tend to leave their households. They also told us that these cases were increasing day by day. So, when asked about the legality of finding these women and returning them to these same violent, neglectful, and controlling households, the police felt that they acted to return the women as they felt afraid for the women. They told us that they strongly felt that in these cases, death (either by suicide or murder) was a likely outcome.

On talking to the women, we strongly felt that this was not likely the real reason for the police's uncharacteristically proactive reason. It was clear to the women and to the Gamana Women's Collective that instead of ensuring the prevention, investigation, or punishment of acts of violence against the women, the police were more interested in catering to the needs of the family. By going after missing women, the police were clearly capitulating to the interests of the family, who were invested in keeping the violence in their families invisible and manageable. By neglecting the calls for help by women when they are being beaten and then pursuing them when they leave the household, the police have one objective: to preserve the sanctity of the family (P. Kumar & Yelne, 2003). Because resistance of the women (in either leaving or calling the police) is seen as defiling the honor of the family, the police do what they can to safeguard the ideology or the "sacredness" of the family (P. Kumar & Yelne, 2003, p. 95). We also realized that women are well aware of these dynamics and often have to strategize to seek justice (whether formally or informally) by ensuring they are seen or deemed to be "good" women. Without this protection of the mantle of a "good" woman, the pathway to justice (as they might define it) can be very rocky.

In fact, even in situations where alternate justice mechanisms such as Nari Adalats (NAs, Women's Courts) are functioning, these interweaving concepts of justice, violence, and identity (especially that of the good woman) are still quite critical (Sharma, 2008). To explore this dynamic further, we examine the community-driven initiative of NAs and the manner in which they are able to articulate and define women's ideas around justice.

ALTERNATIVE FRAMES OF JUSTICE: WOMEN'S COURTS

Nari Adalats, literally translates as "Women's Courts." The idea for these courts came primarily from a governmental program called Mahila Samakhya (MS). The primary purpose of the program was to ensure that women became self-reliant and independent, and created their own pathways for social change through a process of collectivization (for further detail, see Jyotsna et al., 2022). The philosophy of the program was that if provided a space, environment, and time, women would be able to create, facilitate, and sustain an empowering and enriching experience for themselves (Hartsock, 1989; Jandhyala, 2012). True to its philosophy, the program started to investigate the ways in which women themselves could address the violence that they were experiencing. After a series of discussions conducted throughout the country, community models were recognized as a valid way in which women would be able to demand their rights to a violence-free life and access to justice mechanisms (Rajan, 2012). While the initial efforts were focused on informal responses, these soon coalesced into specific committees that would take up issues related to domestic violence, rape, sexual harassment, and other issues related to gender violence. While the mode of operations in the beginning was primarily arbitration and mediation, the main focus of these processes was to give women a sense of control over their situation and to provide a means of validating their experiences (Genn, 1993; Olson & Dzur, 2004).

These processes also enabled the shift from feeling responsible for the violence to having societal support for their experience and to shift the blame to where it belongs—the perpetrator. Because MS realized quite early that (1) deep kinship ties made arbitration a very difficult means of negotiating settlements, and (2) this mechanism should not evolve into an extrajudicial body that operated *away* from the laws of the land, they created formal systems, the NAs (instituted first in Gujarat in 1995). The NAs were designed to ensure that justice was served through a structured set of processes away from the social control of the family or community and within the ambit of formal justice systems (Rajan, 2012). In fact, their defined role was formalized to such an extent that they would only hold these courts/meetings in the same premises as the district courts or in government property, such as the Panchayat office (Rajan, 2012).

The process of NAs follows. Based on the experiences of the women in the collectives, a few strong, articulate women were chosen by the collectives to work exclusively on legal issues. These women would then be trained on counseling and arbitration processes; the legal systems; and how to talk to and negotiate with the police and the court systems. These chosen women would act as advocates, debating the various issues raised by the women. For example, in handling of a case of violence (whether in relation to domestic violence, rape, or custody), notices would be sent to both parties to appear before the court. If they did not appear, postcards would be sent to their addresses, and on further noncompliance, the police would start the formal process of charging the perpetrator. On the day of the meeting, based on the discussions of the women's advocates from the village as well as representation from the perpetrator, the jurors would collectively and through consensus building make a set of decisions that would have to be followed by both the perpetrator and the survivor. Noncompliance with these decisions would trigger the legal process again.

The composition and the process varied significantly from place to place. For example, a research report indicated that in the state of Karnataka, the NA consisted of a four-member jury and at least 20 advocates who debated the issues (Merry, 2006; Rajan, 2012).

This process worked so well that the police often would refer cases that they could not handle to the NAs. This success was due to NAs' ability to tackle a foundational problem. In order for women to be able to open up and speak about their experiences with violence, they needed to be able to speak freely without being ridiculed, shamed, or disbelieved (Hercus, 1999). This is not typically available to them in traditional justice mechanisms. Because NAs was an organic structure that evolved from women's collectivization processes, women were in a better position to understand and trust the process. Moreover, unlike traditional court systems, the NAs also allowed spaces for reflection, analysis, debate, and discussion to emerge within justice mechanisms (Merry, 2006; Rajan, 2012). In fact, apart from working with a feminist interpretation of the law that was prosurvivor (Rajan, 2012), the notions of justice were derived from women themselves.

The NAs were also able to take into consideration the complexity of the social context in which women were often placed. They were able to tackle the predominant issues that women experienced: the fear of the unknown, the (veiled) threats of their families, the rejection by one's natal family or even children, and the uncertainty of sustainability. When necessary, NAs also helped women pursue legal cases. In many ways, NAs acted as a bridge between women's issues and processes of justice. Because NAs were formed and operated by women from within the communities, NAs were able to use the knowledge of local practices (including adjusting meeting times) to gather evidence, to organize meetings, and to negotiate settlements (Merry, 2006). While their legal authority might be limited, they were able to bring to bear the ideas of equality, autonomy, and bodily integrity to a resistant climate of justice. Despite the successes of this alternative justice mechanism, the process of NAs also suffered from the same contextual issues that plague missing women. These are explored in what follows.

ARTICULATING TERMS OF JUSTICE

The foundations of justice are based on the simple idea that all human beings are equal and therefore are worthy of the same social standing or social good as the other (Stumpf et al., 2016). However, when violence is not seen as a law-and-order issue but a family one, or if women are not seen as equal within a family, but are seen as the property of family, then the idea of justice can be quite skewed. One of the reasons for invoking NAs in the context of missing women is because there are several ways in which NAs would have been able to articulate the processes of justice for missing women.

The NAs were effective in ensuring justice because they focused on women's ability to articulate their experience of violence as *violation*. They were able to push against traditional frameworks of justice that tended to revictimize survivors by normalizing the violence. Moreover, because NAs used community forums to articulate both the perpetrator's and survivor's point of view in an open and transparent manner (also visible to the community), they were able to resist a singular narrative of the crime or violation. This nuanced understanding of the violence helped to garner support for survivors of violence, especially if the perpetrator provided false testimony that was refuted (Bhatla & Rajan, 2003). Although NAs emphasized that the survivor's view was heard, NAs, through training and experience, also tried to expand the boundaries of the law. In many ways, they tried to push against, or negotiate, the normative terms of settlement using cues provided by social norms and social culture. In fact, this is often considered the "pragmatic" view and was one of the cornerstones of the NA process.

Another reason NAs were able to tackle the notions of justice resulted from their philosophical stances against violence. For example, unlike Khap or caste-based panchayats,[2] NAs refused to use any means of violence regardless of the provocation. These ethical stances were able to bestow on their processes a different kind of "power"—one that allowed them to let go of vicious cycles of shame, victimhood, and revenge—and created a different framework of legitimacy around the idea and practice of justice.

The NAs also provided pathways to formal channels of justice. One of the foundations of NAs is that they were able to draw from two significant sources: (1) their deep connections to the community and (2) their knowledge and allegiance to the law. Both of these aspects are essential for a framework of justice that is transparent, democratic, and participatory (Cleaver, 1999; Rajan, 2012). The idea is that instead of seeing justice as an "outside" force, it is seen as an integral process that marks every aspect of women's lives. This means that survivors are able to articulate alternate frameworks of justice that look at the actual needs of the women instead of providing a prescriptive answer (which may or may not be implemented or effective).

In general, NAs by their very process were able to create spaces of justice within the community and tried to ensure that women were provided space and a platform so that the processes of justice could be used to push against social norms (Bhatla & Rajan, 2003). However, even in these emancipatory spaces, the emphasis on women's requirements and needs was not necessarily easy to navigate. For example, in cases of bigamy where one woman was duped into marrying an already married man, NAs would often legitimize the first wife's claim, but were always conflicted or ill-equipped to deal with the second wife's contention that she had to suffer the derision of the community at having been abandoned by the person she married. These and other such decisions illustrate the difficulties of defining and affirming justice for disenfranchised women (Kalra, 2016).

Another problem with NAs is that because they are rooted within their communities and there is a tremendous focus on respecting women's choices and voices, the decisions can push against normative feminist understanding of women's rights. For example, when women insist on marrying their rapists, as a way of restoring their honor or the honor of the community, it is not clear to the NAs themselves which decisions they ought to take. In another example, the reprimand to the unwanted advances of the father-in-law to his daughter-in-law was hinged on the idea that the husband has the sole right to a woman's body. In this case, a patriarchal belief system of possession and ownership was used to name a violation. So, NAs cannot be considered as utopian spaces that overcame all structural and systemic barriers of discrimination and inequality. We have to also respect the reality that depending on the circumstance, training, or constitution, they are just as prone to reproducing gender and power hierarchies as traditional or community-driven tribunals.

In fact, one of the most significant ways in which we can unpack this reproduction is to examine the notion of the "good woman." Whether we are examining it in the case of missing women or in the case of NAs, it was clear that women had to fit a certain mold of being a good victim to even be *seen* as deserving of redress. Her conduct, her behavior, and her "virtue" are all scrutinized as a way for the courts and the police to provide her any modicum of justice (Jha et al., 2019; Mitra & Satish, 2014; Roychowdhury, 2015). This is not always the case for men, who, even when their abuse is documented significantly and irrefutably, are seen as "bad" husbands, but never abusive husbands. Therefore, it is not completely surprising that in the cases of missing women, the police rarely prosecute husbands who beat their wives, but will return the wives to their families if and when they leave their abusive situation. Even when women leave relationships, they have to stay on the good side of the good–bad woman dichotomy. Given that not all victims of violence can be good women and survivors of violence does not always coalesce around the primary identity of women, "justice" can be hard to find.

So, even while NAs have been able to create a particular form of feminist politics that provided a collective voice, an institution that helped validate experiences of oppression and gave women the platform to address the reality and structure of oppression (Thomas & Davies, 2005; Dempsey, 2007), it is also important to remember that justice depends on not only systems of oppression but also systems of knowledge. When these knowledge systems are situated within a particularly powerful context (wherein systems of honor influence future life choices or when one's community group is likely to be subject to violence from the state), then commitment to women's notions of justice start to quickly unravel the emancipatory nature of these spaces. In these contested spaces, knowing what is right or wrong can be very difficult to discern. Precisely for these reasons, it is important for all of us to start unpacking notions of justice in practice.

CONCLUSION

Justice can occur simultaneously in many rooms (Braithwaite & Gohar, 2014). If that is true, then we must start to recognize, document, and analyze the different ways in which justice systems (whether traditional or informal) are engaging with women's experience of violence. NAs provide us with a blueprint and a methodology that can help create spaces where meaningful and active participation in justice-seeking mechanisms can take place (Campbell, 2016). It is, perhaps, equally important that we are able to assess the gaps in existing criminal and civil justice provisions and identify mechanisms by which we are able to provide reparations, social, economic, and psychological support and advocate for survivors of violence without resorting to familiar narratives of power and control.

It is indicative of how far we are from our goals of gender justice that the police do not treat domestic violence crimes as crimes, but as "skirmishes" that can be brushed away, and often become the arm of the family in finding missing women as though these women are property. Therefore, we need to create spaces so that women are able to enter these conversations and expand our understanding of the multiple notions of justice and fairness and what is deemed to be "right." Without framing these acceptable notions of justice or the ethical positions one must take against violence, we cannot arrive at claims that can be seen as just or legitimate.

Of course, questions still remain: Will women's notions of justice help against a system that minimizes or rejects the violations for which justice is sought? What is the meaning of justice when free and independent movement away from violence is seen as transgressing boundaries of propriety? It is not clear whether clarifying these notions will resolve our current predicament. However, what is clear is that our understanding of justice is based foundationally on our ideology of what we think is right or wrong. Clearly, this is not always located only in the formal halls of the judiciary. In order to build a new imagination and have it translated within the system, our framework or ideology of justice will reveal "what we value, how we see the world, who we think 'we' are, and whether we like who we are" (Ackerly, 2016, p. 641). In answering these questions, the actions of the state, the police, and ourselves—what we value and who we are—become clearer.

NOTES

1. The report documenting this study will soon be in the public domain but can be made available on request to the author.
2. Khap or caste panchayats are caste-based juries of elders in the village who are distinct from village panchayats. The caste or Khap panchayats are rarely elected and do not serve the needs of all communities, but restrict themselves to matters only related to their own castes.

REFERENCES

Ackerly, B. A. (2016). Raising one eyebrow and re-envisioning justice, gender, and the family. *Hypatia*, *31*(3), 638–650. https://doi.org/10.1111/hypa.12254

Bayley, D. H. (1971a). The police in India. *Economic and Political Weekly*, 2287–2291.

Bayley, D. H. (1971b). The police and political change in comparative perspective. *Law & Society Review*, *6*(1), 91–112.

Bhatla, N., & Rajan, A. (2003). Private concerns in public discourse: Women-initiated community responses to domestic violence. *Economic and Political Weekly*, *38*(17), 1658–1664.

Bhowmik, S. K. (1986). Police and society. *Economic and Political Weekly*, *21*(6), 241–243.

Braithwaite, J., & Gohar, A. (2014). Restorative justice, policing and insurgency: Learning from Pakistan. *Law & Society Review*, *48*(3), 531–561.

Brison, S. J. (2006). Justice and gender-based violence. *Revue internationale de philosophie*, *235*(1), 259–275. https://doi.org/10.3917/rip.265.0259

Campbell, K. (2016). Gender justice beyond the tribunals: From criminal accountability to transformative justice. *American Journal of International Law*, *110*, 227–233. https://doi.org/10.1017/S2398772300009077

Carrillo, D. (2021). Police culture and gender: An evaluation of police officers' practices and responses to domestic abuse. *Journal of Global Faultlines*, *8*(1), 69–80. https://doi.org/10.13169/jglobfaul.8.1.0069

Centre for Budget and Policy Studies. (n.d.). Gender violence in public spaces: Studying the approaches and theorising the pathways of change. Centre for Budget and Policy Studies. https://cbps.in/gender/gender-violence-in-public-spaces-studying-the-app roaches-and-theorising-the-pathways-of-change

Cleaver, F. (1999). Paradoxes of participation: Questioning participatory approaches to development. *Journal of International Development*, *11*(4), 597–612. https://doi.org/ 10.1002/(SICI)1099-1328(199906)11:4<597::AID-JID610>3.0.CO;2-Q

Dempsey, M. M. (2007). Toward a feminist state: What does "effective" prosecution of domestic violence mean? *Modern Law Review*, *70*(6), 908–935. https://doi.org/ 10.1111/j.1468-2230.2007.00670.x

Desai, M. (2009). Red herring in police reforms. *Economic and Political Weekly*, *44*(10), 8–11.

Genn, H. (1993). Tribunals and informal justice. *Modern Law Review*, *56*(3), 393–411.

Hartsock, N. (1989). Postmodernism and political change: Issues for feminist theory. *Cultural Critique*, Winter (14), 15–33. https://doi.org/10.2307/1354291

Hercus, C. (1999). Identity, emotion, and feminist collective action. *Gender & Society*, *13*(1), 34–55. https://doi.org/10.1177/089124399013001003

Iyengar, P. (2016). Adjudicating "litigotiation": Cases filed in the Mumbai Family Court. *Economic and Political Weekly*, *51*(23), 40–49.

Jandhyala, K. (2012). Ruminations on evaluation in the Mahila Samakhya programme. *Indian Journal of Gender Studies*, *19*(2), 211–231.

Jha, J., Ghatak, N., Menon, N., Dutta, P., & Mahendiran, S. (2019). *Women's education and empowerment in rural India*. Routledge.

Jyotsna, J., Niveditha, M., & Ghatak, N. (2022). *The political economy of women's empowerment policies in India* [Working paper]. United Nations University. Retrieved from: https://www.wider.unu.edu/publication/political-economy-women%E2%80%99s-empowerment-policies-india

Kalra, H. (2016). Rights of second wives: Role of informal justice systems. *Economic and Political Weekly*, *51*(25), 16–19.

Karp, A., Marwah, S., & Manchanda, R. (2015). Unheard and uncounted: Violence against women in India [Issue Brief, 5]. Small Arms Survey. https://www.smallarm ssurvey.org/sites/default/files/resources/IAVA-IB5-unheard-and-uncounted.pdf

Kumar, M. (2013). Accountability of Indian police: A historical appraisal. *Indian Journal of Political Science*, *74*(4), 733–742. https://resolver.scholarsportal.info/resolve/00195 510/v74i0004/733_aoipaha.xml

Kumar, P., & Yelne, G. (2003). Women resisting violence: The economic as political. *Sociological Bulletin*, *52*(1), 91–113. https://doi.org/10.1177/0038022920030105

Magar, V. (2012). Rescue and rehabilitation: A critical analysis of sex workers' antitrafficking response in India. *Signs: Journal of Women in Culture and Society*, *37*(3), 619–644. https://doi.org/10.1086/662698

Marx Ferree, M., & McClurg Mueller, C. (2004). Feminism and the women's movement: A global perspective. In D. A. Snow, S. A. Soule, & K. Hanspeter (Eds.), *The Blackwell companion to social movements* (pp. 576–607). Blackwell Publishing.

Merry, S. E. (2006). Transnational human rights and local activism: Mapping the middle. *American Anthropologist*, *108*(1), 38–51. https://doi.org/10.1525/aa.2006.108.1.38

Mitra, D., & Satish, M. (2014). Testing chastity, evidencing rape: Impact of medical jurisprudence on rape adjudication in India. *Economic and Political Weekly, 49*(41), 51–58.

Mukherjee, M. (2022). Karnataka hijab row: The double burden facing India's Muslim women. *The Quint*. https://www.thequint.com/voices/opinion/karnataka-hijab-row-the-double-burden-facing-indias-muslim-women#read-more

Olson, S. M., & Dzur, A. W. (2004). Revisiting informal justice: Restorative justice and democratic professionalism. *Law & Society Review, 38*(1), 139–176. https://doi.org/10.1111/j.0023-9216.2004.03801005.x

Prison Policy Initiative. (2019, May 14). Policing women: Race and gender disparities in police stops, searches, and use of force. Prison Policy Initiative. https://www.prisonpolicy.org/blog/2019/05/14/policingwomen/

Ramachandran, V., Jandhyala, K., & Govinda, R. (2012). Cartographies of empowerment: An introduction. In V. Ramachandran & K. Jandhyala (Eds.), *Cartographies of empowerment: The Mahila Samakhya story* (pp. 12–33). Zubaan Books.

Rajan, A. (2012). Responding to violence and exploring justice through women-centred mechanisms. *Cartographies of empowerment: The Mahila Samakhya story*, 270–307.

Rao, A., & Kelleher, D. (2003). Institutions, organisations and gender equality in an era of globalisation. *Gender & Development, 11*(1), 142–149. https://doi.org/10.1080/741954264

Roychowdhury, P. (2015). Victims to saviors: Governmentality and the regendering of citizenship in India. *Gender & Society, 29*(6), 792–816. https://doi.org/10.1177/0891243215602105

Sarkar, S. (2022). The war over hijab and gendered islamophobia. *Doing Sociology*. https://doingsociology.org/2022/03/02/the-war-over-hijab-and-gendered-islamophobia-swakshadip-sarkar/

Saxena, P. P. (2003). Matrimonial laws and gender justice. *Journal of the Indian Law Institute, 45*(3/4), 33–87.

Scroll Staff. (2022). Full statement: "Give me back my right to live without fear and in peace," says Bilkis Bano. *Scroll*. https://scroll.in/latest/1030721/give-me-back-my-right-to-live-without-fear-and-in-peace-says-bilkis-bano

Sharma, A. (2008). *Logics of empowerment: Development, gender, and governance in neoliberal India*. University of Minnesota Press.

Stumpf, K. H., Becker, C. U., & Baumgärtner, S. (2016). A conceptual structure of justice-providing a tool to analyse conceptions of justice. *Ethical Theory and Moral Practice, 19*(5), 1187–1202. https://doi.org/10.1007/s10677-016-9728-3

Thomas, R., & Davies, A. (2005). What have the feminists done for us? Feminist theory and organizational resistance. *Organization, 12*(5), 711–740. https://doi.org/10.1177/1350508405055945

Verma, A. (2012). A heavy hand: The use of force by India's police [Issue Brief 3]. Small Arms Survey. No. 3; 1–12.

Wilson, K., Ung Loh, J., & Purewal, N. (2018). Gender, violence and the neoliberal state in India. *Feminist Review, 119*(1), 1–6. https://doi.org/10.1057/s41305-018-0109-8

INDEX

For the benefit of digital users, indexed terms that span two pages (e.g., 52–53) may, on occasion, appear on only one of those pages.

Tables and figures are indicated by *t* and *f* following the page number

abolition movement, 5–6
Aboriginal women
   homicide cases against, 116–17, 117*t*
   "kill or be killed" situation, 120
   See also First Nations
abused women, psychological violence and, 52–53
Abusive Behaviour and Sexual Harm (Scotland) Act 2016, 193
American Convention on Human Rights, 234
American Declaration of the Rights and Duties of Man, 234
Ana, Beatriz y Celia González Peréz v. México (2001), 236–37
Andersson, Ulrika, 8–9
anticarceral, feminist positioning feminism, 73
Arizona, RESTORE program, 270
Australia, 2–3
   criminalization of coercive control, 39–40
   criminal offenses of coercive control, 22
   DFV policy and practices, 23
   domestic and family violence and Victoria Police, 172, 176, 177, 181, 184–85
   First Nations women in, 9
   image-based sexual abuse, 65
   immediate police-initiated protection measures, 106
   incarceration of Indigenous, 32, 107
   Indigenous peoples and domestic violence, 99–100
   nonfatal strangulation offense, 10–11
   prison population, 3–4
   research design, 24
   voices of victim-survivors, 7–8
   See also domestic and family violence (DFV)
Australian eSafety Commission, 64–65
Austria, laws on intimate images, 72

Balai Syura, 294
Belem do Pará Convention, 44, 234–35
Belem do Para Inter-American Convention, 55
Bill of Rights Act 1990 (NZ), 156
bipolar disorder, 154–55
Black Bull, Sunrise, 136
blackmail, 49
Bray, Jonnie, 140
Brazil
   benefits and risks on criminalization of psychological violence, 51–55
   civil definition of psychological violence in, 45–47

Brazil (*cont.*)
  criminalization of psychological violence, 47–48
  Maria da Penha Law (MLP), 43
  psychological violence as grounds for civil interventions, 45
  psychological violence in, 8
Brunner, Lisa, 139
B.S. v. Spain, 253
bureaucracy, 287–88
  structural violence, 288
bureaucratic
  term, 287
  term in bureaucratic violence, 287–89
bureaucratic negligence, 286, 295
bureaucratic violence, 286
  "bureaucratic" in, 287–89
  concept of, 11–12, 296
  "grounded" theory of, 286–96
  promises made by the state in the Law, 291–95
  rehabilitation programs, 290, 293–95
  safe houses, 290, 291–93
  state accountability, 295–96
  theory of, 286, 289, 295–96
  "violence" in, 289–90
Burman, Michele, 10–11

Canada
  Circles of Support and Accountability, 273
  sexual offense laws, 80–81
carceral feminism, 73, 217–18
Casa Paula, 242–43
Circles of Support and Accountability, Canada, 273
civil protection order (CPO), domestic and family violence (DFV), 174–75
coercive control
  absence of, 23–24
  causal link with harm caused, 241–42
  criminalization of, 2–3, 4
    Stark, Evan, 2–3
  definition, 2–3
  as illegal constraint, 46
  intimate partner relationships, 209–10
  nonfatal strangulation (NFS) as form of, 209–10
  See also criminalization of coercive control
Cohen, Amy, 281
Cokanasiga, Jojiana, 8–9
collector culture, intimate images, 66
Colville Nation tribe, 9
Colville Reservation, 140, 142–43
Committee on the Elimination of Discrimination Against Women (CEDAW)
  Fiji ratifying, 98–99
  violence against women (VAW) In, 97–98
community awareness, criminalization of coercive control and, 29–30
Comprehensive Organic Law for the Prevention and Eradication of Violence Against Women, 239–40
conscious negligence, 83–84
controlling or coercive behavior, England and Wales, 191
Convention on Elimination of All Forms of Discrimination Against Women (CEDAW), 252, 295–96
Council of Europe, 252–53
Covid-19 pandemic, 4
craftsmanship, gendered digital violence, 66
creepshots, definition, 63
Crimes Act 1961 (NZ), 153
criminalization at the margins
  challenges of, 72–75
  creepshots, 62–64
  downblousing, 61–64
  harms of downblousing, 67–68
  images of breasts otherwise not visible, 71–72
  motive-based criminalization, 70–71
  privacy violations, 68–69
  proof of victim harm, 69
criminalization of coercive control
  ability of justice system to punish perpetrators, 31–34

debates surrounding, 22–24
female participant views on, 26t
impact on improving community
   awareness, 29–30
impact on perpetrator
   accountability, 31–34
impact on victim-survivor safety, 30–31
negative impacts of justice system on
   victim-survivors of DFV, 34–38
participant views on effect of, 28t
recognition of limits of law, 34–38
research design, 24
support alongside recognition of risks, 38–39
survey participants' characteristics, 25t
victim-survivor views on, 24–39
criminalization of psychological violence
benefits and risks on, 51–55, 56t
Brazil, 47–48
criminalizing violence against women,
   consequences of, 2
criminal justice
   human rights and, 233
   reform of the trial process, 152–53
criminal legal system
   actors within, 9–10
   debates in, 79–80
Cripps, Kyllie, 9
Crown Office and Procurator Fiscal
   Service (COPFS), 190, 192, 202–3

de Ávila, Thiago, 8
*Declaration on the Elimination of Violence
   Against Women* (1993), 189
decriminalization, nonfatal strangulation
   (NFS), 221–22
Deer, Sarah, 134–35, 136–37, 138–39, 147n.2
defund the police movement, 5–6
De Graffenreid v. General Motors
   (1976), 249–50
DFV. *See* domestic and family violence (DFV)
disassociation, 36
domestic abuse (DA), Scotland's
   approach, 189
Domestic Abuse (Scotland) Act 2018
   [DA(S)A], 10–11, 190–93

benefits and challenges of, 195–99
data about use of, 193–94
divisional specialists (tier 2), 197
Domestic Abuse Questionnaire
   (DAQ), 198–99
implementation challenges, 192
introduction of, 190–91, 202–3
limited use of, 203
methodology, 194–95
national specialists (tier 3), 197–99
police reflections on, 200–2
police response to, 193
policy definitions, 191
reporting requirement, 192–93
response officers (tier 1), 195–97
stated intentions of, 191
victim-survivor's experience, 200–2
Domestic Abuse Matters Scotland
   (training), 195, 199
domestic and family violence (DFV), 21
adherence to policy, 177–80
bureaucratic violence, 286
conceptualizing the role of
   police, 182–84
definition in Indonesian Law (No. 23/
   2004), 285–86
definition of, 23
expertise on, 40
findings, 177–76
justice system punishing
   perpetrators, 31–34
literature review, 172–75
methodology, 176–77
misidentification in, 33–34
misidentification of women victim-
   survivors as predominant aggressors,
   171–72, 176, 184–86
negative impacts of justice system on
   victim-survivors of, 34–38
perceptions of risk, 180–82
policing policy, 172–74
precautionary policing, 174–75
victim-survivors of, 21–22
Victoria Police, 172, 176, 177, 181, 184–85
See also bureaucratic violence

domestic violence (DV), 3–4
  Committee on the Elimination of Discrimination Against Women (CEDAW), 97–98
  Fiji, 98
  Fiji ratifying CEDAW, 98–99
  Indigenous peoples and, 99–100
  law practice and women's narratives on, 117–19
  nonfatal strangulation (NFS), 209–10
  Pacific countries, 97
  Pacific cultures and, 99
  See also Fiji; nonfatal strangulation (NFS)
domestic violence orders (DVOs), 98
  Australia, 99–100
  Indigenous peoples and, 99–100
domestic violence protection order (DVPO), 99–100
Domestic Violence Restorative Circles (DVRC)
  Men as Peacemakers, 275, 276
  qualitative study of pilot program, 276–77
  safety concerns and support for, 276
  See also restorative justice
domestic violence restraining orders (DVROs), 102–3
  Fiji, 103–6, 104f, 107–9
Douglas, Heather, 10–11
downblousing, 61
  behavior of, 8
  criminalization of, 68
  criminalizing images of breasts otherwise not visible, 71–72
  definition, 62–64
  distinct behaviors, 63–64
  harms of, 67–68
  Hong Kong, 70–71
  laws, 61–62
  Northern Ireland, 70
  online forums of images, 66
  prevalence of, 64–66
  term, 61, 62–63, 65, 74–75
Draft Law on Real and Effective Equality of Trans People, 260–61

due diligence, Inter-American Court of Human Rights (IACtHR), 236–37
dysregulation, 36

Ecuador
  Belém do Pará (1995), 238–40
  Constitution, 238–39
  criminal law-centric models, 240–43
  human rights penalty, 11
  National Survey (2019), 245n.3
  Pact of San José, 239–40
  reduced protection and services, 240–43
  shelter homes for VAW survivors, 242–43
England, domestic violence in, 44–45
English Law Commission
  creepshots, 63
  downblousing, 62–63
  downblousing and upskirting, 66
  imagebased sexual abuse, 63–67, 69–70, 74–75
  prevalence of downblousing, 64–66
Equality Framework Directive (EC), 262–63n.4
Equally Safe, Scotland government strategy, 190
Europe, criminal offenses of coercive control, 22
European Commission, 256, 257
European Court of Human Rights, 232–33, 252–53
European Economic and Social Committee, 263n.5
European Institute for Gender Equality, 249
European Parliament, 254–55, 256, 257, 263n.5
European Union, vulnerable victims and intersectionality, 254–56
Evidence Act 2006 (NZ), 155, 156, 159–60, 162

family violence, 3–4
family violence intervention orders (FVIOs), 174–75, 176, 179–80
Family Violence Reform Implementation Monitor, 185–86

INDEX

Federal District of Brazil, 51–52
feminism
  anticarceral, 73
  feminist positioning, 73
  intersectionality, 250–51
  psychological violence and movements, 53–54
Fernando principles, 119
Fiji
  colonial rule in, 100
  Crimes Act (2009), 101
  Criminal Division of the Magistrate's Court, 103–4, 104*f*, 105, 108–9
  criminalization of DV In, 104–8
  Domestic Violence Act (DV Act), 101, 102–3, 105–6, 108
  domestic violence protection order in, 8–9
  domestic violence restraining orders (DVROs), 103–6, 104*f*, 107–9
  existing data, 103–4
  Family Division of Magistrate's Court, 103–4, 104*f*, 105*f*
  ratifying CEDAW, 98–99
  responding to DV in, 101–4
  Sentencing and Penalties Act (2009), 101
Fiji Women's Crisis Centre (FWCC), 97, 101–2
First Nations, 2
  criminal behaviors and, 32–33
  incarceration of, 3–4
  nonfatal strangulation (NFS) in courts, 223
  overrepresentation in Queensland, 214–15
  prisons and families, 4
  prison sentence remand of, 213–14
Fitzgerald, Robin, 10–11
Fitz-Gibbon, Kate, 7–8
forensic report, legal recognition of psychological violence, 48–50
France, crime of marital harassment, 44–45

Gamana Women's Collective, India, 303–4, 305–6
gender-based violence (GBV), 1
  against Native women in U.S., 134–37
  criminalization of, in U.S., 146
  failing to protect Native women, 9
  feminist critique of law, 233
  legal response to, on Native land, 137–39
  restorative justice options, 274–75
gender mainstreaming, 263n.6
General Crimes Act (1817), 137
Genovese, Ann, 9–10
genuine victim, 10–11
George, Maddesyn, 9, 133, 146
  case of, 139–45
  charges against, 143–44
  defending herself, 143
  as imperfect victim, 143
  plea bargaining, 144–45
  rape of, 140–41
  victimization by White men in U.S., 134–35
  violence against, 140
  See also *United States v. Maddesyn George*
Germany, laws on intimate images, 72
Goodmark, Leigh, 9
Gore, Jody, 115–16
Graber, Kristopher, 9, 133, 146
  criminal history of, 141–42
  dealing drugs on reservation, 134
  death, 145
  George and, 139–40
  history of violence, 145
  See also *United States v. Maddesyn George*
Graham, Stephen, 141–42
Guarantee of the Rights of Lesbian, Gay, Trans, Bisexual, and Intersex People, 260–61

Halley, Janet, 142–43
harm, restorative justice, 272–73
hate crime, 263n.5
Hill, Margo, 134–35
Holloway, Isaiah, 140–41
homicide cases, Aboriginal women in New South Wales, 117*t*
homosociality, gendered digital violence, 66

Hong Kong
    Law Reform Commission, 70–71
    motive-based criminalization, 70–71
Hooper, Shirley, 142–43
human rights
    criminalization and consequences for, 54
    criminal justice and, 233
    moderators of state coercion, 232
    violence against women (VAW), 243
Human Rights Convention, 252–53
human rights penality, 11, 231
Hunter, Rosemary, 5–6

ideal victim, psychological violence and, 52–53
identity of difference, 260–61
I.G. and Others v. Slovakia, 262n.1
illegal constraint, coercive control as, 46
image-based sexual abuse
    concept of, 64
    downblousing, 73–74
    levels of hidden victimization, 65–66
imperfect victims, 9
imprisonment, damaging impacts of, 4
Improving Frontline Responses to Domestic Violence (IMPRODOVA), 194
impunity, Inter-American Court of Human Rights (IACtHR), 235–36
India
    Banwari Devi rape case, 302
    Bilkis Bano case, 300
    caste-based panchayats, 309–10, 313n.2
    concept of justice in, 12
    Gamana Women's Collective, 303–4, 305–6
    Khap, 309–10, 313n.2
    Mahila Samakhya (MS), 302, 306–7
    Ministry of Home Affairs, 301
    Nari Adalats (NAs, Women's Courts), 306–8
    National Crimes Records Bureau, 301
    Nirbhaya murder, 302
    police culture in, 302–4, 312
    resurgence of (Hindu) Right in, 300
    state, family and notions of justice, 301–4
Indonesia
    bureaucratic violence, 11–12
    Elimination of Domestic Violence (the Law), 285–86
    fieldwork data in Banda Aceh, 286–87
    Free Aceh Movement (*Gerakan Aceh Merdeka*), 287
    Ministry of Women's Empowerment and Child Protection, 292–93
    Police Women's and Children's Protection Unit, 292
    See also bureaucratic violence
Indonesia Women's Commission, 291–92
Inter-American Convention on the Prevention, Punishment and Eradication of Violence Against Women, 234
Inter-American Court of Human Rights (IACtHR), 234, 235–36, 237
Inter-American Human Rights System (IAHRS)
    criminal justice, 237–38, 242
    due diligence, 236–37
    functions and virtues of criminal law, 233–34
    human rights penality, 231, 232–33, 243–45
    impunity, 235–36
    violence against women (VAW), 231
International Classification of Diseases (ICD) report, legal recognition of psychological violence, 50
intersectional, word, 261
intersectionality
    concept, 249, 251
    concept of, 258–59
    European Union law, 254–56
    International Human Rights Standards, 252–54
    interpretation of, 262
    issues for research in, 259–62
    as legal concept, 261–62

legal notions of vulnerable victims
and, 251–56
notion of, 260
in Spanish criminal policy on gendered
violence, 256–59
term, 249–50, 256–57
violence against women, 250–51
intimate partner relationships, coercive
control, 209–10
intimate partner sexual violence
complainant vulnerabilities at
trial, 154–56
Connors case, 157, 161
emotional impact of
complainants, 160–61
Farrell case, 160–61, 164
judicial disruption of myths and
misconceptions about, 162–66
judicial interaction with complainants, 156–59
judicial intervention during
questioning, 159–62
Lincoln case, 165
O'Connell case, 162
rape as violence, 151–52
rape trials in New Zealand, 153
reform of the trial process, 152–53
reimagining the judicial role, 166–67
R. v. Keats (2022), 166
intimate partner violence, 3–5
Inventing the Savage (Ross), 136
Ireland
Domestic Violence Act 2018, 22–23
proof of privacy violations, 69
Istanbul Convention (2011), 253–54

Jones, Balawyn, 11–12, 233–34
Judicial Council, Ecuador, 240–41
justice
articulating terms of, 309–12
caste-based panchayats, 309–10, 313n.2
concept of, 12, 299–300
ideology of, 312–13
Khap, 309–10, 313n.2
missing women and
circumventing, 304–6

needs and requirements of women, 300
state, family and notions of, in
India, 301–4
system's ability to punish
perpetrators, 31–34
violation, 309
vision of, 12–13
women's courts as alternative frames
of, 306–8

Kansas Act (1940), 137–38
kill or be killed, situation, 120
Kilroy, Debbie, 4
Kina, Robyn, 118–19

Law, Victoria, 140
law practice, women's narratives of
domestic violence, 117–19
Law Reform Commission, Hong
Kong, 70–71
lesbian, bisexual, trans, nonbinary,
intersex, and queer (LBTIQ), 256
LGBTIQA+ communities, 32
life projects, violence impacting
women's, 2–3

McDonald, Elisabeth, 9–10, 240–41
McGirt v. Oklahoma, 137–38
McGlynn, Clare, 6, 8
Mahila Samakhya (MS), India, 302, 306–7
Major Crimes Act (1885), 137
manipulation, recognition of, 49
Maria da Penha Law (MPL)
Article 7 of, 47
Brazil, 43, 232
definition of psychological violence, 51
legal subsystem around violence against
women, 45
victim and intervention order
request, 46–47
Maria da Penha Maia Fernandes v. Brazil
(2001), 236–37
marital harassment, crime of, in
France, 44–45
mediation, genealogy of, 281

Melanesian countries, 97
Men as Peacemakers, Domestic Violence Restorative Circles (DRVC), 275, 276
Menon, Niveditha, 12
methamphetamine, distribution, 134
#metoo movement, 79–80
Micronesia, 97
Ministry of Home Affairs, India, 301
Minnesota, Veterans Restorative Justice Act (VRJA), 278–79
"missing" women
 circumventing justice, 304–6
 role of police in returning, 12
Monash University Human Research Ethics Committee, 186n.1
MPL. *See* Maria da Penha Law (MPL)
Mubilanzila Mayeka and Kaniki Mitunga v. Belgium, 262n.1
Murri Courts, nonfatal strangulation (NFS), 223

naming, strategy, 51
Nari Adalats (NAs), India, 12, 306–8
National Association for Community and Restorative Justice, 269
National Crimes Records Bureau, India, 301
National DA Task Force, 190
National Network of Shelters, 242–43
Native American women
 gender-based violence against, 134–37
 U.S. military tactic and, 134–35
negligence
 conscious, 83–84
 unconscious, 83–84
negligent rape
 amendment (2018) in Swedish law, 83
 cases from Swedish Supreme Court, 85–90
 complainant, 85, 88–89
 crime of, 8–9
 criminalization in Sweden, 80–81
 defendant, 86, 89
 evidentiary issues, 87, 89–90
 new Swedish crime of, 82–85

premises, 88, 90, 91, 92
presumptions, 86, 87, 88, 90–91, 92
principles, 88, 90, 91, 92
Sweden, 80–81
neutral negligence, 296–97
New Caledonia, 100–1
New South Wales (NSW)
 criminalizing filming "private parts" of another person, 68
 homicide cases against Aboriginal women, 116–17, 117t
New Zealand
 Bill of Rights Act (1990), 156
 complainants in rape trial process, 151–52
 image-based sexual abuse, 65
 judicial disruption of myths and misconceptions about intimate partner rape, 162–66
 judicial interaction with complainants, 156–59
 judicial intervention during questioning, 159–62
 R. v. Keats (2022), 166
 See also intimate partner sexual violence
New Zealand Bill of Rights Act (1990), 156
NFS. *See* nonfatal strangulation (NFS)
nip-slip photographs, 62–63
nonfatal strangulation (NFS), 209–10
 appropriate penalty for, 210–11, 217–18
 business as usual case, 218–21
 consequences for complainants, 215–17
 decriminalization, 221–22
 expectation of prosocial punishment, 219, 223
 First Nations Courts, 223
 First Nations people, 213–15, 220–21
 hybrid approach toward noncarceral responses, 222–23
 implementation of NFS offense, 211–17
 imprisonment, remand and bail refusal, 212–14, 212f
 offenses of, 210, 211
 overrepresentation of First Nations people, 214–15

INDEX

Queensland law in 2016, 210–11
republican approach to sentencing, 222–23
role of criminal law in responding to, 217–23
second convict age in Australia, 220–21
Northern Ireland
motive-based criminalization, 70–71
requiring proof of specific motives, 71–72

Okanogan County, 146–47
Okanogan County police, 140–41
Oklahoma v. Castro-Huerta, 137–38
Oliphant v. Suquamish Indian Tribe (1978), 137–38
overcriminalization, risks of, 33
Oxford English Dictionary, 251

Pacific Island countries
domestic violence legislation, 98–99
experiences of Indigenous peoples, 99–101
immediate police-initiated protection measures, 106
violence against women (VAW), 97–98
See also Fiji
partner violence
restorative justice options, 274–75
See also intimate partner sexual violence
patterns, abuse, 2–3
perceptions of risk, domestic and family violence (DFV), 180–82
perpetrators
accountability of, 31–34
justice system punishing, 31–34
Peterson, Rosanna, 134, 145
Polavarapu, Aparna, 11–12
police
experience with Domestic Abuse (Scotland) Act 2018, 200–2
property training of, 48–49
role of, in domestic and family violence (DFV), 182–84
Police Scotland
Domestic Abuse (Scotland) Act 2018 [DA(S)A], 193

three tiers of DA response, 195
Police Women's and Children's Protection Unit, 292
Polynesia, 97
Portugal, domestic violence in, 44–45
post-traumatic stress disorder (PTSD), 36, 50, 154–55, 159
prank, 66
precaution, domestic and family violence (DFV), 174–75
precautionary policing, domestic and family violence (DFV), 174–75
prevention, domestic and family violence (DFV), 174–75
prisons, move to abolishing, 5–6
privacy violations, criminalization of, 68–69
proof of victim harm, criminalization of, 69
psychological abuse, criminalization of, 2–3
psychological violence
benefits and risks of criminalization of, 51–55, 56*t*
benefits and risks on criminalization of, 51–55
challenges to legal recognition of, 48–50
civil definition of, in Brazil, 45–47
civil intervention in Brazil, 45
criminalization of, 44–45, 47–48
definition of, 45–46
recognition of, 44
symbolic violence, 43–44
Public Law 280 (1953), 137–38

Queensland
analysis of administrative courts, 211–12
consequences of complainants, 215–17
decriminalization of nonfatal strangulation (NFS), 221–22
Domestic Violence (DV), 210–11, 219
domestic violence (DV) taskforce, 210–11
expectation of prosocial punishment, 219

Queensland (*cont.*)
   imprisonment, remand and bail refusal, 212–14, 212*f*
   nonfatal strangulation (NFS) offense, 210
   Office of Department of Public Prosecutions (ODPP), 211–12, 216
   overrepresentation of First Nations people, 214–15
   Queensland Criminal Code 1899 (QCC), 211
   See also nonfatal strangulation (NFS)

Racial Equality Directive (EC), 262–63n.4
racism, psychological violence and, 53
rape
   marital, 151–52
   nonvoluntariness as basis for, 82–83
   See also intimate partner sexual violence; negligent rape
Raquel Martín de Mejía v. Peru (1996), 236, 237
Reeves, Ellen, 10–11
rehabilitation programs, bureaucratic violence, 290, 293–95
relational anaesthesia, phenomenon defined as, 44
restorative justice, 269–70, 280–81
   absorption by the state, 280–81
   accountability in, 273
   consequences of, 273–74
   court, 279–80
   criminal legal system, 271–72, 274
   description of, 270
   harm in, 272–73, 280
   limitations created by the state, 277–79
   process, 279–80
   promise of, 11–12
   responses to sexual and partner violence, 269–70
   role for the state, 274–80
   skepticism in, 273
   survivors of partner violence, 274
   term, 278
   Veterans Restorative Justice Act (VRJA), 278–79
   what and why of, 270–74

RESTORE program, Arizona, 270
revenge porn, 62
revictimization, criminalization creating spaces for, 54–55
Reyna, Luna, 146–47
risk artifacts, domestic and family violence (DFV), 174–75
Ritchie, Andrea, 140–41
Ross, Luana, 136
Royal Commission Into Family Violence (RCFV), 171–72, 177, 185–86
Royal Prerogative of Mercy, 115–16

safe houses
   bureaucratic violence, 290, 291–93
   temporary protection, 291
safety work, 61
Scotland
   approach to domestic abuse, 189–90
   Domestic Abuse Act 2018, 22–23
   domestic abuse offense in, 10–11
   number of interviewees by policing tier and interview sweep, 195*t*
   See also Domestic Abuse (Scotland) Act 2018 [DA(S)A]
Serious Crime Act (2015), England and Wales, 22–23
sexual and partner violence, restorative justice responses, 269–70
sexual harassment, 1
sexual violence in criminal law
   analyzing, 81–82
   premises, 81–82
   presumptions, 81
   principles, 81
   Sweden's treatment of, 79–80
   See also negligent rape
Singapore, laws on intimate images, 72
Smart, Carol, 13–14, 233
Smart, Katie, 161
social entrapment, 115–16
social exclusion, psychological violence and, 53
social isolation, recognizing, 49
social media, survey by Qualtrics, 24

INDEX

Solomon Islands, police safety notices, 106
somatic pathology, 50
South Carolina Department of Corrections, victim-offender dialogues (VODs), 279
Spain
  concept of intersectionality, 260
  domestic violence in, 44–45
  human rights for women in, 11
  identity of difference, 260–61
  intersectionality in criminal policy, 256–59
  Organic Law of Measures of Integral Protection Against Gender-Based Violence, 257
  Organic Law on Integral Guarantee of Sexual Liberty, 257
  Statute of the Victim of Crime, 258
Spanish Congress, 257
Spanish Criminal Code, 258
Spanish Equality Commission (2022), 256
Stalking, as tranquility disturbance, 46
Stark, Evan, 2–3
  coercive control, 2–5, 7
state intervention, gender-based violence, 1
structural violence
  bureaucracy as form, 288
  bureaucratic negligence and, 295
Swan, Yvonne, 142–43
Sweden
  case of unconscious negligence, 88–90
  cases from Swedish Supreme Court, 85–90
  negligent rape criminalization in, 80–81
  new crime of negligent rape, 82–85
  nonvoluntariness as basis for rape, 82–83
  treatment of sexual violence, 79–80
  See also negligent rape

temporary protection
  definition, 291
  safe houses, 290, 291–93
Thuma, Emily, 142–43
Title IX regulations, 269–70
Tonga, police safety notices, 106

tranquility disturbance, stalking as, 46
transformative justice, concept, 280–81
transformative justice movement, 281
trans women, 13–14
tribal lands, legal response to gender-based violence, 137–39

unconscious negligence, 83–84, 88–90
United Kingdom, 2–3
  criminal offenses of coercive control, 22
  image-based sexual abuse, 65
  immediate police-initiated protection measures, 106
United Nations
  decolonization and, 100–1
  human rights violations, 232–33
United Nations Committee on the Elimination of Discrimination Against Women, 252
United States, 2–3
  debate ongoing for justice system, 80
  incarceration of Indigenous women, 107
  intimate partner violence in, 3–4
United States v. Maddesyn George, 133
  case of, 139–45
  facts of, 134
  gender-based violence against Native women in U.S., 134–37
  legal response to gender-based violence on Native land, 137–39
University of Melbourne, 297n.1
upskirting
  criminalization of, 68
  Northern Ireland, 70
  online forums of images, 66
  See also downblousing
Urban Indian Health Institute, 146–47

Valentin Câmpeanu v. Romania, 262n.1
Varona, Gema, human rights, 11
Veterans Restorative Justice Act (VRJA), Minnesota, 278–79
Victim Information and Advice (VIA), 190
victim-offender dialogues (VODs), programs with incarcerated people, 279

victim-survivor(s)
  community awareness of violence, 29–30
  consequences of police contact for, 12–13
  criminalization of coercive control, 39–40
  experience with Domestic Abuse (Scotland) Act 2018, 200–2
  impact on safety of, 30–31
  justice for, 244
  legalistic model of justice and, 233–34
  misidentification as predominant aggressors, 171–72, 176, 184–86
  negative impacts of justice system on, 34–38
  nonfatal strangulation (NFS), 221–22
  prosecution views of, 223–24
  recognizing limits of law on, 34–38
  safety and justice needs of, 13–14
  See also criminalization of coercive control
Victoria Police, domestic and family violence (DFV), 172, 176, 177, 181, 184–85
Victoria Police Centre for Learning for Family Violence, 186n.2
violation, experience as violation, 309
violence, term in bureaucratic violence, 289–90
violence against women (VAW)
  human rights and, 231, 232, 245
  intersectionality, 250–51
  Istanbul Convention (2011), 253–54
  shelter homes for survivors of, in Ecuador, 242–43
Violence Against Women Act (VAWA), 138, 139
VSL. *See* value of a statistical life (VSL)
vulnerability
  concept of, 251, 258–59
  Fineman's theory, 251–52
  institutional, 261–62
vulnerable victims, legal notions on intersectionality and, 251–56

Wanrow, Yvonne, 142–43
Wesler, William, 142–43
Western Australia, Aboriginal women, 115–16
West Papua, 100–1
White Buffalo Calf Women, 136
Williamson County, Texas, transformative justice label, 280–81
women
  creation of crime only against, 53
  feminist politics, 311–12
  missing, 304–6
  notion of 'good woman', 311
  respecting choices and voices of, 310–11
  See also domestic and family violence (DFV); victim-survivor(s)
Women's Courts
  alternative frames of justice, 306–8
  Nari Adalats (NAs), 12, 306–8
World War II, 100–1

Zehr, Howard, 275